Robyn Webb's
MEMORABLE MENUS
MADE EASY

Robyn Webb's
MEMORABLE MENUS
MADE EASY

SIGNATURE MEALS
FOR ENTERTAINING
OR ANY OCCASION

Robyn Webb, MS

Book Acquisitions	Susan Reynolds
Editor	Laurie Guffey
Production Director	Carolyn R. Segree
Production Coordinator	Peggy M. Rote
Book Design & Production	Wickham & Associates, Inc.
Photography	Taran Z
Food Stylist	Lisa Cherkasky
Nutritional Analysis	Nutritional Computing Concepts, Inc.

The suggestions and information contained in this publication are generally consistent with the *Clinical Practice Recommendations* and other policies of the American Diabetes Association, but they do not represent the policy or position of the Association or any of its boards or committees. Reasonable steps have been taken to ensure the accuracy of the information presented. However, the American Diabetes Association cannot ensure the safety or efficacy of any product or service described in this publication. Individuals are advised to consult a physician or other appropriate health care professional before undertaking any diet or exercise program or taking any medication referred to in this publication. Professionals must use and apply their own professional judgment, experience, and training and should not rely solely on the information contained in this publication before prescribing any diet, exercise, or medication. The American Diabetes Association—its officers, directors, employees, volunteers, and members—assumes no responsibility or liability for personal or other injury, loss, or damage that may result from the suggestions or information in this publication.

American Diabetes Association
1660 Duke Street
Alexandria, Virginia 22314

Library of Congress Cataloging-in-Publication Data

Webb, Robyn
    [Memorable menus made easy]
    Robyn Webb's memorable menus made easy / Robyn Webb.
    p.   cm.
    ISBN 0-945448-82-1 (pbk.)
    1. Low-fat diet—Recipes. 2. Food exchange lists. 3. Food composition—Tables. I. Title.
RM237.7.W427 1997
641.5'638—dc21

97-26279
CIP

For my mother, Ruth,

who developed my creative

sense and allowed me to

experiment with food at a very early age;

and my husband, Allan,

my rock and my inspiration.

Robyn Webb's
MEMORABLE MENUS
MADE EASY

❖ ❖ ❖

CONTENTS

i

Robyn Webb's Memorable Menus Made Easy provides an exciting and insightful compilation of sound nutritional information, combined with marvelous menus that range from the purely practical to the absolutely exotic.

There are a few people who still believe that the fitness-conscious person must give up some of the pleasures of fine dining in order to stay on a healthy diet. In this book, Robyn Webb shows us that healthy dishes, properly prepared, can be just as delicious and satisfying as those using high-fat, nutritionally depleted ingredients—and don't require us to spend any extra time or money making them. She has successfully combined nutrition with gastronomy, or the science of food with the art of food, in a most delightful way.

I truly believe that most people are aware of the importance of good nutrition, and are taking positive steps to eat in a healthy way. However, for some strange reason, this effort doesn't seem to extend to entertaining. Party menus routinely include greasy hors d'oeuvres, salads liberally dressed with thick, creamy dressings, outrageously rich entrees, and overly sweet desserts. Even people who really like fresh fruit for dessert wouldn't think of serving it for company without first making it into a gooey pie, and then perhaps topping it with high-fat ice cream.

Now Robyn Webb shows us how to entertain well and not regret it the following day. For your next party, choose her as your catering director and let her fabulous cookbook serve as your guide to innovative, delicious menus.

— *Jeanne Jones*

I always wanted to write a menu cookbook. Through my years as a cooking school owner, the common cry among my students has been, "What do I serve with this?" As I began designing more recipes for people with diabetes, it seemed clear that combining those recipes into delicious, easy-to-prepare menus would be helpful. After all, eating in a healthy way doesn't have to be boring!

I teach my students the importance of four interrelated principles:

◆ Serve meals that are healthy and nutritious
◆ Use fresh, high-quality ingredients
◆ Learn the best cooking techniques to enhance flavor
◆ Adopt smart strategies for quick meal preparation

This book is based on those principles. Each of the 50 mouth-watering menus features:

◆ **Menu Talk:** an informative introduction to each menu describing the origin of some of the ingredients, tips and techniques to ensure preparation success, and helpful serving suggestions

◆ **Market List:** a complete shopping list of everything you'll need to prepare the menu, including refrigerator and pantry items

◆ **Step-by-Step Countdown:** an organized, step-by-step way to work through the menu, so everything's ready when you want it

◆ **Complete and accurate nutritional analysis** for each recipe, including all exchanges (optional ingredients are not included in nutrient analyses)

The menus are very flexible. You can prepare fewer than all five recipes if you like, or mix-and-match recipes from different menus. Consult your meal plan to create the best balance for your day's exchange allotment. You'll notice that you'll have the opportunity to reuse some of the more exotic ingredients in several of the recipes. Also, you'll see many of the same food items appearing on the Market Lists for different menus. That's to make overlapping and menu coordination easier, so you'll be able to create your own personal menu favorites.

Many of the menus are meatless, and in some, the animal protein appears as a condiment rather than a center-stage ingredient. Other menus

offer fish, chicken, or pork as the main dish. Try all the menus to get a good variety of nutrients, flavors, and textures. You'll find plenty of whole grains, with their nutrient-rich bran and germ; an abundance of vegetables, both lightly cooked and raw; an interesting variety of common and exotic fresh fruits; fiber-rich legumes; and light, flavor-rich oils to replace heavy cream and butter.

Each recipe serves six, so you'll either have enough for a fabulous dinner party or be able to enjoy the leftovers the next day. The recipes call for the freshest possible ingredients, and the use of artificial, prepackaged foods is kept to a minimum. I always use Italian (flat leaf) parsley because it has more flavor, but you can use curly parsley if you wish. Always grind fresh pepper with a peppermill, use sea salt instead of table salt (you can use less of it, and it doesn't have a metallic taste), and definitely search out and buy fresh herbs whenever possible.

The Market Lists and Step-by-Step Countdowns will help you feel more organized and confident in the kitchen. As I grew more skilled as a cook, I began to look for ways to save time in the kitchen, so I could add time for exercise and leisure activities to my day. Cooking smart means being both prepared and effective.

Throughout this book, I offer dozens of tips and specific suggestions for the best techniques to use to ensure mealtime success. This kind of help automatically puts you more in charge of your time. Don't be afraid to try something new—I've carefully balanced familiar flavors with more adventurous food combinations, and I provide the guidance for you to feel confident every step of the way.

The information in the book is as fun to read as it is practical. Learning about the wonderful world of food, cooking, and keeping healthy has never been easier or tasted so great! Enjoy.

ACKNOWLEDGMENTS

This book could not have been written without the people who are so special to me. Susan Reynolds allowed me to share my work with others. Laurie Guffey and Peggy Rote helped this book reflect my personal style. Len Boswell demonstrated his usual professionalism, flexibility, and integrity. My publicist, Amy Cubert Katz, continues to keep me strong and visionary. I am thankful for our relationship all these years. Lyn Wheeler did an outstanding job on the nutritional analysis, a critical component of this book. My partners in crime, Austin Zakari and her team, skillfully tested the menus and provided honest feedback to ensure a book filled with good recipes.

My thanks to the authors of the following books, which I consulted while writing *Memorable Menus Made Easy*: Sharon Tyler Herbst's *The New Food Lover's Companion* (Barrons Publishing, 1995); Julie Rosso's *Great Good Food* (Crown Publishing, 1993); and *The Cooking of Italy* and *The Cooking of Spain and Portugal* (Time–Life Books, 1969).

Fiesta Fare

❖ ❖ ❖ ❖ ❖

Crunchy Chicken 3

Crunchy Chicken
Corn Salsa
Chili Rice Pilaf
Stewed Chayote Squash
Mexican Hot Chocolate

Mexican Lasagna 11

Asparagus in Chili Dressing
Mexican Lasagna
Jicama and Carrot Salad
Caramelized Peppers
Pistachio Pudding

Speedy Paella 19

Garlic Soup
Marinated Mushroom Salad
Speedy Paella
Green Beans in Tomato Sauce
Baked Caramel Custard

Andalusian Supper 27

Shrimp Gazpacho
Black and Pinto Bean Salad
Roasted Vegetable Burritos
Tomatillo Salsa
Cool Strawberry Agua

Southwestern Pasta 35

Smoky Tomato and Chili Soup
Southwestern Fusilli
Tomato and Tomatillo Salad
Zucchini and Peppers
Baked Pineapple

Crunchy Chicken

Crunchy Chicken
Corn Salsa
Chili Rice Pilaf
Stewed Chayote Squash
Mexican Hot Chocolate

M E N U   T A L K

Should you buy free-range chickens for this meal? I think they taste better. Free-range chickens are given more freedom to roam outdoors and are fed a special diet that results in a more tender, lean bird. Chicken should be stored in the coldest part of your refrigerator and preferably used within 48 hours. As with all animal products, handle poultry with care. Wash cutting boards and knives with soap and hot water after they have come into contact with raw poultry.

One of my fondest memories of my childhood in upstate New York is of buying fresh corn in the farmer's market on Sunday. We made corn pancakes, muffins, and bread, and enjoyed fresh corn-on-the-cob all week! Yellow corn has a richer taste, but white corn is sweeter. When choosing fresh corn, look for ears with tight-fitting husks. Open the husks and peek inside to view the corn. The kernels should look plump and pack tightly against each other. Frozen corn is perfectly acceptable to use. Fresh corn is best from May to September.

To enhance the natural nutty flavor of rice, I saute it dry, then add the liquid in which it cooks. If you prefer a gentler taste, use mild green chilis, such as cubanelles or Anaheim peppers, instead of jalapenos. These peppers do not emit as much heat as jalapenos but still add a zing to the rice.

Chayote squash, known as christophene in France and mirliton in the southern United States, is a pear-shaped vegetable that can be used instead of summer squash. To use chayote, peel the thin skin and chop or shred the meat. There is a pit in the center that is so soft it can be eaten. Chayote is available mostly in winter months, but some specialty grocers carry it all year long. This vegetable is also popular in Asian cuisine. Look for chayote that is on the small side and unblemished. Store the squash in the refrigerator. Chayote is a mild vegetable, so its flavor stands up well when you add spices and vinegars. This recipe was given to me by one of my first cooking school assistants, Loretta Colom.

Cocoa powder comes from cocoa pods that grow on the tropical cacao tree. Dutch cocoa is richer than cocoa powder. Cocoa powder is low in fat (1 Tbsp contains about 1/2 gram), making it an ideal ingredient to use in your favorite chocolate desserts. If you use Dutch cocoa, which has a sweeter taste, you may find you need less sugar or sweetener in your recipes.

Pantry List

cocoa powder
sugar
ground cinnamon
cinnamon sticks
cornflakes cereal
chili powder
garlic powder
onion powder
olive oil
1 red onion
cumin
red wine vinegar
1 can low-fat, low-sodium chicken
   broth
1 bag rice
1 small can low-sodium tomato
   juice
1 can diced Mexican-style tomatoes

Market List

1 1/2 lb boneless, skinless chicken
   breasts
3 eggs
fresh lime juice
1 small bag frozen corn or 2 large
   ears corn
3 tomatoes
cilantro
2 chayote squash or 1 large zucchini
low-fat sour cream
1 green bell pepper
1 jalapeno pepper
skim milk

STEP-BY-STEP COUNTDOWN

1 Prepare the corn salsa.
2 Prepare the chayote squash.
3 Prepare the chicken.
4 Prepare the rice.
5 Serve the chicken, salsa, chayote squash, and rice.
6 Prepare the hot chocolate and serve it for dessert.

Crunchy Chicken with Corn Salsa

6 Servings

Serving Size:
3 oz

Exchanges

2 1/2 Starch
4 Very Lean Meat

Ingredients

2 cups cornflakes cereal,
   finely crushed
2 tsp chili powder
1 tsp garlic powder
1/2 tsp onion powder
3 eggs, beaten
2 tsp fresh lime juice
1 1/2 lb boneless, skinless chicken
   breasts, halved
2 tsp olive oil
2 cups fresh corn kernels
2 small tomatoes, diced
1/4 cup minced red onion
2 Tbsp minced cilantro
1 tsp cumin
2 Tbsp red wine vinegar
1 Tbsp fresh lime juice

Preparation—25 minutes

1 Preheat the oven to 350 degrees. Mix together the cornflakes, chili powder, garlic powder, and onion powder in a shallow pan or pie plate.
2 In a medium bowl, beat together the eggs and lime juice. Dip each chicken breast into the egg mixture, then roll in the cornflakes to coat. Place all chicken breasts on a cookie sheet. Drizzle the chicken with oil. Bake for 30–35 minutes or until the chicken is opaque.
3 While the chicken is baking, combine the remaining ingredients. Refrigerate until serving time, then serve with the chicken.

Calories	357
Calories from Fat	65
Total Fat	7 g
Saturated Fat	2 g
Cholesterol	175 mg
Sodium	406 mg
Carbohydrate	40 g
Dietary Fiber	3 g
Sugars	6 g
Protein	33 g

Chili Rice Pilaf

6 Servings

Serving Size:
1/2 cup

Exchanges

2 1/2 Starch
1 Vegetable

Ingredients

2 tsp olive oil
1/2 cup diced onion
2 cloves garlic, minced
1/2 cup chopped green bell pepper
1 1/2 cups rice
2 tsp minced jalapeno pepper
1/2 cup low-sodium tomato juice
2 1/2 cups low-fat, low-sodium
   chicken broth
1/2 cup diced canned tomatoes,
   Mexican-style, drained and
   chopped
Chopped cilantro

Preparation—10 minutes

1 Heat the oil in a skillet over medium-high heat. Add the onion and saute for 5 minutes. Add the garlic and saute for 2 minutes. Add the green bell pepper and rice and saute for 5 minutes.
2 Add the jalapeno pepper and saute for 1 minute. Add the juice and broth, bring to a boil, lower the heat, cover, and simmer until the rice has absorbed the liquid, about 20 minutes.
3 Add the chopped tomatoes, garnish with cilantro, and serve.

Calories	211
Calories from Fat	26
Total Fat	3 g
Saturated Fat	1 g
Cholesterol	0 mg
Sodium	82 mg
Carbohydrate	42 g
Dietary Fiber	1 g
Sugars	3 g
Protein	5 g

Stewed Chayote Squash

6 Servings

Serving Size:
1/2 cup

Exchanges

2 Vegetable
1/2 Saturated Fat

Ingredients

1 tsp olive oil
2 Tbsp low-fat, low-sodium chicken
   broth
1/2 cup diced red onion
2 cloves garlic, minced
3 cups diced chayote squash (or use
   zucchini)
1 medium tomato, diced
2 tsp chili powder
1/2 cup low-fat sour cream

Preparation—20 minutes

1 Heat the oil and broth in a skillet over medium-high heat. Add the onion and saute for 4 minutes. Add the garlic and saute for 2 minutes. Add the chayote and tomato.
2 Cover and simmer until the chayote is tender, about 25 minutes.
3 Sprinkle the mixture with chili power and cook uncovered for 5 minutes. Add the sour cream and serve.

Calories	65
Calories from Fat	25
Total Fat	3 g
Saturated Fat	1 g
Cholesterol	7 mg
Sodium	35 mg
Carbohydrate	10 g
Dietary Fiber	3 g
Sugars	6 g
Protein	2 g

Mexican Hot Chocolate

6 Servings

Serving Size:
1/2 cup

Exchanges

1 Carbohydrate

Ingredients

3 cups skim milk
1/4 cup cocoa powder
1/4 cup sugar
1 tsp ground cinnamon
Cinnamon sticks

Preparation—5 minutes

Warm the milk in a saucepan, then pour it into a blender. Add the cocoa, sugar, and ground cinnamon and process until frothy. Serve in warmed mugs with a cinnamon stick.

Calories	83
Calories from Fat	6
Total Fat	1 g
Saturated Fat	0 g
Cholesterol	2 mg
Sodium	63 mg
Carbohydrate	16 g
Dietary Fiber	1 g
Sugars	14 g
Protein	5 g

☞ WHY DON'T YOU . . .

When entertaining, consider serving each course in a different room. Choose a menu that can be easily eaten in rooms without tables.

Mexican Lasagna

Asparagus in Chili Dressing
Mexican Lasagna
Jicama and Carrot Salad
Caramelized Peppers
Pistachio Pudding

MENU TALK

Instead of a soup or green salad, why not enjoy crunchy stalks of asparagus as a first course? Color is important when presenting balanced menus. The green of the asparagus is set off by red tomatoes and slices of yellow lemon. Feed your eyes as well as your stomach! Other colors can add to or detract from the dining experience. Did you ever wonder why the walls of a fast-food restaurant are never painted a restful blue? Hot, stimulating colors, such as red or orange, encourage customers to eat more and faster. For a more pleasurable dining experience, choose pretty plates and a fresh centerpiece, and serve the meal in a room decorated with subdued, calming colors.

Chipotle peppers are actually dried, smoked jalapenos. Their skin is wrinkled and they taste almost like chocolate. Chipotles can be purchased in packages or cans. For this lasagna, you can use any spicy pepper. Chop a fresh jalapeno, or use ground chili powder. Try making this lasagna with raw, uncooked pasta. Simply layer all ingredients, cover, and place in the refrigerator overnight, and the juices from the sauce and cheese will "cook" the noodles and soften them. The next day, just bake the lasagna. This method comes in particularly handy when you want really even slices.

Jicama, a large, round, brown-skinned root vegetable, is also often referred to as the Mexican potato. Prized for its sweetness and crunch, it is better eaten raw. When jicama is cooked, it loses its sweet taste. Jicama is also a good source of vitamin C. Jicama is available November through

See color photo after p. 80.

May, although you can sometimes find it during the summer months. Its skin should be peeled before you use it. One of my very favorite ways to eat jicama is to cut thin slices, sprinkle them with a little lime juice, and dust just a little chili powder on top. The sweet taste of the jicama, the tartness of the lime, and the little bit of heat from the chili powder create an unbelievable taste sensation.

Caramelizing vegetables is a delicious way to prepare them. Just a touch of sugar draws out the natural sweetness in many vegetables and creates a nice glaze. It is a low-fat way to add great taste! Caramelized vegetables are great on top of pasta and rice.

Pistachios are cultivated in the United States, Italy, Turkey, and Iran. The nut is green and is encased in a brown shell. Pistachios require a little effort to eat, so it's harder to overindulge in them. Creme de menthe adds a fresh mint flavor to complement this dessert.

Pantry List

sherry vinegar
olive oil
garlic
chili powder
sugar
1 yellow onion
1 box lasagna noodles
1 small can black olives
1 4-oz pkg fat-free, sugar-free
   pistachio pudding
macaroons
green creme de menthe
pistachio nuts
chipotle peppers

Market List

1/2 lb ground turkey breast
   (97% fat-free)
2 bunches asparagus
1 lemon
cilantro
fresh lime juice
1 container part-skim ricotta cheese
1 cup low-fat cottage cheese
1 cup low-fat jack cheese
1 small jicama
1 carrot
1 mango
fresh orange juice
7 tomatoes
1 serrano pepper
1 each red and yellow bell pepper
1 cup low-calorie whipped topping

low-calorie margarine
green onions
nonfat milk

Asparagus in Chili Dressing

6 Servings

Serving Size:
5 spears with sauce

Exchanges

1 Vegetable

Ingredients

30 spears asparagus, ends trimmed
1/3 cup sherry vinegar
2 Tbsp lime juice
1 tsp olive oil
1 clove garlic, minced
1 tsp chili powder
1 tsp sugar
Thin slices lemon
12 tomato wedges

Preparation—10 minutes

1 Blanch the asparagus in boiling water for 3 minutes. Drain, plunge into ice water, and drain again. Set the asparagus aside.
2 Whisk together the vinegar, lime juice, olive oil, garlic, chili powder, and sugar for the dressing.
3 Plate 5 spears of asparagus per person. Drizzle with dressing and surround with lemon slices and tomato wedges.

Calories	40
Calories from Fat	11
Total Fat	1 g
Saturated Fat	0 g
Cholesterol	0 mg
Sodium	16 mg
Carbohydrate	7 g
Dietary Fiber	2 g
Sugars	4 g
Protein	2 g

❧ WHY DON'T YOU . . .

Start off the evening with the dishwasher empty, so you can load dishes after each course.

Mexican Lasagna

6 Servings

Serving Size:
1 6-inch square

Exchanges

3 Starch
1 Vegetable
3 Lean Meat
1/2 Saturated Fat

Ingredients

2 tsp olive oil
3 cloves garlic, minced
1/2 cup minced onion
1/2 lb ground turkey breast
(97% fat-free)
5 large tomatoes, diced
2 whole red chipotle peppers,
rehydrated and chopped
(or 1 tsp cayenne pepper)
2 Tbsp minced cilantro
3 Tbsp fresh lime juice
2 cups part-skim ricotta cheese
1 cup low-fat cottage cheese
1 cup shredded low-fat jack cheese
10 cooked lasagna noodles
1/4 cup sliced ripe black olives
2 Tbsp low-fat jack cheese

Preparation—30 minutes

1 Preheat the oven to 350 degrees. Heat the oil in a medium skillet over medium-high heat. Add the garlic and saute for 30 seconds. Add the onion and saute for 4 minutes. Add the ground turkey and saute for 5 minutes.
2 Add the tomatoes, bring to a boil, and lower the heat. Simmer for 5 minutes. Add the chipotle peppers or cayenne pepper. Simmer for 10 minutes.
3 In a large bowl, mix together the cilantro, lime juice, and all the cheeses. Layer some of the sauce on the bottom of a narrow, long casserole dish. Add a layer of noodles, a layer of the cheese mixture, and a layer of sauce.
4 Repeat the layers, ending with the sauce. Decorate the top with sliced olives and an additional 2 Tbsp of jack cheese.
5 Cover the casserole and bake for 35 minutes. Remove the cover and bake until the cheese is melted, about 10 minutes. Let the casserole stand for 15 minutes before cutting into squares and serving.

Calories	464
Calories from Fat	118
Total Fat	13 g
Saturated Fat	7 g
Cholesterol	62 mg
Sodium	431 mg
Carbohydrate	52 g
Dietary Fiber	4 g
Sugars	1 g
Protein	35 g

Jicama and Carrot Salad

6 Servings

Serving Size:
1/2 cup

Exchanges

1/2 Fruit
1 Vegetable

Ingredients

1 1/2 cups diced, peeled jicama
1 cup sliced carrots
1/2 cup diced, peeled mango
   (or papaya)
1/4 cup fresh lime juice
3 Tbsp fresh orange juice
1 tsp olive oil
1 serrano or jalapeno pepper, seeded
   and diced

Preparation—15 minutes

1 Toss the jicama, carrots, and mango together in a salad bowl.
2 In a blender, combine the remaining ingredients. Toss with the jicama salad. Refrigerate 1 hour and serve.

Calories	46
Calories from Fat	8
Total Fat	1 g
Saturated Fat	0 g
Cholesterol	0 mg
Sodium	9 mg
Carbohydrate	10 g
Dietary Fiber	3 g
Sugars	6 g
Protein	1 g

Caramelized Peppers

6 Servings

Serving Size:
1/2 cup

Exchanges

1 Vegetable

Ingredients

1 Tbsp low-calorie margarine
3 cups sliced red and yellow
  bell peppers
2 Tbsp minced green onions
1 Tbsp sugar

Preparation—10 minutes

1 Melt the margarine in a skillet over high heat. Add the peppers and saute for 5–6 minutes. Add the green onions and saute for 4 minutes.
2 Add the sugar and continue to saute until peppers are caramelized. Serve warm.

Calories	35
Calories from Fat	9
Total Fat	1 g
Saturated Fat	0 g
Cholesterol	0 mg
Sodium	17 mg
Carbohydrate	7 g
Dietary Fiber	1 g
Sugars	4 g
Protein	1 g

SPEAKING OF SPICES

Chili Peppers

Chili peppers are capsicums, in the same family as bell peppers and paprika pods. They range in flavor from sweet to fiery hot. When using chilis, remember to combine them with other spices so your dish will have full, rounded flavors. Here are heat ratings for some of the chili peppers used in these recipes.

Heat Ratings in Scoville Units
Jalapeno   55,000
Cayenne   40,000
Crushed Red Pepper 20,000
Chipotle Pepper   15,000
Ancho Pepper   3, 000

Pistachio Pudding

6 Servings

Serving Size:
1/2 cup

Exchanges

1 Carbohydrate
1 Saturated Fat

Ingredients

1   4-serving-size pkg fat-free, sugar-
      free pistachio pudding mix
2   cups skim milk
1   cup low-calorie whipped cream
3   macaroons, crushed
1   tsp green cream de menthe
2   Tbsp toasted pistachio nuts

Preparation—10 minutes

1   Prepare the pudding mix according to package directions using skim milk. Refrigerate to set.
2   When the pudding is set, mix the whipped cream with the macaroons and cream de menthe. Layer the pudding and whipped cream mixture in parfait glasses. Garnish each glass with nuts and serve.

Calories	121
Calories from Fat	31
Total Fat	3 g
Saturated Fat	3 g
Cholesterol	1 mg
Sodium	273 mg
Carbohydrate	17 g
Dietary Fiber	1 g
Sugars	10 g
Protein	3 g

❖ ❖ ❖

Speedy Paella

Garlic Soup
Marinated Mushroom Salad
Speedy Paella
Green Beans in Tomato Sauce
Baked Caramel Custard

M E N U   T A L K

Sopa de ajo, garlic soup, is a classic dish from central Spain. It's simple to prepare—lots of garlic, bread, and a bit of oil all simmered together—but its flavor is fantastic! It is light enough to be the first course for a hearty paella dish. Use stale bread for best results.

Marinated mushrooms are another favorite *tapa*, or appetizer, in Spain and Latin America. Many different tapas are prepared and served in restaurants and bars during long, festive evenings. Friends come together to enjoy food and conversation. In fact, tapas are so popular, many Spaniards just make a meal of them and skip dinner. Serve the marinated mushrooms before the soup if you wish, perhaps in your living room or rec room. Pierce the mushrooms with fancy frill picks and let your guests settle in and enjoy a few moments with you. You can also serve the mushrooms as a salad with dinner.

Fresh tomatoes are a must for these green beans. Tomatoes are members of the nightshade family. The French call tomatoes "love apples" in reference to their reputed power as aphrodisiacs. Place any unripe tomatoes in a paper bag, add an apple, and leave the tomatoes for several days at room temperature to ripen. Try to use tomatoes still attached to the vine–they are the most flavorful.

The colorful paella, probably the best-known Spanish food outside Spain, gets its name from the two-handled pan in which it is cooked. Paella has many variations, but rice, saffron, and olive oil are always used. To reduce fat, I have omitted the traditional chorizo sausage and used less oil. In Spain, paella is cooked outdoors on open fires. Some people think paella is complicated to prepare, but it's not: just chop everything up and throw it into one big pot.

This version of baked caramel custard, or flan, is lower in fat and cholesterol. Flan is the light and perfect finish to a hearty, spicy meal.

Pantry List

dry white wine
olive oil
garlic
1 small loaf Italian bread
paprika
5 cans low-fat, low-sodium
   chicken broth
cayenne pepper
balsamic vinegar
1 yellow onion
sugar
1 bag brown rice
saffron threads
1 can evaporated skim milk
port wine
vanilla

Market List

12 oz boneless, skinless chicken
   breasts
12 oz fresh shrimp
2 eggs
1 carton egg substitute
2 pints mushrooms
green onions
rosemary
1 head romaine lettuce
2 red bell peppers
1 green bell pepper
3 tomatoes
1 lb green beans
parsley
1 zucchini
1 bunch asparagus

1 bag frozen peas
skim milk

STEP-BY-STEP COUNTDOWN

1 Prepare the dessert and the mushroom salad the night before. Keep custards in cups overnight.
2 The next day, prepare step 1 of the paella. Prepare the remaining ingredients to be added in step 2.
3 Prepare the green beans.
4 Prepare the ingredients for the soup, but do not cook them.
5 Add the remaining ingredients to the paella.
6 Prepare the garlic soup.
7 Serve the soup.
8 Serve the mushroom salad.
9 Serve the paella and green beans.
10 Unmold the dessert and serve.

Garlic Soup

6 Servings

Serving Size:
1 cup

Exchanges

1 Starch
1 Fat

Ingredients

1/2 cup white wine
2 tsp olive oil
3 Tbsp minced garlic
3 cups coarsely crumbled Italian
    bread, crusts removed
1 tsp paprika
6 cups low-fat, low-sodium chicken
    broth
1/2 tsp cayenne pepper (optional)
1 egg, lightly beaten

Preparation—15 minutes

1 Heat the wine and oil in a stockpot over high heat. Add the garlic and saute for 3 minutes. Add the bread and cook until the bread is golden. Do not let it burn.
2 Add the paprika, broth, and cayenne pepper. Bring to a boil, lower the heat, and simmer.
3 Mash the bread until it is pulverized. Add the egg and cook only 1 minute. Do not let the mixture boil. Serve immediately.

Calories	122	
Calories from Fat	49	
Total Fat	5	g
Saturated Fat	1	g
Cholesterol	36	mg
Sodium	239	mg
Carbohydrate	15	g
Dietary Fiber	1	g
Sugars	3	g
Protein	6	g

Marinated Mushroom Salad

6 Servings

Serving Size:
1/2 cup

Exchanges

1 Vegetable
1/2 Monounsatur-
ated Fat

Ingredients

3 cups whole small mushrooms,
   well cleaned, stems trimmed
5 cloves garlic, minced
2 Tbsp minced green onions
1/2 cup minced parsley
1/2 cup dry white wine
2 Tbsp balsamic vinegar
2 tsp olive oil
2 Tbsp minced rosemary
6 large romaine lettuce leaves
1/2 cup minced red bell pepper

Preparation—10 minutes

1 Combine all ingredients except the romaine lettuce and red bell pepper. Refrigerate overnight.
2 Place a lettuce leaf on each serving plate. Mound the mushroom mixture on top, garnish with minced pepper, and serve.

Calories	40
Calories from Fat	16
Total Fat	2 g
Saturated Fat	0 g
Cholesterol	0 mg
Sodium	7 mg
Carbohydrate	4 g
Dietary Fiber	1 g
Sugars	2 g
Protein	1 g

❖ ❖ ❖ ❖ ❖ ❖ ❖

⤳ WHY DON'T YOU . . .

*Allow someone else to do part
of the cooking. (Who says you
have to do everything?)*

Speedy Paella

6 Servings

Serving Size:
2 oz chicken
2 oz shrimp
1/2 cup rice
1/2 cup vegetables

Exchanges

2 1/2 Starch
1 Vegetable
3 Very Lean Meat
1 Monounsaturated
  Fat

Ingredients

2 Tbsp olive oil
3 cloves garlic, minced
1 medium onion, minced
1/2 cup each red and green bell
   pepper
1 1/2 cups brown rice, rinsed
3 1/2 cups low-fat, low-sodium
   chicken broth
1 tsp saffron threads
1/2 cup sliced zucchini
1/2 cup sliced asparagus tips
1/2 cup diced tomato
1/2 cup frozen peas, thawed
12 oz cooked chicken breast, cut
   into cubes
12 oz peeled and deveined shrimp
Fresh ground pepper
Dash salt (optional)

Preparation—25 minutes

1 Heat the oil in a large paella pan or skillet over medium-high heat. Add the garlic and onion and saute for 5 minutes. Add the peppers and saute for 4 minutes. Add the rice and saute for 4 minutes.
2 Add the broth and saffron. Bring to a boil, lower the heat, cover, and simmer for about 40 minutes.
3 Add the zucchini, asparagus, tomatoes, and peas. Cook, covered, over medium-low heat for 8 minutes.
4 Add the chicken and shrimp. Cook, covered, for 5 minutes until the shrimp turns pink. Add the pepper and salt and serve.

Calories	376
Calories from Fat	76
Total Fat	8 g
Saturated Fat	2 g
Cholesterol	118 mg
Sodium	171 mg
Carbohydrate	44 g
Dietary Fiber	4 g
Sugars	5 g
Protein	31 g

 WHY DON'T YOU . . .

*Begin indoors and end up on
the patio with dessert.*

Green Beans in Tomato Sauce

6 Servings

Serving Size:
1/2 cup

Exchanges

2 Vegetable

Ingredients

3 cups sliced green beans
2 tsp olive oil
1/2 cup minced onion
3 cloves garlic, finely minced
2 tomatoes, minced
2 Tbsp minced parsley
1 tsp sugar
Fresh ground pepper
Dash salt (optional)

Preparation—10 minutes

1 Blanch the green beans for 2 minutes in a pot of boiling water. Drain, splash them with cold water, and set aside.
2 Heat the oil in a skillet over medium-high heat. Add the onion and garlic and saute for 3 minutes. Add the tomatoes, bring to a boil, lower the heat, and simmer for 5 minutes.
3 Add the parsley and sugar and simmer for 2 minutes. Add the green beans and simmer for 5 minutes. Add the pepper and salt and serve.

Calories	57
Calories from Fat	17
Total Fat	2 g
Saturated Fat	0 g
Cholesterol	0 mg
Sodium	8 mg
Carbohydrate	10 g
Dietary Fiber	3 g
Sugars	4 g
Protein	2 g

Baked Caramel Custard

6 Servings

Serving Size:
1/2 cup

Exchanges

2 Carbohydrate

Ingredients

1 1/2 cups evaporated skim milk
1 1/2 cups skim milk
1/3 cup plus 2 Tbsp sugar
1 cup egg substitute
1 egg yolk
2 tsp port wine
2 tsp vanilla

Preparation—10 minutes

1 Preheat the oven to 350 degrees. Scald the milks together in a heavy saucepan. Remove from the heat.
2 Caramelize the sugar in a skillet over medium heat until it melts and turns brown. Slowly add the milks to the sugar, stirring constantly until the sugar dissolves.
3 In a medium bowl, beat the egg substitute and egg yolk together until it is lemon-colored. Add the milk mixture, port, and vanilla and stir well.
4 Pour the mixture into 6 custard cups and place them into a baking dish. Pour boiling water into the baking dish so that the water comes halfway up the sides of the cups. Place in the oven and bake until set, about 35–40 minutes.
5 Remove the custard cups from the oven and cool completely in the refrigerator. When they are chilled, place a dessert plate on top of each custard cup and invert. Serve immediately.

Calories	146
Calories from Fat	10
Total Fat	1 g
Saturated Fat	0 g
Cholesterol	39 mg
Sodium	125 mg
Carbohydrate	26 g
Dietary Fiber	0 g
Sugars	24 g
Protein	9 g

Andalusian Supper

Shrimp Gazpacho
Black and Pinto Bean Salad
Roasted Vegetable Burritos
Tomatillo Salsa
Cool Strawberry Agua

MENU TALK

Gazpacho, a simple concoction of seeded tomatoes, cucumbers, and peppers, is a classic favorite of those living in the hot climate of Andalusia, in the southern part of the Iberian peninsula. Gazpacho is mentioned in Roman and Greek literature as a drinkable food, and it appears in both testaments of the Bible. There are as many versions of gazpacho as there are cooks—here is yet another version! I incorporate the classic elements, but add diced cooked shrimp to each soup bowl for a more elegant look. Grace your table with refreshing gazpacho on those hot summer days.

A tomatillo is one of my favorite vegetables. This small, underripe Mexican tomato with its papery husk can be found in most supermarkets today. If you like the taste of a Granny Smith apple, you will probably like the tomatillo's combination sweet and tart flavor. Just remove the tomatillo's husk, wash, and chop. Use them alone to replace tomatoes in salsa and gazpacho or use them in combination with tomatoes. Choose medium, firm tomatillos with tight-fitting husks. Tomatillos are found in stores on and off all year long. They are more acidic than tomatoes and are rich in vitamin A.

I like to serve combinations of beans to add visual interest. Beans are a great source of fiber, calcium, and iron. Canned beans are fine for most purposes—just drain and rinse them well to avoid unnecessary sodium.

Roasting vegetables brings out their natural sweetness and makes their flavor spectacular. Almost any vegetable can be roasted. My favorites are tomatoes, portobello mushrooms, zucchini, yellow squash, and carrots. Tortillas will keep for a few months in the freezer, but they will lose flavor if kept several days in the refrigerator, so plan on using them quickly.

Try not to prewash strawberries or they will turn mushy. You can wipe them off with a damp paper towel or wash them just before using them. Remove the cottony center inside the strawberry with the tip of a sharp knife. Insert the tip of the knife into the strawberry, make a circle around the underside of the stem, then pull out the cap. The cottony center should pull out with the cap. Strawberries, along with their berry friends blueberries, raspberries, boysenberries, and blackberries, are an excellent source of fiber (one of the highest in fruit land) and vitamin C.

Pantry List

sugar
1 red onion
tomato juice
2 cans low-fat, low-sodium chicken
   broth
hot pepper sauce
cayenne pepper
red wine vinegar
garlic
olive oil
chili powder
cumin
1 can black beans
1 can pinto beans

Market List

6 oz fresh shrimp
1 cucumber
3 red bell peppers
1 green bell pepper
1 bunch green onions
4 tomatoes
thyme
3 jalapeno peppers
cilantro
lemon juice
1 yellow squash
1 zucchini
flour tortillas
low-fat Jack or cheddar cheese
8 tomatillos
parsley
lime juice
1 1/2 pints fresh strawberries

STEP-BY-STEP COUNTDOWN

1 Prepare the gazpacho, but do not place the shrimp on top. You may prepare the gazpacho the night before.
2 Prepare the salsa and refrigerate. You may prepare the salsa the night before.
3 Prepare the bean salad.
4 Prepare step 1 of the burrito recipe.
5 When the gazpacho, salsa, and bean salad have chilled thoroughly, proceed with the rest of the burrito recipe.
6 Serve the gazpacho with the shrimp on top.
7 Serve the burritos, bean salad, and salsa.
8 Have everyone join in to prepare the Cool Strawberry Agua.

Shrimp Gazpacho

6 Servings

Serving Size:
1 cup

Exchanges

1 Starch
(or 3 Vegetable)
1 Very Lean Meat

Ingredients

1 medium cucumber, peeled, seeded, and diced
1 each red and green bell pepper, seeded and diced
1/2 cup minced red onion
1/4 cup minced green onions
2 large tomatoes, diced
2 cups low-sodium tomato juice
2 cups low-fat, low-sodium chicken broth
2 tsp minced thyme
1 small jalapeno pepper, minced
3 Tbsp fresh lime juice
6 oz medium shrimp, cooked and coarsely chopped
Hot pepper sauce to taste
Sprigs of cilantro

Preparation—20 minutes

1 Combine all the ingredients except the shrimp, hot pepper sauce, and cilantro sprigs.
2 Puree one half of the mixture in batches in a blender. Add this mixture to the remaining chopped vegetables.
3 Refrigerate the soup for 3–4 hours. Add hot pepper sauce to taste.
4 For each serving, ladle the soup into bowls and add 1 oz of shrimp on top. Garnish with cilantro sprigs.

Calories	93	
Calories from Fat	14	
Total Fat	2	g
Saturated Fat	0	g
Cholesterol	55	mg
Sodium	117	mg
Carbohydrate	14	g
Dietary Fiber	3	g
Sugars	9	g
Protein	9	g

Black and Pinto Bean Salad

6 Servings

Serving Size:
1/2 cup

Exchanges

1 Starch

Ingredients

1 cup black beans, drained and rinsed
1 cup pinto beans, drained and rinsed
1 cup diced red bell pepper
1/2 cup minced green onions
1/4 tsp cayenne pepper
2 Tbsp red wine vinegar
1 Tbsp fresh lemon juice
2 Tbsp minced cilantro

Preparation—10 minutes

Combine all ingredients. Refrigerate for 1 hour before serving.

Calories	85	
Calories from Fat	3	
Total Fat	0	g
Saturated Fat	0	g
Cholesterol	0	mg
Sodium	108	mg
Carbohydrate	16	g
Dietary Fiber	5	g
Sugars	2	g
Protein	5	g

 WHY DON'T YOU . . .

Retreat to a small room after dinner. Small rooms encourage coziness and warmth.

Roasted Vegetable Burritos

6 Servings

Serving Size:
1 burrito

Exchanges

1 1/2 Starch
1 Vegetable
1 1/2 Monounsatur-
ated Fat

Ingredients

2 cloves garlic, minced
1 medium red bell pepper, seeded
   and thinly sliced
1/2 cup julienned yellow squash
1/2 cup julienned zucchini
1/2 cup chopped red onion
1/2 cup low-fat, low-sodium
   chicken broth
2 Tbsp olive oil
1 Tbsp lime juice
2 tsp chili powder
2 tsp cumin
2 Tbsp minced cilantro
Fresh ground pepper
Dash salt (optional)
6 flour tortillas, each 7–8 inches
   across
1/2 cup shredded low-fat Jack or
   cheddar cheese

Preparation—30 minutes

1 Preheat the oven to 350 degrees. In a casserole dish, add all the ingredients except the tortillas and the cheese. Roast, covered, until tender, about 35–40 minutes. Uncover and roast for 10 minutes.
2 Wrap the tortillas in aluminum foil and heat them in the oven for 5–8 minutes.
3 Add some of the vegetable filling to each burrito. Fold the ends over and roll up. Garnish each burrito with a sprinkling of cheese and serve.

Calories	203
Calories from Fat	78
Total Fat	9 g
Saturated Fat	2 g
Cholesterol	5 mg
Sodium	236 mg
Carbohydrate	25 g
Dietary Fiber	2 g
Sugars	3 g
Protein	7 g

Tomatillo Salsa

Ingredients

8 medium tomatillos, husks removed, skin washed, and coarsely chopped
2 tomatoes, coarsely chopped
1/2 cup minced onion
2 Tbsp minced green onions
3 Tbsp minced cilantro
2 jalapeno peppers, minced
3 Tbsp minced parsley
2 Tbsp red wine vinegar
2 Tbsp fresh lime juice

Preparation—20 minutes

Combine all ingredients. Refrigerate for 1–2 hours and serve with the burritos.

Calories	24
Calories from Fat	3
Total Fat	0 g
Saturated Fat	0 g
Cholesterol	0 mg
Sodium	5 mg
Carbohydrate	5 g
Dietary Fiber	1 g
Sugars	3 g
Protein	1 g

❖ ❖ ❖ ❖ ❖ ❖

➤ WHY DON'T YOU . . .

Entertain "down-home" style. Prepare the foods you and your family love most; then invite your friends over, use fancier plates, and place a simple arrangement in the center of table. Your guests will appreciate your sharing a bit of yourself with them.

Cool Strawberry Agua

4 Servings

Serving Size:
I cup

Exchanges

I Carbohydrate

Ingredients

2 1/4 cups strawberries, rinsed
2 Tbsp sugar
2 Tbsp fresh lime juice
2 1/2 cups water
Additional fresh strawberries, sliced
    almost through

Preparation—2 minutes

1 Puree the 2 1/4 cups strawberries in a blender. Add the sugar and lime juice and blend.
2 In a pitcher, add the puree to the water. Serve in glasses with a sliced strawberry placed on the rim of each glass.

Calories	51
Calories from Fat	3
Total Fat	0 g
Saturated Fat	0 g
Cholesterol	0 mg
Sodium	3 mg
Carbohydrate	13 g
Dietary Fiber	2 g
Sugars	10 g
Protein	I g

❖ ❖ ❖ ❖ ❖ ❖
VINEGARS

Balsamic Vinegar

Balsamic vinegar is made from Trebbiano grapes. It gets its dark color from aging in wooden barrels over a number of years. The more aged the vinegar, the more expensive it is. Good balsamic vinegar is very potent and has a smooth taste. Balsamic vinegar is great with legume dishes, chicken, and pasta. Start with small drizzles, and add more to taste.

Southwestern Pasta

Smoky Tomato and Chili Soup
Southwestern Fusilli
Tomato and Tomatillo Salad
Zucchini and Peppers
Baked Pineapple

Pan-roasting tomatoes imparts a lovely, smoky flavor. Be sure to use a nonstick skillet, so you can catch all the tasty tomato juices. I find it helpful to use tweezers to peel off the tomato skin. Do this to avoid tomato skins floating on the surface of your soup! Look for a canned broth that is low in fat and sodium. Ideally, the broth should contain less than 140 mg of sodium per serving. You can also try some of the vegetable broths on the market.

The bean and corn mixture topping the Southwestern Fusilli is almost a meal in itself. You can prepare this portion of the recipe and serve it cold over greens for a light spring or summer salad. Fusilli pasta are corkscrew shaped, and their grooves help trap the chunky topping. There is a difference between chili powder and chili peppers. Chili pepper is composed of chili pods that have been dried, then powdered. Chili powder is a ground mixture of chili peppers and other spices, usually cumin, garlic, and oregano. For really hot taste, use ground chili peppers; to regulate the heat, use mild chili powders.

The combination of tart tomatillos and sweet tomatoes is visually as well as gastronomically appealing. If tomatillos are not available, use all tomatoes. This dressing can be used on green salads as well. Use any combination of greens—I like Boston and bibb lettuces.

Zucchini should only be cooked to the tender-crisp stage. Be careful—it overcooks very quickly! Use yellow squash or chayote in this recipe (for a discussion of chayote squash, see page 3). When you use strong spices and herbs such as chili powder and oregano, the need for fat is minimized. I only need a teaspoon of oil to help carry the taste of the chili powder and oregano. The trick to low-fat, high-flavor foods is to use the freshest produce, meats, spices, and herbs in the right proportions. You'll find yourself less and less dependent on fats to add flavor to your cooking.

The pineapple is native to Central and South America. Hawaii now produces most of the world's supply. Fresh pineapples are found year-round, but are best between March and July. Pick only ripe ones that yield to light pressure. Look for leaves that stand upright with no yellowing or browning. Pineapple is delicious grilled or baked—a great change from serving it cold. Pineapples are a good source of vitamin C. Feel free to omit the rum from this recipe if you prefer.

Pantry List

garlic
1 yellow onion
1 red onion
4 large tomatoes
olive oil
2 cans low-fat, low-sodium
     chicken broth
1 can evaporated skim milk
chili powder
cumin
1 can stewed tomatoes
1 can black beans
1 box fusilli pasta
1/2 lb tomatillos
dried oregano
brown sugar
dark rum
cinnamon
1 ancho chili pepper

Market List

1 bunch cilantro
1 jalapeno pepper
1 small package yellow corn or
     1 ear fresh corn
fresh oregano
1 serrano pepper
parsley
fresh lime juice
fresh lemon juice
6 cups mixed greens of choice
1 medium zucchini
1 large red pepper
1 large pineapple

STEP-BY-STEP COUNTDOWN

1 Prepare the pineapple. Be sure to turn off the heat when you're finished.
2 Prepare the soup, but do not add the milk. Turn the heat off after simmering the tomatoes in the soup.
3 Cook the fusilli pasta.
4 While the pasta cooks, prepare the tomato and tomatillo salad, but do not mix in the dressing. Drain the fusilli.
5 Prepare the zucchini and peppers, but do not cook them.
6 Finish preparing the fusilli.
7 Finish preparing the zucchini and peppers.
8 Add the milk to the soup. Simmer for 5 minutes and serve.
9 Toss the tomatillos and tomatoes with the dressing and serve.
10 Serve the pasta with the zucchini and peppers.
11 Serve the pineapple.

Smoky Tomato and Chili Soup

6 Servings

Serving Size:
1 cup

Exchanges

1 Starch
1/2 Monounsaturated Fat

Ingredients

1 ancho chili pepper
3 cloves garlic
1 medium onion, quartered
3 large tomatoes
1/4 cup lime juice
1 Tbsp olive oil
1/4 cup cilantro
3 cups low-fat, low-sodium chicken broth
1 cup evaporated skim milk
Fresh ground pepper
Dash salt (optional)

Preparation—10 minutes

1 Soak the ancho chili pepper in warm water for 15 minutes.
2 While the pepper is soaking, cook the garlic, onion, and tomatoes in a dry nonstick skillet over high heat. With tongs, char the tomatoes on all sides, about 10 minutes. Remove from the pan and let cool. Cut each tomato in half, peel, and discard the seeds.
3 Drain the ancho chili pepper and coarsely chop it. Combine the tomatoes, garlic, and onions in a blender. Add the chili, lime juice, oil, and cilantro. Process for 30 seconds.
4 Heat the broth in a stockpot. Add the tomato mixture and simmer for 5 minutes. Add the milk and simmer for 5 minutes. Add the pepper and salt and serve.

Calories	104
Calories from Fat	35
Total Fat	4 g
Saturated Fat	1 g
Cholesterol	2 mg
Sodium	113 mg
Carbohydrate	15 g
Dietary Fiber	2 g
Sugars	9 g
Protein	6 g

Southwestern Fusilli

6 Servings

Serving Size:
1 cup
1/2 cup beans

Exchanges

3 1/2 Starch
1 Vegetable

Ingredients

2 tsp olive oil
2 garlic cloves, minced
1/4 cup minced onion
2 tsp minced jalapeno pepper
1/2 tsp chili powder
2 tsp cumin
1 cup stewed tomatoes, drained
1/2 cup low-fat, low-sodium
      chicken broth
1/2 cup corn kernels
1 1/2 cups black beans, drained
      and rinsed
1 Tbsp fresh minced oregano
Fresh ground pepper
Dash salt (optional)
6 cups hot cooked fusilli

Preparation—15 minutes

1 Heat the oil in a skillet over medium-high heat. Add the garlic and onion and saute for 4 minutes. Add the jalapeno peppers, chili powder, and cumin and saute for 3 minutes.
2 Add the stewed tomatoes and broth and bring to boil. Lower the heat and add the corn and black beans. Simmer for 5 minutes. Add the oregano, salt, and pepper.
3 Toss the bean and corn mixture with the pasta and serve.

Calories	301
Calories from Fat	29
Total Fat	3 g
Saturated Fat	0 g
Cholesterol	0 mg
Sodium	199 mg
Carbohydrate	61 g
Dietary Fiber	7 g
Sugars	5 g
Protein	12 g

Tomato and Tomatillo Salad

6 Servings

Serving Size:
1/2 cup

Exchanges

1 Vegetable
1 Monounsaturated
    Fat

Ingredients

1/4 cup diced red onion
2 tsp minced serrano pepper
1 cup diced tomatillos
1 1/2 cups diced tomatoes
2 Tbsp minced cilantro
2 tsp minced parsley
3 Tbsp fresh lime juice
2 tsp fresh lemon juice
1 1/2 Tbsp olive oil
1 tsp cumin
2 tsp minced garlic
Fresh ground pepper
Dash salt (optional)
6 cups mixed greens

Preparation—10 minutes

1 Combine the onion, pepper, tomatillos, tomatoes, cilantro, and parsley in a large salad bowl.
2 In a blender, combine the lime juice, lemon juice, oil, cumin, garlic, pepper, and salt.
3 Toss the salad with the dressing and mound the salad over mixed greens on individual plates.

Calories	61
Calories from Fat	35
Total Fat	4 g
Saturated Fat	1 g
Cholesterol	0 mg
Sodium	13 mg
Carbohydrate	7 g
Dietary Fiber	2 g
Sugars	4 g
Protein	1 g

Zucchini and Peppers

6 Servings

Serving Size:
1/2 cup

Exchanges

1 Vegetable

Ingredients

1 1/2 cups zucchini slices
1 1/2 cups diced red pepper
1/2 cup diced onion
2 cloves garlic, minced
1 Tbsp lemon juice
1 tsp olive oil
1 tsp chili powder
1/4 tsp oregano
Fresh ground pepper
Dash salt (optional)

Preparation—15 minutes

1   Steam together the zucchini, red pepper, onion, and garlic on top of boiling water, covered, for about 4 minutes. Drain.
2   Combine the lemon juice, oil, chili powder, oregano, pepper, and salt. Sprinkle over the cooked vegetables and serve.

Calories	31
Calories from Fat	8
Total Fat	1 g
Saturated Fat	0 g
Cholesterol	0 mg
Sodium	7 mg
Carbohydrate	6 g
Dietary Fiber	1 g
Sugars	3 g
Protein	1 g

❧ WHY DON'T YOU . . .

Invite people you really like to dinner. Think about who mixes well together for a more successful gathering.

Baked Pineapple

6 Servings

Serving Size:
1/2 cup

Exchanges

1 Fruit

Ingredients

1　large ripe pineapple
2　tsp brown sugar
2　Tbsp dark rum
2　Tbsp lime juice
1/2　tsp cinnamon

Preparation—20 minutes

1　Cut the pineapple in half. With a sharp knife, cut around the rim of the pineapple and remove the core. Cut the fruit into bite-sized pieces. Toss the cut fruit with the sugar, rum, lime juice, and cinnamon.

2　Pile the fruit into the two pineapple shells and wrap the shells in aluminum foil. Bake at 350 degrees for 25 minutes.

Calories	62
Calories from Fat	4
Total Fat	0 g
Saturated Fat	0 g
Cholesterol	0 mg
Sodium	2 mg
Carbohydrate	15 g
Dietary Fiber	1 g
Sugars	13 g
Protein	0 g

Pastabilities

❖ ❖ ❖ ❖

Penne Portofino 45

Sun-Dried Tomato Spread with Grissini
Green Leaf Salad with Blue Cheese Dressing
Penne Portofino
Braised Fennel
Peaches and Macaroons

Classic Capellini 53

Mini Crab Cakes with Roasted Red
   Pepper Sauce
Fresh Chopped Salad
Capellini with Hot Garlic Sauce
Onion-Topped Broccoli
Peach Melba Sauce with Frozen Yogurt

Herbed Bow Ties 61

Tuna Crostini
Cucumber and Mint Salad
Bow Tie Pasta with Roasted Peppers and Basil
Gratin of Zucchini
Granita

Porcini Tagliatelle 69

Asparagus in Balsamic Vinegar
Fresh Clam Soup
Porcini Tagliatelle
Spinach with Pine Nuts
Banana Strawberry Cream

Lemon Fettucine 77

Cream of Wild Mushroom Soup
Red Romaine Salad with Tomato-
   Honey Dressing
Lemon Fettucine with Salmon and Baby Peas
Sauted Baby Vegetables
Peach Mousse

Chicken Peanut Pasta 85

Sugar Snap Pea and Carrot Salad
Spicy Chicken Peanut Pasta
Zucchini and Squash Noodles
Sauted Watercress
Carambolas and Raspberries

❖ ❖ ❖

Penne Portofino

Sun-Dried Tomato Spread with Grissini
Green Leaf Salad with Bleu Cheese Dressing
Penne Portofino
Braised Fennel
Peaches and Macaroons

MENU TALK

I have always loved using sun-dried tomatoes with their rich, earthy taste. Here, tomatoes combine with other flavorful ingredients in a creamy, low-fat spread. I buy sun-dried tomatoes in cellophane bags and rehydrate them in water. *Grissini* is Italian for bread stick, but not the fat bread sticks Americans are used to. Grissini are thin, long bread sticks that are very crisp. Many grocery stores carry grissini, or choose another low-fat cracker for this appetizer.

Bleu cheese contains molds that form blue veins. It's very strong and adds great flavor (and very little fat) to salad dressings. Use gorgonzola, Roquefort, or stilton cheese. Buttermilk is made by adding enzymes to skim or low-fat milk, which give buttermilk its characteristic tang. Use small-curd cottage cheese for dressings and sauces—it seems to contain less water; hence, a creamier sauce or dressing is created. Creamy cottage cheese has 4–8% milk fat, low-fat cottage cheese has 1–2% milk fat, and nonfat cottage cheese has no fat. Using low-fat cottage cheese in combination with more flavorful ingredients will work fine. Store cottage cheese in the coldest part of the refrigerator.

Arugula is a lively green popular among Italians and is still making itself known to American palates. Arugula has a peppery flavor and can be cooked or eaten raw. This green has a very dirty leaf and should be washed thoroughly. Arugula is sold in small bunches and is a rich source of iron. If you find the taste of arugula too strong, you can substitute spinach for this recipe. Pasta means "paste" in Italian, referring to the paste of semolina flour and water. When choosing pasta for Italian meals, use only imported pasta. Imported pasta does not absorb too much water, unlike the American counterpart, so the pasta is slightly chewier. Quill-shaped penne pasta is ideal to catch chunky sauces and bits of vegetables.

Fennel, also known as finocchio in Italian, is cultivated in Europe and the United States. Fennel looks like a fat, short stalk of celery. The base and stems can be eaten raw in a salad or cooked. The flavor of cooked fennel is mild and sweet. Like dill, the feathery greenery on the stems can be snipped into foods. Refrigerate fennel in a sealed bag for up to five days. Fennel is a good source of vitamin A.

Fruit was a staple dessert among the ancient Romans. Peaches came from Persia, dates from Africa, and apricots from Armenia. Look for peaches that are very fragrant and that give just a little when you apply pressure. To ripen peaches, place them in a paper bag, pierce the bag several times, and leave the bag at room temperature for several days. Refrigerate the ripe peaches and use within five days. Peaches are available from May to October, although peaches are at their peak during the summer months. Peaches are a good source of vitamins A and C.

Pantry List

anchovy paste
sun-dried tomatoes
garlic
Grissini bread sticks
1 red onion
1 yellow onion
dry white wine
1 can low-fat, low-sodium
    chicken broth
1 box penne pasta
sugar
olive oil
macaroons
lite mayonnaise

Market List

1 1/2 lb shrimp
nonfat cream cheese
Parmesan cheese
2 heads green leaf lettuce
1 pint cherry tomatoes
1/4 lb white mushrooms
low-fat yogurt
low-fat cottage cheese
low-fat buttermilk
blue cheese
mint sprigs
2 oz Canadian bacon
1 each small red and yellow
    bell peppers
1/2 lb arugula
basil
Italian parsley
1 large fennel bulb

STEP-BY-STEP COUNTDOWN

1 Prepare the tomato spread and refrigerate.
2 Prepare and bake the dessert. Remove the
   dessert from the oven and cover it with foil.
3 Prepare the salad and dressing, but do not mix
   them together.
4 Prepare the fennel.
5 Boil the pasta. While the pasta cooks, finish
   preparing the rest of this dish.
6 Serve the tomato spread.
7 Toss the salad with the dressing and serve.
8 Serve the pasta and fennel.
9 Serve the dessert.

3 peaches
low-calorie margarine
1 carton egg substitute

47

Sun-Dried Tomato Spread with Grissini

6 Servings

Serving Size:
1/2 oz bread
1 Tbsp spread

Exchanges

1/2 Starch

Ingredients

1/2 cup nonfat cream cheese
2 Tbsp Parmesan cheese
1 Tbsp anchovy paste (optional)
1/4 cup lite mayonnaise
6 sun-dried tomatoes, rehydrated,
   finely minced
2 cloves garlic, finely minced
Grissini bread sticks (2 per person)

Preparation—15 minutes

Mix all ingredients except the bread sticks in a food processor until smooth, but thick. Place the spread in a bowl or crock and serve with Grissini bread sticks.

Calories	59
Calories from Fat	14
Total Fat	2 g
Saturated Fat	0 g
Cholesterol	2 mg
Sodium	257 mg
Carbohydrate	9 g
Dietary Fiber	1 g
Sugars	1 g
Protein	2 g

❖ ❖ ❖ ❖ ❖

OILS

Sesame Seed Oil

Sesame seed oil, extracted from sesame seeds, comes in light and dark varieties. Light sesame seed oil is used in salad dressings and sauteing. Dark sesame seed oil is much heavier; it's typically added to foods at the end of the cooking time to impart a nutty flavor. Add dark sesame seed oil to stir-frys or cooked vegetables.

Green Leaf Salad with Bleu Cheese Dressing

6 Servings

Serving Size:
1 cup lettuce
1/2 cup vegetables
1 Tbsp dressing

Exchanges

1 Vegetable
1/2 Saturated Fat

Ingredients

6 cups torn green leaf lettuce
1 pint cherry tomatoes, halved
1 small red onion, sliced into thin rings
1/2 cup white mushrooms, well cleaned, thinly sliced
1/4 cup low-fat yogurt
1/4 cup low-fat cottage cheese
4 Tbsp low-fat buttermilk
2 Tbsp bleu cheese
Fresh ground pepper
Mint sprigs

Preparation—10 minutes

1 Combine the lettuce, tomatoes, onion, and mushrooms in a large bowl. Mound the mixture on individual plates.
2 In a medium bowl, combine the yogurt, cottage cheese, buttermilk, and blue cheese and mix by hand until smooth. Add the pepper. Drizzle the dressing over each salad. Garnish with mint and serve.

Calories	55
Calories from Fat	11
Total Fat	1 g
Saturated Fat	1 g
Cholesterol	3 mg
Sodium	96 mg
Carbohydrate	8 g
Dietary Fiber	2 g
Sugars	5 g
Protein	4 g

Penne Portofino

6 Servings

Serving Size:
1 cup pasta
1/2 cup vegetables
3 oz shrimp

Exchanges

3 Starch
2 Very Lean Meat

Ingredients

2 oz Canadian bacon, diced
2 cloves garlic, minced
1/2 cup minced onion
1/4 cup dry white wine
1 each red and yellow bell peppers, julienned
1 1/2 cups arugula leaves, washed and torn
1 1/2 lb medium shrimp, peeled and deveined
1/2 cup low-fat, low-sodium chicken broth
2 tsp minced basil
1 Tbsp minced Italian parsley
Fresh ground pepper
Dash salt (optional)
6 cups cooked penne pasta

Preparation—30 minutes

1 Saute the bacon in a skillet over medium-high heat. Remove the bacon from the skillet, leaving the drippings in the pan.
2 Add the garlic, onions, and wine to the skillet and saute for 4 minutes. Add the peppers and saute for 6–7 minutes.
3 Add the arugula, shrimp, and broth and cover. Cook until the arugula wilts and the shrimp turns pink, about 3–4 minutes. Add the basil, bacon, parsley, pepper, and salt.
4 Toss the pasta with the sauce and serve.

Calories	324
Calories from Fat	25
Total Fat	3 g
Saturated Fat	1 g
Cholesterol	165 mg
Sodium	312 mg
Carbohydrate	46 g
Dietary Fiber	3 g
Sugars	4 g
Protein	27 g

Braised Fennel

Ingredients

1 tsp olive oil
1 large fennel bulb, julienned
1 cup low-fat, low-sodium
   chicken broth
2 Tbsp sugar

Preparation—10 minutes

1 Heat the oil in a skillet over medium heat. Add the fennel and saute for 5 minutes. Add the broth, bring to a boil, cover, and reduce the heat to medium low. Braise until the fennel is soft, about 10 minutes.

2 Remove the cover and bring the fennel to a boil. Cook over medium-high heat until the liquid is almost absorbed.

3 Add the sugar and continue to cook and stir until the fennel is caramelized. Serve.

Calories	39
Calories from Fat	11
Total Fat	1 g
Saturated Fat	0 g
Cholesterol	0 mg
Sodium	38 mg
Carbohydrate	7 g
Dietary Fiber	2 g
Sugars	5 g
Protein	1 g

 WHY DON'T YOU . . .

Consider hiring help to clean the house before a dinner party when you just can't do it yourself. There is nothing wrong with occasionally spending money for help, especially if it frees you to cook and feel more relaxed.

Peaches and Macaroons

6 Servings

Serving Size:
1/2 peach

Exchanges

1 1/2 Carbohydrate
1 Saturated Fat

Ingredients

3 large peaches
3 macaroons, crushed in a blender
2 Tbsp sugar
3 Tbsp low-calorie margarine
2 Tbsp egg substitute
1/2 cup dry white wine

Preparation—15 minutes

1 Preheat the oven to 375 degrees. Blanch the peaches in boiling water for 1–2 minutes. Drain and splash with cold water. Peel the peaches, cut in half, and remove the pits.

2 Scoop out the peach meat, leaving a shell. There should be enough meat left in the peach for the shell to hold its shape. Dice the peach meat and combine with the crushed macaroons, sugar, margarine, and egg substitute. Fill each peach shell with 1/6 of the mixture.

3 Pour the wine into a baking dish. Set the peaches, cut side up, in the baking dish. Bake until the peaches are soft, about 20 minutes.

Calories	129
Calories from Fat	44
Total Fat	5 g
Saturated Fat	2 g
Cholesterol	0 mg
Sodium	70 mg
Carbohydrate	20 g
Dietary Fiber	2 g
Sugars	16 g
Protein	1 g

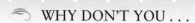

❖ ❖ ❖ ❖ ❖ ❖ ❖

WHY DON'T YOU . . .

Feed your children and baby-sitter before your guests arrive.

Classic Capellini

Mini Crab Cakes with Roasted Red Pepper Sauce
Fresh Chopped Salad
Capellini with Hot Garlic Sauce
Onion-Topped Broccoli
Peach Melba Sauce with Frozen Yogurt

MENU TALK

Lump crabmeat is whole pieces of white crabmeat, the most tasty of all crabmeat. Saltwater crabs are the most plentiful source of meat. Dungeness crab comes from the Pacific coast, snow crab from the north Pacific, and stone crab from Florida. Crabmeat is expensive, so use it on special occasions. Canned crabmeat is a poor substitute for the real thing.

This recipe can be used with flaked salmon (canned salmon, unlike canned crab, works well) or tuna instead of crab. You can also try tiny or small chopped shrimp. Make bigger crab cakes to serve the family as a main course. The roasted red pepper sauce can be tossed into pasta or used as a sauce to top grilled chicken. Fines herbs is a blend of chervil, parsley, chives, and tarragon. It comes dried and mixed, and is used for sauces, eggs, salads, and sauted vegetables.

One of the best chopped salads I ever had was at the Beverly Hills Hotel in California. Almost any vegetable can be used in a great chopped salad, as long as it is chopped fine enough to fit on a fork. Choose a variety of greens to act as a bed for the salad. Add color by choosing red cabbage or radicchio.

Capellini are thin pasta, thicker than angel hair, but thinner than spaghetti. The thinner the pasta, the less the cooking time, which should be welcome! Very thin pasta should not be drowned out with heavy sauces. This sauce is more like a light topping, but with flavors bold enough to perk up the pasta. Use less crushed red pepper or omit it entirely for a milder taste. The garlic used here should be fresh. Do not substitute garlic powder, granules, or salt.

When purchasing onions, make sure they are heavy for their size and feel dry. Any signs of moistness or bruising should be avoided. Onions should be stored in a cool, dry place. When chopping, avoid moving the knife in half circles to chop. This will release the onion fumes and your tears will flow! To cut an onion properly, cut it in half so it lies flat. Remove the skin. Make several horizontal cuts into the onion, but do not cut all the way through (leave the root end on). Then make several vertical slices. Then chop downward to yield uniform pieces of onion, with no need to chop further. If the onion smells very strong, freeze it for 20 minutes before chopping. This should help decrease the fumes.

Dame Nellie Melba was the recipient of this dessert, created for her by the famous Chef Escoffier. My variation is lower in fat but just as delicious. Instead of halved peaches topped with ice cream and melba sauce, I chop peaches, add them to raspberry sauce, and serve the sauce over nonfat, sugar-free frozen yogurt. Serve the sauce warm or cold. You can make it ahead of time and keep it in the refrigerator for 1–2 days.

Pantry List

1 red onion
hot pepper sauce
bread crumbs
dry white wine
garlic
4 roasted red bell peppers
   (use from the jar)
1 box capellini pasta
Dijon mustard
sherry vinegar
olive oil
walnut oil
fines herbs
cornstarch or arrowroot powder
1 small yellow onion
dried basil
dried oregano
crushed red pepper
evaporated skim milk

Market List

12 oz lump crabmeat
1 small red bell pepper
1 small yellow bell pepper
chives
dill
1 egg
1 peach
orange juice
lemon juice
1/2 pint fresh raspberries
nonfat, sugar-free frozen yogurt
1 1/2 lb fresh broccoli
low-calorie margarine

Parmesan cheese
parsley
1 small carrot
1/4 lb fresh green beans
1 small zucchini
1 small avocado
1 small tomato
6 cups mixed greens of choice

STEP-BY-STEP COUNTDOWN

1 Prepare the dessert and let the sauce refrigerate.
2 Prepare, but do not bake, the crab cakes. Place formed crab cakes on the cookie sheet (or on a plate; then transfer later to a cookie sheet) and refrigerate them. Prepare the sauce, which can remain in a saucepan on the stove with the heat off.
3 Prepare the salad, but do not toss the salad with the dressing.
4 Boil the water for the capellini. While the pasta is boiling, assemble the remaining ingredients.
5 Prepare the ingredients for the broccoli, but do not cook the broccoli.
6 Finish preparing the capellini and turn off the heat.
7 Prepare the broccoli and turn off the heat.
8 Broil the crab cakes, reheat the sauce, and serve.
9 Toss the salad with the dressing and serve.
10 Gently reheat the pasta and broccoli if necessary and serve.
11 Scoop yogurt into dessert dishes and top with sauce. You may reheat the sauce if desired.

Mini Crab Cakes with Roasted Red Pepper Sauce*

6 Servings

Serving Size:
1/6 recipe

Exchanges

1/2 Starch
2 Very Lean Meat

Ingredients

1 tsp olive oil
3 Tbsp each minced red and
       yellow pepper
1/4 cup minced red onion
1 Tbsp minced fresh chives
2 tsp minced dill
2 tsp hot pepper sauce
12 oz fresh lump crabmeat,
       cartilage removed
1 egg, beaten
1/2 cup fresh bread crumbs
1/4 cup dry white wine
1/4 cup minced red onion
4 roasted red bell peppers
2 cloves garlic, minced
2–3 Tbsp evaporated skim milk
2 tsp fines herbs
Fresh ground pepper

Preparation—25 minutes

1 Heat the oil in a skillet over medium heat. Add the peppers and onion and saute for 5 minutes. Remove from the heat. Add the chives, dill, and hot pepper sauce.
2 Add the crabmeat and mix well. Add the egg and bread crumbs. Shape into small patties and place on a plate in the refrigerator while you prepare the sauce.
3 Heat the wine in a skillet over medium-high heat. Add the onion and saute for 5 minutes. Add the roasted peppers and saute for 5 minutes. Add the garlic and saute for 2 minutes.
4 Remove the mixture from the skillet and pour into a blender. Add the evaporated skim milk, fines herbs, and pepper and puree. Keep the mixture warm on a low flame in a saucepan.
5 Place the crab cakes on a nonstick cookie sheet and broil, turning once, for a total of 10 minutes. Serve the crab cakes on a platter with a dish of the warm sauce in the center.

Calories	114
Calories from Fat	21
Total Fat	2 g
Saturated Fat	0 g
Cholesterol	60 mg
Sodium	632 mg
Carbohydrate	8 g
Dietary Fiber	1 g
Sugars	5 g
Protein	14 g

* This dish is high in sodium.

Fresh Chopped Salad

6 Servings

Serving Size:
1 cup greens
1/2 cup chopped
    vegetables

Exchanges

1 Vegetable
1 Monounsaturated
    Fat

Ingredients

1/2 cup diced carrots
1/2 cup diced green beans
1/2 cup diced red onion
1/2 cup diced zucchini
1/2 cup diced avocado
1/2 cup diced tomato
2 Tbsp Dijon mustard
1/4 cup sherry vinegar
1 Tbsp olive oil
1 tsp walnut oil
Fresh ground pepper
Dash salt (optional)
6 cups mixed greens (try to include
    radicchio, romaine, and green
    leaf lettuce)

Preparation—20 minutes

1 In a pot of boiling water, blanch the carrots and green beans for 1 minute and drain. Plunge into ice water and drain again. Toss the carrots and green beans with the onion, zucchini, avocado, and tomato.
2 Whisk together the mustard, vinegar, olive and walnut oils, pepper, and salt. Drizzle a little of this mixture on the chopped vegetables.
3 Place the salad greens on individual plates. Drizzle the remaining dressing on the greens. Top the greens with the chopped vegetables.

Calories	79
Calories from Fat	49
Total Fat	5 g
Saturated Fat	1 g
Cholesterol	0 mg
Sodium	76 mg
Carbohydrate	7 g
Dietary Fiber	3 g
Sugars	4 g
Protein	2 g

Capellini with Hot Garlic Sauce

6 Servings

Serving Size:
1 cup

Exchanges

2 1/2 Starch
1/2 Monounsat-
urated Fat

Ingredients

1   Tbsp olive oil
4   cloves garlic, minced
1/2   cup minced onion
1/2   each red and yellow bell
      peppers, thinly sliced
3   tsp crushed red pepper
1   cup dry white wine
Fresh ground pepper
Dash salt (optional)
6   cups hot cooked capellini
1/4   cup Parmesan cheese
1/4   cup minced Italian parsley

Preparation—25 minutes

1   Heat the oil in a skillet over medium-high heat. Add the garlic and onion and saute for 5 minutes. Add the peppers and saute for 5 minutes.
2   Add the crushed red pepper and wine and bring to a boil. Simmer for 5–7 minutes. Season with pepper and salt and toss with the hot capellini. Garnish with Parmesan cheese and parsley.

Calories	219
Calories from Fat	28
Total Fat	3 g
Saturated Fat	0 g
Cholesterol	0 mg
Sodium	5 mg
Carbohydrate	38 g
Dietary Fiber	2 g
Sugars	4 g
Protein	6 g

Onion-Topped Broccoli

6 Servings

Serving Size:
1/2 cup

Exchanges

1 Vegetable

Ingredients

3 cups broccoli florets
2 Tbsp low-calorie margarine
1/4 cup diced onion
1 tsp dried basil
1/2 tsp dried oregano
Fresh ground pepper
Dash salt (optional)

Preparation—5 minutes

1 Blanch the broccoli in boiling water and drain.
2 Melt the margarine in a skillet over medium-high heat. Add the onion and saute for 4 minutes. Add the basil, oregano, pepper, and salt.
3 Sprinkle the mixture over the broccoli and serve.

Calories	30
Calories from Fat	18
Total Fat	2 g
Saturated Fat	0 g
Cholesterol	0 mg
Sodium	40 mg
Carbohydrate	3 g
Dietary Fiber	1 g
Sugars	1 g
Protein	1 g

☞ WHY DON'T YOU . . .

Have a brunch party instead of a dinner party. Ask the guests to arrive around noon. Plan on serving no later than 1 p.m.—you don't want guests to be starving.

Peach Melba Sauce with Frozen Yogurt

6 Servings

Serving Size:
1/2 cup

Exchanges

2 Carbohydrate

Ingredients

1 medium peach, peeled, pitted,
  and diced
1/3 cup fresh orange juice
1 Tbsp sugar
2 Tbsp lemon juice
1 cup fresh raspberries
1 Tbsp cornstarch or arrowroot
  powder
1/4 cup water
3 cups any flavor nonfat, sugar-free
  frozen yogurt

Preparation—20 minutes

1 Combine the peach and orange juice in a
saucepan. Cook over medium-low heat for
10 minutes. Add the sugar and lemon juice and
cook for 5 minutes. Add the raspberries and
cook for 5 minutes.
2 Dissolve the cornstarch or arrowroot powder in
the water and add to the sauce. Cook over medium-
low heat until thickened.
3 Refrigerate the sauce for 1 hour. Serve over
yogurt. If desired, you can serve the sauce hot over
the yogurt, but you will have to serve dessert
immediately.

Calories	130
Calories from Fat	1
Total Fat	0 g
Saturated Fat	0 g
Cholesterol	0 mg
Sodium	66 mg
Carbohydrate	28 g
Dietary Fiber	2 g
Sugars	10 g
Protein	4 g

❖ ❖ ❖

Herbed Bow Ties

Tuna Crostini
Cucumber and Mint Salad
Bow Tie Pasta with Roasted Peppers and Basil
Gratin of Zucchini
Granita

MENU TALK

Using tuna in a dip is a welcome change from tuna sandwiches! This spread can be used as a sandwich filling; it's much more flavorful than plain old tuna with mayonnaise. You can use other fishes such as salmon, smoked or flaked trout, or tiny shrimp. Look for the nonfat variety of ricotta cheese that works very well when combined with other ingredients.

This cucumber and mint salad is light and very refreshing. Use an English cucumber (for a discussion of English cucumbers, see page 319) instead of regular cucumbers if you wish. This salad should not be made ahead of time. The cucumbers are too porous a vegetable, drinking in any liquid you add to them. You need this salad to be crispy.

The pasta sauce is also delicious on rice or couscous or tossed over cooked broccoli, asparagus, zucchini, carrots, or cauliflower. Bow tie pasta, or farfelle in Italian, can be found in most supermarkets. If farfelle is not available, use any other shaped pasta. You might want to prepare this dish using a number of different shapes of pasta for variety and eye appeal. This dish is delicious served cold as a salad. You may also add any leftover meat to it.

Au gratin dishes have been topped with cheese or bread crumbs and browned under a broiler. Au gratin casserole dishes are sold in specialty cooking shops, but any shallow casserole dish will do. Use yellow squash in place of zucchini if you like, or use a combination of both.

Ice or granita in Italian and granite in France is a term to describe a frozen mixture of sugar, water, and flavorings. Granitas are fun to make.

Experiment with other fruits and add flavorings such as almond, pineapple, coconut, or even chocolate extracts. Light and refreshing, when served in a fluted champagne glass they can turn the ending of any simple dinner into a grand finale.

Pantry List

1 7-oz can water-packed tuna
1 can evaporated skim milk
Dijon mustard
capers
1 jar black olives
crushed red pepper
1 small loaf Italian bread
balsamic vinegar
dry white wine
1 box bow tie pasta
garlic
1 red onion
olive oil
sugar

Market List

part-skim ricotta cheese
low-fat cream cheese
Italian parsley
3 cucumbers
1 green bell pepper
green onions
mint
lemon juice
2 red bell peppers
2 yellow bell peppers
2 tomatoes
basil
Parmesan cheese
1 large zucchini
part-skim mozzarella cheese
1 pint strawberries or raspberries

STEP-BY-STEP COUNTDOWN

1 Prepare the granita. This can be done one day or several days in advance. (Be sure you remove the granita from the freezer before serving and allow it to defrost enough at room temperature so it will easily scrape into dessert dishes.)
2 Prepare the first step of the bow tie pasta recipe.
3 Prepare the tuna crostini and bake.
4 Prepare the zucchini.
5 Boil the pasta.
6 Prepare the cucumber and mint salad, but do not add the dressing.
7 Finish preparing the pasta recipe.
8 Serve the tuna crostini.
9 Pour the dressing over the cucumbers and serve.
10 Serve the pasta and zucchini.
11 Serve the dessert.

Tuna Crostini

6 Servings

Serving Size:
1/2 oz bread
2 Tbsp spread

Exchanges

1 Starch
1 Very Lean Meat

Ingredients

1 7-oz can water-packed tuna,
    drained
1/2 cup part-skim ricotta cheese
1/2 cup low-fat cream cheese
1/4 cup evaporated skim milk
2 tsp Dijon mustard
2 tsp capers
2 Tbsp chopped black olives
2 Tbsp minced Italian parsley
1 tsp crushed red pepper
Fresh ground pepper
Dash salt (optional)
3 oz Italian bread, sliced

Preparation—20 minutes

1 Preheat the oven to 400 degrees. In a food processor, combine the tuna with the cheeses and milk. Add the mustard and process until smooth, but thick.
2 By hand, fold in the capers, olives, parsley, red pepper, ground pepper, and salt. Toast the bread slices in the oven for 2–3 minutes.
3 Serve the tuna in a crock placed in the middle of a platter with the toast arranged around the crock.

Calories	118
Calories from Fat	10
Total Fat	1 g
Saturated Fat	0 g
Cholesterol	18 mg
Sodium	405 mg
Carbohydrate	11 g
Dietary Fiber	0 g
Sugars	3 g
Protein	15 g

Cucumber and Mint Salad

6 Servings

Serving Size:
1 cup

Exchanges

1 Vegetable
1/2 Monounsatur-
ated Fat

Ingredients

6   cups sliced cucumbers
1   small green bell pepper, diced
3   green onions, sliced
1/4 cup minced mint
1/4 cup lemon juice
1   Tbsp olive oil
2   Tbsp balsamic vinegar
Fresh ground pepper
Dash salt (optional)

Preparation—15 minutes

1   Combine the cucumbers, peppers, onions, and mint in a salad bowl.
2   In a separate bowl, whisk together the remaining ingredients. Toss with the vegetables and serve.

Calories	45
Calories from Fat	22
Total Fat	2 g
Saturated Fat	0 g
Cholesterol	0 mg
Sodium	7 mg
Carbohydrate	6 g
Dietary Fiber	2 g
Sugars	4 g
Protein	1 g

⤳ WHY DON'T YOU . . .

Scout out antique stores for eclectic bowls, platters, and dishes made with colored glass. Who says all your tableware has to match? In fact, if tastefully done, your finds can be the subject of dinner conversation.

Bow Tie Pasta with Roasted Peppers and Basil

6 Servings

Serving Size:
1 cup

Exchanges

3 Starch
1 Vegetable

Ingredients

2 red bell peppers
2 yellow bell peppers
1 Tbsp olive oil
2 cloves garlic, minced
1/2 cup dry white wine
1/2 cup fresh basil leaves
Dash crushed red pepper
Fresh ground pepper
Dash salt (optional)
6 cups cooked bow tie pasta
Grated fresh Parmesan cheese

Preparation—20 minutes

1 Core, seed, and halve the peppers. Place the peppers skin side up on a broiler pan set 4 inches from the heat source and broil until blackened. Remove the peppers from the oven and place into a plastic bag. Seal the bag and set aside.
2 When the peppers are cool, remove the charred skin with your fingertips, rinsing to remove any excess. Don't worry if you cannot remove it all; the skin is tasty! Slice the peppers.
3 Heat the oil in a skillet over medium-high heat. Add the garlic and saute for 30 seconds. Add the peppers and saute for 3 minutes. Add the wine, bring to a boil, reduce the heat, and simmer for 5 minutes.
4 Add the basil and simmer for 4 minutes. Add the crushed red pepper, ground pepper, and salt. Serve the sauce over the pasta and garnish with grated fresh Parmesan cheese.

Calories	274
Calories from Fat	34
Total Fat	4 g
Saturated Fat	1 g
Cholesterol	1 mg
Sodium	19 mg
Carbohydrate	50 g
Dietary Fiber	3 g
Sugars	4 g
Protein	9 g

Gratin of Zucchini

6 Servings

Serving Size:
1/2 cup

Exchanges

1 Vegetable
1 Very Lean Meat

Ingredients

2 tsp olive oil
1 red onion, diced
2 cloves garlic, minced
1 1/2 cups sliced zucchini
1 1/2 cups sliced tomato
3 oz shredded part-skim
    mozzarella cheese
Fresh ground pepper
Dash salt (optional)

Preparation—20 minutes

1 Preheat the oven to 350 degrees. Heat the oil in a skillet over medium-high heat. Add the onion and garlic and saute for 5 minutes.
2 In a casserole dish, make a bottom layer of some of the zucchini. Add a layer of tomatoes. Add some of the onion mixture. Repeat layers until all the ingredients are used up.
3 Sprinkle the cheese on top and season with pepper and salt. Bake, covered, for 20–25 minutes. Uncover and bake 5 minutes.

Calories	66
Calories from Fat	15
Total Fat	2 g
Saturated Fat	0 g
Cholesterol	2 mg
Sodium	106 mg
Carbohydrate	7 g
Dietary Fiber	2 g
Sugars	5 g
Protein	6 g

Granita

6 Servings

Serving Size:
1/2 cup

Exchanges

1 Carbohydrate

Ingredients

1 cup water
1/3 cup sugar
2 cups fresh strawberries or
    raspberries, pureed, seeds
    removed through a sieve
2 Tbsp fresh lemon juice

Preparation—10 minutes

1 Boil the water and sugar until the sugar dissolves. Continue to cook for 5 minutes. Remove from the heat.
2 When the mixture has cooled, add the berries and lemon juice. Freeze in a container (an ice cube tray works well) for 4 hours, stirring every 1/2 hour. To serve, scrape into dessert dishes.

Calories	61
Calories from Fat	2
Total Fat	0 g
Saturated Fat	0 g
Cholesterol	0 mg
Sodium	1 mg
Carbohydrate	16 g
Dietary Fiber	2 g
Sugars	13 g
Protein	0 g

❖ ❖ ❖ ❖ ❖ ❖

⌒ WHY DON'T YOU . . .

Use placemats instead of a tablecloth, especially for informal entertaining. On top of a really nice wooden dining room table, colorful mats add a festive feel.

Porcini Tagliatelle

Asparagus in Balsamic Vinegar
Fresh Clam Soup
Porcini Tagliatelle
Spinach with Pine Nuts
Banana Strawberry Cream

MENU TALK

Add vegetables such as broccoli, cauliflower, and green beans to this asparagus, double the dressing, and you have a cold vegetable side dish! Choose thin asparagus for this appetizer; it will be easier to eat. Try to avoid using canned asparagus—it has a mushy texture and a dull color.

There are two main varieties of clams, hard shell and soft shell. Hard shell is the type you want for this soup. Hard-shell clams come in three sizes: small, or littleneck clams; medium, or cherrystone clams; and large, or chowder clams. Razor clams and steamer clams are examples of soft-shell clams. When you buy hard-shell clams, make sure the shell is tightly closed. Store live clams for up to two days in the refrigerator. Clams are high in protein with some calcium and iron. This soup is best eaten very fresh.

Porcini mushrooms are also called cepes. They are a wild mushroom, pale brown in color. Fresh porcini mushrooms are hard to come by in the United States, so we often have to rely on the dried variety. Choose porcinis that are still relatively whole, avoiding those that have bits broken off or look powdered. Porcini mushrooms have a rich taste. Porcinis are expensive, so think about using them in combination with other mushrooms so your supply will last longer. Substitute other wild mushrooms, such as portobello or shiitake, in this recipe, or use plain white mushrooms. Tagliatelle are long, wide noodles. Use any other shape of pasta you like in this recipe.

Pine nuts are also called pignoli nuts. The nuts grow inside pine cones. The pine cone is heated and each nut is removed. Cultivating pine nuts is a labor-intensive job; hence, pine nuts are more expensive than other nuts. Buy them in bulk in natural food stores or in bags at gourmet stores. Keep them in the refrigerator to prevent them from turning rancid.

Bananas are excellent when frozen. To freeze, peel the skin, place the banana in a zippered plastic bag, and freeze overnight. For a very simple snack or dessert, just wrap the bottom of a frozen banana with a napkin and eat it like a popsicle! Or, if you wish, freeze them and then puree them in a blender or food processor and eat them like a custard. The creamy texture of ricotta cheese give this dessert its appealing consistency. My friend and colleague, Sara Blumenthal, gave me this recipe.

Pantry List

olive oil
garlic
dry white wine
dry red wine
1 red onion
1 pkg dried porcini mushrooms
1 can crushed tomatoes
1 box tagliatelle
balsamic vinegar
1 sun-dried tomato
1 jar roasted red bell peppers
1 pkg pine nuts
sugar
1 macaroon
1 banana

Market List

2 1/2 dozen small hard-shell clams
parsley
1 red bell pepper
1 carrot
basil
rosemary
2 bundles asparagus
7 medium tomatoes
1 lemon
1 banana
2 1/2 lb spinach
1/2 cup strawberries
1 container part-skim ricotta cheese
orange juice

STEP-BY-STEP COUNTDOWN

1 Prepare the dessert.
2 Prepare step 1 of the asparagus recipe and refrigerate the dressing.
3 Prepare the ingredients for the pasta, but do not cook it.
4 Prepare the ingredients for the spinach, but do not cook it.
5 Prepare the soup.
6 While the clams are steaming, cook the pasta and drain it. Cook the sauce, but do not combine the pasta and sauce. Turn off the heat on the sauce.
7 Finish preparing the asparagus and serve.
8 Serve the soup.
9 When guests have almost finished their soup, cook the spinach.
10 Reheat the pasta sauce and combine it with the pasta. Serve the pasta and spinach.
11 Remove the dessert from the freezer and let it stand at room temperature for 10 minutes. Scoop into dessert dishes, top with macaroon crumbles, and serve.

Asparagus in Balsamic Vinegar

6 Servings

Serving Size:
5 medium spears
   with dressing

Exchanges

1 Vegetable

Ingredients

30 medium spears asparagus, tough
   ends removed
2 Tbsp balsamic vinegar
1 tsp olive oil
1 Tbsp minced sun-dried tomato
2 tsp minced parsley
2 tsp finely minced garlic
Fresh ground pepper
Dash salt (optional)
Thin slices lemon
Strips of roasted red bell pepper
   (use from the jar)

Preparation—10 minutes

1 Whisk together the vinegar, oil, sun-dried tomato, parsley, garlic, pepper, and salt and refrigerate for 1/2 hour.
2 Blanch the asparagus in a large pot of boiling water for 3 minutes, until the asparagus is just lightly cooked and still crisp. Drain, plunge into ice water, and drain again.
3 Plate 5 spears of asparagus per person. Drizzle with some dressing, garnish with lemon and roasted red bell pepper strips, and serve.

Calories	29
Calories from Fat	9
Total Fat	1 g
Saturated Fat	0 g
Cholesterol	0 mg
Sodium	36 mg
Carbohydrate	4 g
Dietary Fiber	2 g
Sugars	2 g
Protein	2 g

Fresh Clam Soup

6 Servings

Serving Size:
1 cup

Exchanges

2 Vegetable
1 Very Lean Meat

Ingredients

1 tsp olive oil
3 tsp minced garlic
3/4 cup dry white wine
5 1/2 cups ripe tomatoes, seeded
    and coarsely chopped
2 1/2 dozen small hard-shell clams,
    rinsed
1 3/4 cups boiling water
2/3 cup minced parsley
Fresh ground pepper

Preparation—20 minutes

1 Heat the oil in a saucepan over medium heat. Add the garlic and saute for 30 seconds. Add the wine and tomatoes and bring to a boil, lower the heat, and simmer for 5 minutes.
2 Boil the clams in the boiling water with 1/4 cup of the parsley, covered, until the shells open, about 5–10 minutes.
3 Place the clams into individual soup bowls. Strain the remaining liquid left by the clams and add to the tomato-wine mixture. Cook for 1–2 minutes. Ladle the tomato mixture over the clams, sprinkle with remaining parsley, season with pepper, and serve.

Calories	90
Calories from Fat	16
Total Fat	2 g
Saturated Fat	0 g
Cholesterol	15 mg
Sodium	45 mg
Carbohydrate	10 g
Dietary Fiber	2 g
Sugars	6 g
Protein	7 g

Porcini Tagliatelle

6 Servings

Serving Size:
1 cup

Exchanges

3 Starch
1 Vegetable
1/2 Monounsatur-
    ated Fat

Ingredients

1 Tbsp olive oil
2 cloves garlic, minced
1/2 red onion, minced
1/2 cup julienned red bell pepper
1/2 cup julienned carrot
1/2 cup dry red wine
1 cup rehydrated porcini
    mushrooms
1 1/2 cups crushed tomatoes
2 tsp minced basil
1 tsp minced rosemary
Fresh ground pepper
Dash salt (optional)
6 cups cooked tagliatelle (wide
    noodles)

Preparation—10 minutes

1 Heat the oil in a skillet over medium heat. Add the garlic and onion and saute for 4 minutes. Add the red bell pepper and carrots and saute for 4 minutes.
2 Add the wine, raise the heat, and boil for 1 minute. Lower the heat to medium low, add the mushrooms, and cook for 3 minutes.
3 Add the tomatoes, basil, and rosemary. Simmer for 15–20 minutes. Season with pepper and salt. Serve the sauce over the cooked tagliatelle noodles.

Calories	285
Calories from Fat	44
Total Fat	5 g
Saturated Fat	1 g
Cholesterol	53 mg
Sodium	191 mg
Carbohydrate	49 g
Dietary Fiber	4 g
Sugars	7 g
Protein	9 g

Spinach with Pine Nuts

6 Servings

Serving Size:
1/2 cup

Exchanges

1 Vegetable
1 Monounsaturated
  Fat

Ingredients

2 1/2 lb fresh spinach leaves
2 tsp olive oil
2 Tbsp toasted pine nuts
1 tsp finely minced garlic
Fresh ground pepper

Preparation—10 minutes

1 Wash the spinach, but allow the water to cling to the leaves. Cook the spinach until it wilts in a skillet over medium-high heat, about 3 minutes.
2 Heat the oil in a skillet over medium-high heat. Add the spinach, pine nuts, and garlic and cook for 2 minutes. Season with pepper and serve.

Calories	65
Calories from Fat	32
Total Fat	4 g
Saturated Fat	1 g
Cholesterol	0 mg
Sodium	101 mg
Carbohydrate	6 g
Dietary Fiber	4 g
Sugars	0 g
Protein	5 g

 WHY DON'T YOU . . .

Set the table the night before. This is an easy task, and you'll feel good it's behind you.

Banana Strawberry Cream

6 Servings

Serving Size:
1/3 cup

Exchanges

1 Carbohydrate

Ingredients

1 ripe frozen banana
1/2 cup sliced strawberries
1 Tbsp orange juice
2 Tbsp sugar
3/4 cup part-skim ricotta cheese
2 macaroons, crumbled

Preparation—5 minutes

1 Puree the frozen banana with the berries, juice, and sugar in a blender. Fold in the cheese.
2 Place the mixture in a pint container and freeze for several hours. Allow the mixture to stand at room temperature for 10 minutes. Using an ice cream scoop, scoop into dessert dishes, top with crumbled macaroons, and serve.

Calories	79
Calories from Fat	7
Total Fat	1 g
Saturated Fat	1 g
Cholesterol	10 mg
Sodium	30 mg
Carbohydrate	14 g
Dietary Fiber	1 g
Sugars	11 g
Protein	4 g

❖ ❖ ❖

Lemon Fettucine

Cream of Wild Mushroom Soup
Red Romaine Salad with Tomato-Honey Dressing
Lemon Fettucine with Salmon and Baby Peas
Sauted Baby Vegetables
Peach Mousse

MENU TALK

This low-fat, creamy, wild mushroom soup is a great beginning to this fresh spring menu. The combination of mushroom flavors makes this soup unique. Cremini mushrooms are a darker, fuller-flavored white mushroom. The portobello is its more mature version. Although it is a time-saver to precut vegetables, mushrooms darken too quickly, so slice them just before you are ready to cook. When reheating leftovers of this soup, be sure to use a low flame to avoid curdling the milk.

The radish is the root of a plant in the mustard family. Its flavor is slightly peppery. Radishes should be hard and not yield to pressure. They are sold cleaned and ready for consumption or still attached to the greens. To keep radishes crisp, store them in a bowl of ice water until ready to eat. The dressing for this salad is slightly sweet. The tomato gives it good body and rich flavor, so very little oil is needed. Try to obtain the wonderfully aromatic Hungarian paprika for this dressing.

Look for flavored pastas in supermarkets and gourmet shops. Vegetables and fruits are exotic additions to otherwise ordinary pasta. Pastas flavored with lemon are quite popular, but if you can't find lemon fettucine, just use the regular variety. Salmon is rich in omega-3 fatty acids, a fatty acid structure considered helpful in elevating good cholesterol levels. Any type of salmon will do for this dish; fresh is preferable, but canned red salmon will do in a pinch. If you prefer to use less wine for poaching the salmon, use half wine and half broth, or use all broth and eliminate the wine.

Baby vegetables, once appearing only on restaurant menus, are now yours to enjoy at home. Baby zucchini and yellow squash are about the size of a long finger. If you can't find baby zucchini and yellow squash, slice the large versions of them. Baby carrots have become America's favorite snack food. These vegetables only require a brief cooking time to preserve their delicate flavor.

Serve this delicious peach mousse in long, fluted champagne glasses and garnish with a mint sprig. You can use nectarines or apricots instead of peaches if you like. This mousse is light, yet tastes rich enough to satisfy any palate.

Pantry List

dry sherry
1 can low-fat, low-sodium chicken broth
3 cans evaporated skim milk
unbleached white flour
2 red onions
1 sweet onion
honey
paprika
olive oil
nutmeg
garlic
dry white wine
capers
1 box lemon fettucine or regular fettucine
unflavored gelatin
peach nectar
ground ginger

Market List

14 oz salmon fillet
1 lb mixed wild mushrooms (cremini, oyster, shiitake, or regular white mushrooms)
thyme
chives
2 large heads red romaine lettuce
3 oz radishes
1 yellow bell pepper
parsley
1 small tomato
1 small bag frozen baby peas
12 baby zucchini

12 baby carrots
12 baby yellow squash
3 fresh peaches or 1 can water-packed peaches
1 cup plain nonfat yogurt
1 small container low-fat cottage cheese
1 container low-calorie whipped topping
low-calorie margarine
fresh lemon juice
1 lemon

1 Prepare the dessert. This can be done the night before.
2 Prepare the salad and dressing, but do not combine them.
3 Prepare the soup through step 3 and turn off the heat.
4 Prepare the fettucine, but do not cook the pasta. Keep the salmon mixture in the skillet, covered.
5 Prepare the baby vegetables, but do not cook them.
6 Boil the fettucine almost all the way and turn off the heat.
7 Prepare the baby vegetables and turn off the heat.
8 Drain the fettucine.
9 Finish preparing the soup and serve.
10 Toss the salad with the dressing and serve.
11 Toss the hot salmon mixture with the pasta. Serve the pasta with the baby vegetables (reheat them if necessary).
12 Spoon dessert into dishes and serve.

Cream of Wild Mushroom Soup

6 Servings

Serving Size:
1 cup

Exchanges

1 1/2 Starch

Ingredients

5 cups sliced wild mushrooms (use shiitake, cremini, oyster, or regular white mushrooms, if wild are not available)
1/4 cup dry sherry
1/2 cup minced red onion
1/4 cup low-fat, low-sodium chicken broth
1 tsp minced chives
4 cups evaporated skim milk
1/3 cup unbleached white flour
Fresh ground pepper

Preparation—30 minutes

1 Combine the mushrooms, sherry, onion, and broth in a stockpot over medium-high heat. Cook until mushrooms are browned, about 5 minutes.
2 Add the chives and cook for 2 minutes. Add 3 1/2 cups of the milk. Lower the heat and simmer for 5 minutes.
3 Combine the remaining 1/2 cup of milk and flour. Add to the soup, stirring until smooth and thick, about 4 minutes. Add the pepper and serve.

Calories	119
Calories from Fat	19
Total Fat	2 g
Saturated Fat	1 g
Cholesterol	2 mg
Sodium	137 mg
Carbohydrate	19 g
Dietary Fiber	2 g
Sugars	9 g
Protein	9 g

Red Romaine Salad with Tomato-Honey Dressing

Ingredients

6 cups red romaine lettuce, washed
    and torn
1 red onion, thinly sliced
1/2 cup sliced radishes
1/2 cup sliced yellow bell pepper
1 ripe tomato, seeded and chopped
    fine
2 Tbsp minced onion
2 Tbsp honey
1 tsp paprika
1 tsp olive oil
1 Tbsp minced parsley
Dash nutmeg
2 cloves garlic, minced

Preparation—10 minutes

1 Combine the lettuce, onion, radishes, and bell pepper in a large salad bowl.
2 Process the remaining ingredients in a food processor or blender until smooth.
3 Drizzle the dressing over the salad and serve.

Calories	60
Calories from Fat	10
Total Fat	1 g
Saturated Fat	0 g
Cholesterol	0 mg
Sodium	11 mg
Carbohydrate	12 g
Dietary Fiber	3 g
Sugars	9 g
Protein	2 g

Lemon Fettucine with Sauted Salmon and Baby Peas

6 Servings

Serving Size:
1 cup pasta
2 oz salmon

Exchanges

3 Starch
2 Lean Meat
1/2 Monounsatur-
ated Fat

Ingredients

1 Tbsp olive oil
1 garlic clove, minced
1/2 cup minced onion
14 oz fresh salmon filet, cubed
1 cup dry white wine
1/4 tsp lemon peel
2 tsp capers
1 cup baby peas, thawed
2 Tbsp minced parsley
6 cups cooked lemon fettucine (or
    use regular fettucine)
Fresh ground pepper
Dash salt (optional)

Preparation—20 minutes

1 Heat the oil in a skillet over medium heat. Add the garlic and onion and saute for 3 minutes. Add the salmon and saute on all sides for a total of about 2 minutes.
2 Add the wine, lemon peel, and capers. Let the salmon poach in the wine for 5 minutes. Remove the salmon pieces. Boil the wine until reduced by one-third.
3 Add the baby peas and parsley. Cook for 5 minutes.
4 Toss the salmon mixture with the cooked fettucine. Season with pepper and salt and serve.

Calories	387
Calories from Fat	94
Total Fat	10 g
Saturated Fat	2 g
Cholesterol	94 mg
Sodium	85 mg
Carbohydrate	46 g
Dietary Fiber	4 g
Sugars	5 g
Protein	23 g

Sauted Baby Vegetables

6 Servings

Serving Size:
1/2 cup

Exchanges

1 Vegetable

Ingredients

1 Tbsp low-calorie margarine
12 baby zucchini
12 baby carrots
12 baby yellow squash
1/4 cup low-fat, low-sodium
     chicken broth
Fresh ground pepper
Dash salt (optional)

 SPEAKING OF SPICES

Cinnamon

It takes 20–30 years before cinnamon can be harvested from a tree. The inner bark is removed and curls into quills. Cinnamon sticks are low in flavor. To make the more flavorful ground cinnamon, large chunks of lower bark are removed. China Cassia cinnamon is the world's finest cinnamon. Native to Southeast Asia, this variety is strong and sweet. Ceylon cinnamon or true cinnamon is less sweet and more like citrus; it is used most often in England and Mexico.

Preparation—10 minutes

1 Melt the margarine in a skillet over medium-high heat. Add the vegetables and saute for 2 minutes.
2 Add the broth and saute for 4 minutes. Season with pepper and salt and serve.

Calories	29
Calories from Fat	10
Total Fat	1 g
Saturated Fat	0 g
Cholesterol	0 mg
Sodium	36 mg
Carbohydrate	5 g
Dietary Fiber	2 g
Sugars	2 g
Protein	1 g

Peach Mousse

Ingredients

1 1/2 cups diced peaches (either canned and drained or fresh and peeled)
2 Tbsp lemon juice
1/2 cup plain nonfat yogurt, stirred
1/2 cup low-fat cottage cheese
1 packet unflavored gelatin
1/4 cup water
1/4 cup peach nectar
1 tsp ground ginger
1/4 cup sugar
1/2 cup low-calorie whipped topping

Preparation—10 minutes

1 Puree the peaches and lemon juice in a food processor. Mix together the yogurt and cottage cheese. Stir the mixture by hand into the pureed fruit.
2 Dissolve the gelatin in the water in a small saucepan over low heat. Add the nectar, ginger, and sugar. Cook for about 2 minutes.
3 Add the peach mixture to the gelatin. Mix well. Place the mixture into a pint container and freeze until the mixture looks thick, about 30 minutes.
4 Fold the whipped topping into the peach mixture and refrigerate for several hours. Spoon into individual dessert dishes and serve.

Calories	98
Calories from Fat	6
Total Fat	1 g
Saturated Fat	1 g
Cholesterol	1 mg
Sodium	89 mg
Carbohydrate	18 g
Dietary Fiber	1 g
Sugars	16 g
Protein	5 g

❖ ❖ ❖

Chicken Peanut Pasta

Sugar Snap Pea and Carrot Salad
Spicy Chicken Peanut Pasta
Zucchini and Squash Noodles
Sauted Watercress
Carambolas and Raspberries

M E N U   T A L K

The sugar snap pea is a sweet pea that is completely edible, pod and all! It is a cross between the English pea and the snow pea. The best seasons for sugar snap peas are spring and fall. The pods should be plump and crisp. These peas are best eaten raw or very lightly cooked. They are so sweet and crispy that any prolonged cooking will destroy them. Use snow peas if sugar snap peas are unavailable.

This pasta dish is very rich! The sauce is great served on any other Asian dish. Steam some vegetables and use the sauce to coat them; serve this dish hot. Blanch some vegetables, shock them in cold water, and serve the vegetables cold, using the sauce as a dip. Pour the sauce over brown rice or couscous. If you can't find Asian chili sauce, substitute hot pepper sauce instead.

To get long strands of zucchini and yellow squash that look like noodles, use the julienne blade of a food processor or a mandoline. A mandoline is a hand-operated machine that has many blades for thin or thick slicing and for julienne or french-fry cuts. While I'm not a believer in having every kitchen gadget available, a mandoline is very useful, especially since it takes up less room than a food processor and is ideal for small amounts of chopping and slicing. Mandolines can be purchased in most kitchen specialty stores. Mirin is a low-alcohol, golden wine made from sticky rice. Mirin, also called rice wine, adds sweetness to foods and is available in some supermarkets and Asian grocery stores.

This watercress recipe is very versatile. You can substitute any other green, such as spinach, bok choy, chard, kale, mustard greens, or Chinese cabbage, for the watercress. Just a touch of cooking is all these leafy greens need, making them ideal as last-minute side dishes. This recipe is a good base to add to other stir-fried vegetables. Try the watercress dish cold, with a little rice vinegar splashed on—it's delicious!

The showstopper of this meal is a star—actually, a star fruit. Carambolas, which form a striking star shape when cut crosswise, are beautiful to behold and more spectacular to eat. Carambolas have five broad ribs that run the length of the fruit. The skin does not have to be peeled. Carambolas range in taste from sweet to somewhat tart. They are best in the summer, and should be used within three days of purchase. These carambolas are particularly striking set against the ruby red raspberries. Feel free to omit the Drambuie if you wish.

Pantry List

brown sugar
crystallized ginger
Drambuie
sesame oil
1 yellow onion
cayenne pepper
Asian chili sauce
1 can low-fat, low-sodium chicken
   broth
hoisin sauce
mirin or rice vinegar
peanut oil
garlic
lite soy sauce
low-fat peanut butter
1 can lite coconut milk
1 box capellini pasta

Market List

1 1/2 lb boneless, skinless
   chicken breasts
3 large carrots
1/4 lb sugar snap peas
orange juice
1 head red leaf lettuce
1 lemon
ginger root
1 bunch green onions
jalapeno peppers
parsley
1 yellow squash
1 zucchini
1 red bell pepper
1/4 lb shiitake mushrooms

cilantro
watercress
1 pint raspberries
2 carambolas (star fruit)

STEP-BY-STEP COUNTDOWN

1 Prepare step 1 of the sugar snap pea recipe and set aside.
2 Prepare the sauce for the pasta. Keep the sauce in the skillet.
3 Prepare the ingredients for the squash and the watercress, but do not cook them.
4 Prepare step 1 of the dessert recipe. Let the raspberries stand.
5 While the pasta boils, cook the squash and turn off the heat.
6 Drain the pasta.
7 Toss the sugar snap peas with the dressing.
8 Cook the watercress and turn off the heat.
9 Serve the sugar snap peas.
10 Toss the pasta with the peanut sauce.
11 Briefly reheat the squash and the watercress. Serve the pasta and both vegetables.
12 Place carambolas on each serving of raspberries and serve.

Sugar Snap Pea and Carrot Salad

6 Servings

Serving Size:
1/2 cup

Exchanges

1 Vegetable

Ingredients

1 1/2 cups thinly sliced carrots
1 1/2 cups sugar snap peas, ends
    removed
1 Tbsp lite soy sauce
1 clove garlic, minced
1/2 tsp sesame oil
1 Tbsp orange juice
red leaf lettuce leaves
lemon slices

Preparation—10 minutes

1 Blanch the carrots for 3 minutes in boiling water. After 1 minute, add the sugar snap peas. Drain, plunge the vegetables into cold water, and drain again.
2 Whisk together the soy sauce, garlic, oil, and juice. Toss with the carrots and sugar snap peas.
3 Place the lettuce leaves on individual plates. Mound the vegetables on top, garnish with lemon, and serve.

Calories	36
Calories from Fat	5
Total Fat	1 g
Saturated Fat	0 g
Cholesterol	0 mg
Sodium	162 mg
Carbohydrate	7 g
Dietary Fiber	2 g
Sugars	4 g
Protein	1 g

Spicy Chicken Peanut Pasta

6 Servings

Serving Size:
1 cup

Exchanges

3 Starch
3 Lean Meat

Ingredients

2 tsp peanut oil
3 cloves garlic, minced
2 tsp minced ginger
2 Tbsp minced green onions
2 Tbsp minced jalapeno peppers
2 Tbsp lite soy sauce
1/4 cup low-fat peanut butter
1 cup lite coconut milk
1/2 tsp Asian chili sauce
1 Tbsp brown sugar
1/4 cup low-fat, low-sodium
      chicken broth
1 1/2 lb boneless, skinless chicken
      breasts, halved and cut into
      2-inch cubes
1/2 cup sliced shiitake mushrooms
1/2 cup julienned red pepper
1/2 cup sliced carrots
6 cups cooked capellini pasta

Preparation—20 minutes

1 Heat the oil in a heavy skillet over medium-high heat. Add the garlic, ginger, green onions, and jalapenos and saute for 4 minutes.
2 Add the soy sauce, peanut butter, coconut milk, chili sauce, and sugar. Bring to a boil, lower the heat, and simmer for 5 minutes. Set the sauce aside.
3 Heat the broth in another skillet over medium-high heat. Saute the chicken in the broth for 5 minutes.
4 Add the mushrooms, red peppers, and carrots. Saute until the chicken is done and vegetables are crisp, about 5–8 minutes.
5 Add the chicken and vegetable mixture to the sauce. Toss the peanut sauce with the capellini and serve.

Calories	425
Calories from Fat	98
Total Fat	11 g
Saturated Fat	3 g
Cholesterol	69 mg
Sodium	347 mg
Carbohydrate	46 g
Dietary Fiber	3 g
Sugars	8 g
Protein	34 g

Zucchini and Yellow Squash Noodles

6 Servings

Serving Size:
1/2 cup

Exchanges

1 Vegetable

Ingredients

1/2 cup low-fat, low-sodium chicken broth
1 1/2 cups long strands of zucchini
1 1/2 cups long strands of yellow squash
2 Tbsp finely diced carrots
2 tsp mirin (sweet rice wine) or rice vinegar
2 Tbsp minced parsley
2 tsp minced cilantro

Preparation—5 minutes

1 Heat the broth in a skillet over medium-high heat. Add the zucchini, yellow squash, and carrots. Cover and steam for 5 minutes.
2 Add the mirin or rice vinegar, parsley, and cilantro. Serve.

Calories	18
Calories from Fat	3
Total Fat	0 g
Saturated Fat	0 g
Cholesterol	0 mg
Sodium	13 mg
Carbohydrate	4 g
Dietary Fiber	1 g
Sugars	2 g
Protein	1 g

Sauted Watercress

6 Servings

Serving Size:
1/2 cup

Exchanges

1/2 Fat

Ingredients

5 bunches fresh watercress
1 Tbsp sesame oil
2 Tbsp minced onion
Dash cayenne pepper

Preparation—10 minutes

1 Cut any coarse stems off the watercress. Wash the watercress leaves and thoroughly dry them.
2 Heat the oil in a skillet over high heat. Add the onion and saute for 1 minute. Add the watercress and stir-fry, stirring constantly, for 1–2 minutes. Add the cayenne pepper and serve.

Calories	33
Calories from Fat	20
Total Fat	2 g
Saturated Fat	0 g
Cholesterol	0 mg
Sodium	39 mg
Carbohydrate	2 g
Dietary Fiber	1 g
Sugars	0 g
Protein	2 g

 WHY DON'T YOU . . .

Set out fresh, colorful towels in the bathroom. Make sure all bathrooms are tidy (guests love to check out bathrooms). Get rid of any dead plants. Close and lock any rooms that are off-limits.

Carambolas and Raspberries

6 Servings

Serving Size:
1/2 cup

Exchanges

1/2 Carbohydrate

Ingredients

2 cups fresh raspberries
1 Tbsp brown sugar
1 Tbsp Drambuie (optional)
1 Tbsp finely diced crystallized
   ginger
2 medium carambolas (star fruit),
   sliced into 1/2–inch slices

Preparation—5 minutes

1 Mix together the raspberries, sugar, liqueur, and crystallized ginger. Let the mixture stand for 1/2 hour.
2 Place the raspberries in wide-mouthed wine glasses or dessert bowls. Top each serving with some slices of carambola and serve.

Calories	45	
Calories from Fat	3	
Total Fat	0	g
Saturated Fat	0	g
Cholesterol	0	mg
Sodium	1	mg
Carbohydrate	11	g
Dietary Fiber	4	g
Sugars	7	g
Protein	1	g

Seafood Bounty

❖ ❖ ❖ ❖

Drunken Shrimp 95

Watercress, Papaya, and Avocado Salad
Tequila Honey Shrimp
Ancho Chili Salsa
Grilled Corn with Cilantro
Honeydew Cooler

Sesame Seafood 103

Tree Oyster Mushroom Soup
Sesame Sole with Scallion Sauce
Udon Noodles with Slivered Vegetables
Bok Choy, Carrots, and Green Beans
Orange Pudding

Marinated Trout 111

Marinated Trout
Peach Salsa
Coconut Rice
Spinach Salad with Raisin-Mango
    Chutney Dressing
Creamy Soft Custard

Halibut on Dal 119

Mint Dip
Halibut on Dal
Cauliflower with Turmeric
Roasted Cumin Seed and Cucumber Salad
Bananas with Cardamom Cream

California Seafood Salad 127

Chilled Cream of Tomato Soup
California Seafood Salad
Cucumber and Fennel Relish
Herbed Bagel Crisps
Peach Smoothies

❖ ❖ ❖

Drunken Shrimp

Watercress, Papaya, and Avocado Salad
Tequila Honey Shrimp
Ancho Chili Salsa
Grilled Corn with Cilantro
Honeydew Cooler

MENU TALK

Watercress is a member of the mustard family. Its flavor is slightly bitter, with a peppery flip. You can find watercress, typically sold in small bunches, all year. To store watercress, place the entire bouquet in a glass of water, stem side down. Cover with a plastic bag and store in the refrigerator. Watercress is great cold in salads and sandwiches or cooked quickly as a side dish.

Avocados were first grown in this country in Florida, but almost all of the crop comes from California today. There are many varieties of avocados, but the two principal ones are the black, pebbly-skinned Haas and the green, smooth-skinned Fuerte. Inside the avocado lies a soft, buttery meat. When choosing avocados, look for ones that yield to pressure. To ripen avocados at home, place them in a brown paper bag and leave at room temperature for several days. Avocados do have fat, but they also provide vitamins A and C, thiamine, and riboflavin. Just a few slices of this rich fruit go a long way.

See color photo after p. 80.

Tequila originated in Tequila, Mexico. It is a pale-colored liquor made from the agave plant. You may omit the tequila from this seafood recipe if you wish. There are many species of shrimp. Generally, they fall into two classifications, warm water and cold water. Cold-water shrimp are usually smaller and sweeter. Shrimp should be cooked just until they turn pink, then immediately removed from the heat source. Because shrimp are not cheap, make sure your cooking methods will help the shrimp retain its juiciness. Fresh shrimp is best, but frozen shrimp will do in a pinch.

Ancho chili peppers are sweet, rich, and fruit flavored. Poblanos are fresh anchos. You can find ancho peppers in most supermarkets and Mexican markets. They rehydrate in as little as 10 minutes. Anchos impart a smoky, as well as sweet, taste. This salsa needs very few other spices—the ancho will provide all the flavor you need.

Grilling corn is one of my favorite ways to prepare it. The husk serves the same purpose as aluminum foil and it won't go up in flames! Grill the corn until the husk is covered with grill marks and the corn is cooked through. Let the husk cool down a bit before peeling it back to reveal the slightly charred kernels. The cilantro and chili really add to the overall flavor, but this corn is also delicious plain.

Honeydew melons are grown in California and parts of the Southwest. Honeydew is best from July to September, but is available year-round. Honeydews should be heavy for their size and have smooth skin. Honeydew melons are a good source of vitamin C. Cantaloupe may be substituted for the honeydew melon in this recipe.

Mexican Lasagna Dinner, see page 11

Drunken Shrimp Dinner, see page 95

Pantry List

sugar
allspice
olive oil
honey
tequila
dried ancho chili
1 red onion
red wine vinegar
garlic
chili powder
paprika

Market List

1 1/2 lb fresh shrimp
2 bunches watercress
5 tomatoes
1 papaya
1 avocado
fresh lime juice
cilantro
butter
parsley
6 ears corn
1 honeydew melon
low-calorie margarine

STEP-BY-STEP COUNTDOWN

1 Prepare the salsa.
2 Prepare the salad, but not the avocado and dressing.
3 Prepare the corn and grill.
4 Prepare the shrimp and immediately turn off the heat.
5 Add the avocado to the salad, drizzle on the dressing, and serve.
6 When the corn is completed, serve the shrimp (reheat just briefly, if necessary); corn; and salsa.
7 Prepare the dessert and serve.

Watercress, Papaya, and Avocado Salad

6 Servings

Serving Size:
1/2 cup

Exchanges

1/2 Fruit
1 Vegetable
1 Monounsaturated
Fat

Ingredients

1 1/2 cups watercress, washed
1 1/2 cups thinly sliced papaya,
    peeled and seeded
12 thin slices avocado
12 tomato wedges
1/4 cup fresh lime juice
2 tsp sugar
1 Tbsp minced cilantro
1/4 tsp allspice
1 tsp olive oil

Preparation—15 minutes

1 Arrange the watercress on individual plates. Arrange the papaya on the watercress in a spoke pattern. Garnish each salad with avocado and tomato.
2 Whisk together the remaining ingredients and drizzle over each salad to serve.

Calories	95
Calories from Fat	56
Total Fat	6 g
Saturated Fat	1 g
Cholesterol	0 mg
Sodium	12 mg
Carbohydrate	11 g
Dietary Fiber	3 g
Sugars	5 g
Protein	2 g

❖ ❖ ❖ ❖ ❖ ❖

〜 WHY DON'T YOU . . .

Buy good oven-to-table cookware. I personally like the French white cookware. It looks great on the table and means less pot-washing afterward.

Tequila Honey Shrimp

6 Servings

Serving Size:
3 oz

Exchanges

1/2 Carbohydrate
3 Very Lean Meat

Ingredients

2 tsp olive oil
1 tsp butter
2 cloves garlic, minced
1 1/2 lb peeled and deveined
    medium shrimp
2 Tbsp honey
2–3 Tbsp tequila

Preparation—10 minutes

1 Heat the oil and butter in a skillet over medium-high heat. Add the garlic and saute for 30 seconds. Add the shrimp and saute for 3–4 minutes or until the shrimp turn pink.
2 Add the honey and tequila and cook for 1–2 minutes. Serve immediately.

Calories	134
Calories from Fat	27
Total Fat	3 g
Saturated Fat	1 g
Cholesterol	163 mg
Sodium	192 mg
Carbohydrate	6 g
Dietary Fiber	0 g
Sugars	6 g
Protein	7 g

Ancho Chili Salsa

8 Servings

Serving Size:
1/4 cup

Exchanges

1 Vegetable

Ingredients

1 dried ancho chili
1 lb firm tomatoes, seeded and
   coarsely chopped
1/2 cup minced red onion
2 Tbsp minced parsley
3 cloves garlic, minced
2 Tbsp lime juice
1 Tbsp red wine vinegar

Preparation—10 minutes

1 In a small heatproof bowl, pour boiling water over the dried chili. Let the chili soften for 20 minutes, then drain and chop the chili.
2 Combine the remaining ingredients. Add the chili and mix again. Refrigerate for 1 hour before serving.

Calories	22
Calories from Fat	2
Total Fat	0 g
Saturated Fat	0 g
Cholesterol	0 mg
Sodium	7 mg
Carbohydrate	5 g
Dietary Fiber	1 g
Sugars	3 g
Protein	1 g

Grilled Corn with Cilantro

6 Servings

Serving Size:
1 small ear

Exchanges

1 Starch
1/2 Fat

Ingredients

6 small ears corn
3 Tbsp low-calorie margarine
2 tsp finely minced garlic
2 Tbsp finely minced cilantro
1/4 tsp chili powder
1/4 tsp paprika

Preparation—5 minutes

1 Pull back the husk of each piece of corn and remove the silks.
2 Melt the margarine in a skillet over medium heat. Add the garlic and cilantro and saute for 2 minutes. Add the chili powder and paprika.
3 Spread each ear of corn with the cilantro mixture. Pull the husks back over the corn.
4 Grill the corn over medium hot coals for about 20 minutes, turning frequently. Remove from the heat and let cool slightly. Peel back the husk and serve.

Calories	102	
Calories from Fat	26	
Total Fat	3	g
Saturated Fat	0	g
Cholesterol	0	mg
Sodium	44	mg
Carbohydrate	20	g
Dietary Fiber	2	g
Sugars	2	g
Protein	3	g

VINEGARS

Sherry Vinegar

Sherry vinegar is made from the Spanish palomino grape. It is aged in white oak, resulting in a rich, fruity taste. Sherry vinegar can be used instead of balsamic vinegar; it is common in Spanish cuisine. Try a splash of it over leafy greens.

Honeydew Cooler

6 Servings

Serving Size:
3/4 cup

Exchanges

1 Carbohydrate

Ingredients

4 cups diced honeydew melon
1/2 cup cold water
1/4 cup sugar
3 Tbsp lime juice

Preparation—5 minutes

Process all ingredients in a blender until smooth.
Serve immediately.

Calories	74
Calories from Fat	1
Total Fat	0 g
Saturated Fat	0 g
Cholesterol	0 mg
Sodium	12 mg
Carbohydrate	19 g
Dietary Fiber	1 g
Sugars	18 g
Protein	1 g

 WHY DON'T YOU . . .

Jazz up your brunch table country style! Use folded bandanas as napkins, serve rolls and breads from baskets, and drink from sturdy goblets.

Sesame Seafood

Tree Oyster Mushroom Soup
Sesame Sole with Scallion Sauce
Udon Noodles with Slivered Vegetables
Bok Choy, Carrots, and Green Beans
Orange Pudding

MENU TALK

Tree oyster mushrooms are fan-shaped and beige, with grayish white stems. When eaten raw, their flavor is strong; when cooked, their flavor mellows. Canned tree oyster mushrooms are also available. If you can't find either fresh or canned oyster mushrooms, substitute white mushrooms.

Sole is ideal for pan sauteing, as in this recipe. Be careful when you turn the fish over: use a wide spatula to hold the fish easily and a nonstick skillet so the fish stays together. Peanut oil is a great choice to use when sauteing this fish. Its high smoking point makes it ideal for fast cooking. Other fish that would work equally well include flounder, orange roughy, perch, cod, and turbot.

Udon noodles are made from brown rice flour and wheat flour. I like to think of udon noodles as Asian fettucine, because the noodles are flat and long. You can substitute regular spaghetti or fettucine if you can't find udon. To julienne vegetables, first make 1/8-inch slices. Then stack the slices and make 1/8-inch strips. Julienned foods look very pretty, so take time to practice this technique.

Bok choy, also known as Chinese white cabbage, resembles a wide bunch of celery with long leaves. Bok choy is usually available all year. For a real treat, Asian markets sell baby bok choy, which is extremely tender. Bok choy has a very mild taste and a light texture and is a good source of calcium. In addition to dairy foods, there are many wonderful and tasty vegetables that can provide significant amounts of calcium. Try collard greens, kale, turnip greens, cress, endive, mustard greens, dandelion greens, and spinach as well as bok choy. Recently the guidelines for calcium intake have changed. Adults need an average of 1300 mg of calcium a day. You can obtain this by eating low-fat dairy products and choosing calcium-rich vegetables.

Tapioca is the starch substance extracted from the root of the cassava plant. Every supermarket carries tapioca. You may want to venture out to an Asian market where they sell jewel-colored tapioca. For many, tapioca pudding is the ultimate comfort food.

Pantry List

pearl tapioca
sugar
4 cans low-fat, low-sodium
    chicken broth
garlic
sesame oil
white pepper
unbleached white flour
sesame seeds
peanut oil
lite soy sauce
honey
dry sherry
cornstarch or arrowroot powder
dry white wine
1 pkg udon noodles
1 can water chestnuts

Market List

1 1/2 lb sole filets
1/2 lb fresh tree oyster mushrooms
    or shiitake mushrooms
1/2 lb white mushrooms
green onions
ginger root
2 eggs
3 carrots
1 red bell pepper
1 yellow squash
1 red chili pepper
1/2 lb green beans
1/2 lb bok choy
1 orange
shallots

Tree Oyster Mushroom Ginger Soup

6 Servings

Serving Size:
1 cup

Exchanges

1/2 Starch

Ingredients

6 cups low-fat, low-sodium chicken broth
1 tsp sesame oil
1 cup fresh tree oyster mushrooms or shiitake mushrooms
1 cup sliced white mushrooms
2 cloves garlic, minced
2 Tbsp minced green onions
1 Tbsp minced ginger
Fresh ground white pepper

Preparation—5 minutes

1 Heat 1/2 cup of the broth and the oil in a stockpot over high heat. Add both kinds of mushrooms and saute for 5 minutes. Add the garlic and saute for 1 minute.

2 Add the green onions, the remaining broth, and the ginger. Simmer for 15 minutes. Sprinkle with fresh ground white pepper and serve.

Calories	47
Calories from Fat	29
Total Fat	3 g
Saturated Fat	1 g
Cholesterol	0 mg
Sodium	108 mg
Carbohydrate	6 g
Dietary Fiber	1 g
Sugars	3 g
Protein	4 g

Sesame Sole with Scallion Sauce

6 Servings

Serving Size:
3 oz

Exchanges

1 Starch
3 Very Lean Meat
1 1/2 Fat

Ingredients

1/4 cup flour
Fresh ground pepper
1 1/2 lb sole filets
2 eggs, beaten
1/2 cup toasted sesame seeds
1 Tbsp peanut oil
1/2 cup low-fat, low-sodium
     chicken broth
2 Tbsp lite soy sauce
1 Tbsp honey
1 Tbsp dry sherry
2 tsp cornstarch or
     arrowroot powder
3 Tbsp minced green onions

Preparation—25 minutes

1 Combine the flour and pepper in a zippered plastic bag. Add the filets and shake well to coat.
2 Place the beaten eggs in a shallow bowl. Dip each filet into the egg, then roll it in the toasted sesame seeds. Place all the filets on a plate and place in the refrigerator to set for 1/2 hour.
3 Heat the peanut oil in a nonstick skillet over medium-high heat. Add the filets and saute on each side for about 4 minutes. Remove the filets from the skillet and keep warm.
4 Combine the remaining ingredients in a saucepan and cook over medium heat until thickened. Serve the sole with the sauce.

Calories	257
Calories from Fat	103
Total Fat	11 g
Saturated Fat	2 g
Cholesterol	131 mg
Sodium	327 mg
Carbohydrate	12 g
Dietary Fiber	2 g
Sugars	5 g
Protein	27 g

Udon Noodles with Slivered Vegetables

6 Servings

Serving Size:
1/2 cup

Exchanges

1 1/2 Starch
1 Vegetable

Ingredients

1/2 cup dry white wine
1 large carrot, julienned
1 red bell pepper, julienned
1/2 cup water chestnuts, sliced
1/2 cup yellow squash, julienned
3 cups cooked udon noodles
1 tsp sesame oil
2 Tbsp lite soy sauce
1 tsp honey

Preparation—15 minutes

1 Heat the wine in a skillet or wok over high heat. Add the vegetables, cover, and steam for 5 minutes. Toss in the cooked udon noodles.
2 Combine the remaining ingredients and add to the noodles. Toss well and serve.

Calories	144
Calories from Fat	12
Total Fat	1 g
Saturated Fat	0 g
Cholesterol	0 mg
Sodium	218 mg
Carbohydrate	27 g
Dietary Fiber	3 g
Sugars	5 g
Protein	4 g

❖ ❖ ❖ ❖ ❖ ❖

⤜ WHY DON'T YOU . . .

Copy recipes you like from books or magazines, then post them on your kitchen cupboards near your work area. This prevents books from taking up valuable counter space, and you can write notes on the recipe as you work.

Bok Choy, Carrots, and Green Beans

6 Servings

Serving Size:
1/2 cup

Exchanges

1 Vegetable

Ingredients

1 tsp peanut oil
2 small shallots, minced
1 small red chili pepper, minced (optional)
2 medium carrots, sliced diagonally
1 cup cut green beans
1 cup chopped bok choy
1/3 cup low-fat, low-sodium chicken broth
1 Tbsp lite soy sauce

Preparation—15 minutes

1 Heat the oil in a wok or skillet over high heat. Add the shallots and chili pepper and saute for 3 minutes. Add the carrots and stir-fry for 3 minutes.
2 Add the green beans and stir-fry for 2 minutes. Add the bok choy and stir-fry for 2 minutes.
3 Add the broth and simmer for 2 minutes. Add the soy sauce and serve.

Calories	37
Calories from Fat	9
Total Fat	1 g
Saturated Fat	0 g
Cholesterol	0 mg
Sodium	137 mg
Carbohydrate	7 g
Dietary Fiber	2 g
Sugars	2 g
Protein	2 g

Orange Pudding

6 Servings

Serving Size:
1/2 cup

Exchanges

1 1/2 Carbohydrate

Ingredients

1/2 cup pearl tapioca
2 1/2 cups water
1/4 cup sugar
1 orange, peeled and sectioned

Preparation—5 minutes

1 Combine the tapioca with 1/2 cup of the water and the sugar. Mix well, then let stand for 2 hours.
2 Boil 2 cups of water and add the tapioca mixture. Cook until tapioca is creamy, about 2–3 minutes. Add the orange sections and cook for 2 minutes.

Calories	92
Calories from Fat	0
Total Fat	0 g
Saturated Fat	0 g
Cholesterol	0 mg
Sodium	0 mg
Carbohydrate	23 g
Dietary Fiber	1 g
Sugars	11 g
Protein	0 g

❖ ❖ ❖

Marinated Trout

Marinated Trout
Peach Salsa
Coconut Rice
Spinach Salad with Raisin-Mango Chutney Dressing
Creamy Soft Custard

MENU TALK

Trout is a great fish to grill. Sturdy and hearty, it stands up well to the intense heat of an outdoor grill. The best-known variety of trout is rainbow trout. You can also use swordfish or tuna for this recipe. As with all fish recipes that call for marinating, the longest you should marinate is 2 hours. Otherwise, the fish "cooks" in the marinade and will not turn out very well. This is good news for those of you who want a great dinner, but are short on time. Fish can marinate in as little as 20 minutes and still be full of flavor.

Think creatively when you think of salsa. Salsa can be made from fruits as well as the traditional tomato base. Peaches are delicious as a base for salsa. The salmon color of the peach, red of the pepper, and green of the cilantro and jalapeno all contribute to a salsa with great eye appeal. Mangoes, pineapples, kiwi, papaya, bananas, and plums can all be used for salsa, either as the main ingredient or in combination with each other. The strong flavor of this salsa complements the mild fish.

Jazz up plain rice with a little coconut! Just a small amount of toasted coconut enlivens the flavor of bland rice. I like to think of rice as a blank canvas. Almost anything you add to it can give it good flavor. The crunchiness of the coconut also adds an interesting texture.

The dressing for the salad can be used as a chutney for chicken, fish, pork, and seafood. The spinach and romaine are good sources of fiber and vitamins A and C.

The secret to this creamy, light custard is using evaporated skim milk, which provides richness without the fat. This is a soft custard rather than a baked custard. Try using almond extract instead of vanilla for a whole new taste.

Pantry List

2 cans evaporated skim milk
cornstarch or arrowroot powder
cinnamon
vanilla extract
raisins
walnut oil
mango chutney
ground ginger
basmati rice
2 cans low-fat, low-sodium chicken
  broth
currants
unsweetened coconut
sugar
olive oil
chili powder
2 red onions

Market List

1 1/2 lb trout filets
2 peaches
1 red bell pepper
1 bunch cilantro
1 jalapeno pepper
spinach leaves
1 large head romaine lettuce
1 pint cherry tomatoes
low-calorie margarine
egg substitute
lime juice
lemon juice

1 Prepare the custard several hours in advance or
  the day before.
2 Marinate the trout. Prepare and refrigerate
  the salsa.
3 Prepare the salad and dressing, but do not
  mix them.
4 Prepare the rice and turn off the heat.
5 Grill the fish.
6 Toss the dressing with the salad and serve.
7 Plate the fish, salsa, and rice and serve.
8 Serve the dessert.

Marinated Trout with Peach Salsa

6 Servings

Serving Size:
3 1/2 oz

Exchanges

1/2 Fruit
4 Very Lean Meat
1 Monounsaturated
   Fat

Ingredients

1 1/2 lb trout filets
1 Tbsp olive oil
1 Tbsp fresh lemon juice
1/4 tsp chili powder
2 peaches, peeled and coarsely
   chopped
3 Tbsp finely minced red onion
3 Tbsp finely minced red bell
   pepper
1 Tbsp finely minced cilantro
3 Tbsp fresh lime juice
2 tsp sugar
1 tsp minced jalapeno pepper

Preparation—15 minutes

1 In a glass pan, combine the trout with the oil, lemon juice, and chili powder. Marinate in the refrigerator for 2 hours.
2 Combine the remaining salsa ingredients and refrigerate.
3 Prepare an outdoor grill with the rack set 6 inches above the coals. On a gas grill, place the setting on medium-high.
4 Place the trout on the hot grill and grill the filets until flaky, about 5–6 minutes per side. Remove the trout from the grill and serve with the salsa.

Calories	213
Calories from Fat	82
Total Fat	9 g
Saturated Fat	2 g
Cholesterol	66 mg
Sodium	64 mg
Carbohydrate	8 g
Dietary Fiber	1 g
Sugars	6 g
Protein	24 g

Coconut Rice

6 Servings

Serving Size:
1/2 cup

Exchanges

3 Starch

Ingredients

1 1/2 cups basmati rice, rinsed
3 cups low-fat, low-sodium chicken broth or water
3 Tbsp currants, dried
3 Tbsp unsweetened shredded coconut, toasted (Place the coconut in a dry skillet over medium heat. Shake the pan until the coconut is toasted, about 5 minutes.)
2 tsp sugar

Preparation—10 minutes

1 Combine the rice and broth in a heavy saucepan. Bring to a boil, lower the heat, cover, and simmer for 10 minutes.
2 Add the currants to the rice and simmer until the rice is tender, about 10 minutes.
3 Stir in the coconut and sugar.

Calories	228
Calories from Fat	27
Total Fat	3 g
Saturated Fat	2 g
Cholesterol	0 mg
Sodium	56 mg
Carbohydrate	47 g
Dietary Fiber	2 g
Sugars	6 g
Protein	6 g

 SPEAKING OF SPICES

Nutmeg

Nutmeg is one of the world's oldest spices. Nutmeg grows in Indonesia and in the West Indies, particularly in Grenada. Nutmeg trees grow very tall, up to 50 feet high. The tree produces two spices: nutmeg, and its lacy outer covering, mace. Tree climbers collect the spices by hand. Nutmeg and mace are becoming more widely used now, with the emerging popularity of Caribbean cooking.

Spinach Salad with Raisin-Mango Chutney Dressing

6 Servings

Serving Size:
1 cup

Exchanges

1/2 Carbohydrate
1 Vegetable
1 Polyunsaturated
  Fat

Ingredients

4 cups spinach leaves, torn
2 cups romaine lettuce, torn
1 medium red onion, thinly sliced
1 cup cherry tomatoes, halved
3 Tbsp raisins
1/4 cup boiling water
2 Tbsp walnut oil
3 Tbsp lemon juice
1/4 cup mango chutney
1/2 tsp ground ginger
Fresh ground pepper to taste

Preparation—10 minutes

1 Combine the spinach, romaine, onion, and tomatoes and set aside.
2 Pour boiling water over the raisins, let them stand for 10 minutes, and drain.
3 Combine the drained raisins with the remaining ingredients in a food processor and blend well.
4 Toss the salad and dressing together and serve.

Calories	109
Calories from Fat	44
Total Fat	5 g
Saturated Fat	0 g
Cholesterol	0 mg
Sodium	59 mg
Carbohydrate	16 g
Dietary Fiber	2 g
Sugars	13 g
Protein	2 g

Creamy Soft Custard

6 Servings

Serving size:
1/3 cup

Exchanges

1 1/2 Carbohydrate

Ingredients

2   cups evaporated skim milk
1   cup egg substitute
3   Tbsp cornstarch or arrowroot
    powder
1/2 cup sugar
2   Tbsp low-calorie margarine
1   tsp cinnamon
1   tsp vanilla extract

Preparation—10 minutes

1   In a blender, combine the milk, egg substitute, cornstarch or arrowroot powder, and sugar. Blend until smooth.
2   Pour the mixture into a double boiler over simmering water. Cook, stirring constantly, until the mixture thickens. Remove from the heat and add the remaining ingredients.
3   Pour the custard into a bowl. Place a sheet of waxed paper or plastic wrap over the bowl to prevent a skin from forming over the custard.
4   Refrigerate several hours. Before serving, dust the custard with additional cinnamon.

Calories	146	
Calories from Fat	19	
Total Fat	2	g
Saturated Fat	0	g
Cholesterol	3	mg
Sodium	202	mg
Carbohydrate	21	g
Dietary Fiber	0	g
Sugars	14	g
Protein	11	g

OILS

Walnut Oil

To me, walnut oil is the finest. It's expensive, but you can buy a small bottle or split a larger one with a friend. Its taste is incomparable in salads. Just a small amount lends a rich flavor. Try hazelnut oil as well; you'll only need a little. Refrigerate these oils, because you will probably not go through them very fast.

Halibut on Dal

Mint Dip
Halibut on Dal
Cauliflower with Turmeric
Roasted Cumin Seed and Cucumber Salad
Bananas with Cardamom Cream

MENU TALK

Yogurt is more than just a quick American breakfast or lunch. It is a central ingredient in much of the world's cuisine, including this Indian menu. Indians prefer to make their own yogurt. Commercially prepared yogurt is a little thinner than the Indian version, so if you'd like a thicker texture without the fat, use 1/4 cup low-fat sour cream for every 3/4 cup of plain low-fat yogurt for sauces and dips. Yogurt is a good source of calcium, protein, and vitamins. People who have a hard time digesting milk often find yogurt tolerable. The cool mint is a nice foil to the tartness of yogurt in this recipe.

Everyone knows about Spanish black bean soup, Middle Eastern hummus, and the ever-popular American chili with beans, but many people are not aware that Indians use legumes in many ways and were familiar with bean cookery long before inhabitants of many other parts of the world. The most popular of the Indian bean dishes is dal. Most dal dishes are pureed and range in consistency from thin to thick. Lentils are often used in dal. They are first cooked, then mashed with spices. Dal is very simple to prepare and can be served as a side or main dish. Red lentils create a beautiful dal; to find them, go to a natural grocery store or an Indian market. You can substitute yellow split peas if you can't find red lentils.

Cauliflower is a member of the cruciferous, cancer-fighting vegetable family. Its color should be creamy white with no browning or yellowing.

The head should be compact and the leaves should look crisp. Cauliflower is a good source of vitamin C and is best used within five days of purchase. Cauliflower is a popular vegetable in Indian cooking. The brilliant color of turmeric makes this dish very attractive. Roasting spices increases their flavor, as you'll see when roasting the cumin seed for this menu's salad. Whole cumin seeds will stay fresh for about one year.

This menu's salad recipe comes from one of my testers, Zack, who has travelled extensively through India. It's delicious with chicken, too.

Try baking bananas for a soft, creamy, simply delicious dessert. Here, a very small amount of cardamom is used in the cream. Cardamom seeds are contained in small pods. Each pod contains about 17–20 seeds. Cardamom, like ginger, imparts a warm, spicy, sweet flavor. For the very best flavor, consider purchasing cardamom in the pod and grinding it yourself with an electric or spice grinder.

Pantry List

1 yellow onion
sugar
canola oil
dry white wine
1 can low-fat, low-sodium chicken
   broth
1 bag red lentils
dried chilis
bay leaves
turmeric
paprika
coriander
cayenne pepper
cumin seeds
juice-sweetened marmalade
ground cardamom
1 can evaporated skim milk

Market List

1 1/2 lb halibut steaks
3 cups plain yogurt
ginger root
mint
cilantro
fresh lemon juice
fresh lime juice
green chili
1 large head cauliflower
2 English cucumbers
3 bananas
orange juice
4 oz low-fat cream cheese
1 lemon

STEP-BY-STEP COUNTDOWN

1 Prepare the dip and salad and refrigerate.
2 Prepare the dessert. Refrigerate the cream and turn off the oven after the bananas have baked for 10 minutes. Remove the bananas from the oven.
3 Prepare the halibut and dal. While the halibut is grilling, prepare the cauliflower.
4 Remove the halibut from the grill. Place the fish in a 250-degree oven, covered. Keep the dal in a pot, covered.
5 Serve the dip.
6 Serve the salad.
7 Serve the halibut, dal, and cauliflower.
8 Serve the dessert.

Mint Dip

6 Servings

Serving Size:
2 Tbsp

Exchanges

I Vegetable

Ingredients

1 cup plain yogurt, stirred
1 Tbsp minced onion
1/2 tsp minced ginger
1/4 cup minced mint
2 Tbsp minced cilantro
1 tsp sugar

Preparation—10 minutes

Mix all ingredients together and serve with raw vegetables or crackers.

Calories	24
Calories from Fat	0
Total Fat	0 g
Saturated Fat	0 g
Cholesterol	I mg
Sodium	32 mg
Carbohydrate	4 g
Dietary Fiber	0 g
Sugars	4 g
Protein	2 g

 WHY DON'T YOU . . .

Invest in a "buffet" range. Provided you have an outlet nearby, place the soup that has to simmer for hours on the range, so you can free up a burner.

Halibut on Dal

6 Servings

Serving Size:
4 oz fish
1/2 cup dal

Exchanges

12 Starch
4 Very Lean Meat

Ingredients

1 1/2 Tbsp canola oil
1/2 cup white wine
1/2 cup low-fat, low-sodium
  chicken broth
1 Tbsp fresh lemon juice
2 tsp minced cilantro
1 1/2 lb halibut steaks
3 cups water
1 cup red lentils
2 tsp sugar
3 whole dried chilis
2 bay leaves
1/2 cup sliced onions
2 Tbsp lime juice
2 tsp minced cilantro

Preparation—15 minutes

1 Combine 1 Tbsp oil, wine, broth, lemon juice, and cilantro and pour over the fish. Marinate for 30 minutes at room temperature.
2 Combine the water and lentils in a saucepan and bring to a boil. Cover and simmer for 20 minutes. Add the sugar and stir until the mixture resembles a puree.
3 Heat 1/2 Tbsp oil in a skillet over high heat. Add the chilis and bay leaves and fry until the chilis blacken. Add the onion, lower the heat, and fry until the onions are browned. Add to the lentils and stir. Add the lime juice and cilantro.
4 Grill the halibut on each side for a total of 10–12 minutes. Serve the grilled fish over the dal.

Calories	266
Calories from Fat	44
Total Fat	5 g
Saturated Fat	1 g
Cholesterol	36 mg
Sodium	68 mg
Carbohydrate	22 g
Dietary Fiber	10 g
Sugars	4 g
Protein	33 g

Cauliflower with Turmeric

6 Servings

Serving Size:
1/2 cup

Exchanges

1 Vegetable

Ingredients

2 tsp canola oil
2 tsp minced ginger
2 tsp minced green chili
3 cups cauliflower florets
1 tsp turmeric
1/2 cup low-fat, low-sodium
    chicken broth

Preparation—15 minutes

1 Heat the oil in a skillet over high heat. Add the ginger and chili and stir-fry for 1 minute.
2 Add the cauliflower, turmeric, and broth. Cover and steam until the cauliflower is tender, yet firm, about 6–7 minutes.

Calories	29
Calories from Fat	17
Total Fat	2 g
Saturated Fat	0 g
Cholesterol	0 mg
Sodium	24 mg
Carbohydrate	3 g
Dietary Fiber	1 g
Sugars	1 g
Protein	1 g

Roasted Cumin Seed and Cucumber Salad

6 Servings

Serving Size:
1/2 cup

Exchanges

1 Vegetable

Ingredients

1 1/2 cups plain yogurt, stirred
1/8 tsp turmeric
1/4 tsp paprika
1/2 tsp coriander
1/8 tsp cayenne pepper
1 1/2 English cucumbers, peeled, seeded, and diced
3 tsp cumin seeds
1 Tbsp minced cilantro
Green leaf lettuce (optional)

Preparation—10 minutes

1 Combine the yogurt, turmeric, paprika, coriander, and cayenne. Add the cucumbers and refrigerate for 1 hour.
2 Roast the cumin seeds in a dry, nonstick skillet until the seeds begin to brown. Top the cucumber salad with the seeds. Sprinkle with cilantro and serve over green leaf lettuce, if desired.

Calories	42
Calories from Fat	3
Total Fat	0 g
Saturated Fat	0 g
Cholesterol	1 mg
Sodium	50 mg
Carbohydrate	6 g
Dietary Fiber	1 g
Sugars	5 g
Protein	4 g

Bananas with Cardamom Cream

6 Servings

Serving Size:
1/2 banana

Exchanges

2 Carbohydrate

Ingredients

3 large bananas, halved lengthwise
3 Tbsp orange juice
2 Tbsp lime juice
8 oz low-fat cream cheese
2 Tbsp fruit-sweetened marmalade
3 Tbsp evaporated skim milk
1 tsp sugar
1/4 tsp cardamom
1 1/2 tsp lemon zest (optional)

Preparation—15 minutes

1 Preheat the oven to 350 degrees. Place the bananas in a casserole dish. Sprinkle with the juices. Bake, covered, for 10 minutes.
2 Meanwhile, combine the cream cheese, marmalade, milk, sugar, and cardamom in a mixing bowl. Using electric beaters, beat well.
3 Cut each long half of banana into two pieces and place in a dessert dish. Top with cream, sprinkle with grated lemon zest, and serve.

Calories	150
Calories from Fat	4
Total Fat	0 g
Saturated Fat	0 g
Cholesterol	5 mg
Sodium	227 mg
Carbohydrate	31 g
Dietary Fiber	2 g
Sugars	21 g
Protein	8 g

❖ ❖ ❖

California Seafood Salad

Chilled Cream of Tomato Soup
California Seafood Salad
Cucumber and Fennel Relish
Herbed Bagel Crisps
Peach Smoothies

M E N U   T A L K

The tomato is a versatile vegetable, delicious in any form—whether eaten straight from the vine, crushed for a sauce, or pureed for this soup. You can use this basic recipe to create cream of carrot soup instead. Try it hot or cold: simply omit the tomatoes and tomato juice, substitute 1 lb cooked, pureed carrots, and add the milk. You can also add pureed roasted red peppers to the tomato soup. Add 1/2 cup pureed peppers to the tomato mixture and chill before proceeding with the rest of the recipe.

Halibut is a low-fat, firm, mild-flavored fish. Halibut is available all year long and does well with any cooking method. Orange roughy comes from New Zealand and has become popular in this country. Mild flavored and low in fat, it is almost always sold to markets frozen and then defrosted, so avoid refreezing it or the fish will toughen. Haddock is closely related to cod. It is mild, white, and low in fat. It can also be prepared in any manner. I particularly like it in soups and stews. Bass is a general term that describes a number of fish with spiny fins including striped, rock, and red eye. Bass is particularly good grilled. Try any of the above fish in this light and refreshing salad.

Cucumbers are members of the gourd family. Although they contribute little in the way of nutrition, cucumbers add texture to many foods and are a crisp remedy to summer's heat. Cucumbers are available all year. Choose smooth, firm cucumbers, and store them in the refrigerator for up to 10 days. Seed the cucumber if you don't want excess moisture in your dish.

127

Although arguably the best bagels come from New York, bagel shops have sprouted up all over the United States. For a chewier bagel, buy water bagels. Because they are made without eggs, they are lower in cholesterol, and their texture is not as soft as egg bagels. Try whole-wheat bagels for extra fiber. Be careful with daily consumption—bagel sizes have "swelled" over the years, making them quite caloric. Try to purchase smaller ones. Making your own bagel crisps is easy, and they're lower in fat than commercially prepared bagel crisps. Kids will love making this recipe with you.

Smoothies, first popular in California, are a great snack or dessert. Any fruit, some milk, a flavored extract, and a bit of sweetener make this thick, healthy shake. Have a smoothie party, and experiment with many different combinations!

Pantry List

1 small can low-sodium
   tomato juice
2 cans low-fat, low-sodium
   chicken broth
1 can evaporated skim milk
cloves
garlic salt
olive oil
sherry vinegar
garlic
1 red onion
1/2 lb baby red potatoes
capers
1 small can black olives
white wine vinegar
sugar
3 bagels
dried basil
dried oregano
paprika
garlic powder
almond extract

Market List

1 1/2 lb halibut, haddock,
   orange roughy, or bass
basil
parsley
fresh lemon juice
2 lb plum tomatoes
2 tomatoes
1 avocado
2 cucumbers
1 fennel bulb

2 peaches
skim milk
blueberries

STEP-BY-STEP COUNTDOWN

1 Prepare the soup and refrigerate. This can be done the day before.
2 Cook the fish for the salad, using any cooking method desired.
3 Prepare the relish.
4 Prepare the bagel crisps.
5 Finish preparing the seafood salad.
6 Serve the soup.
7 Serve the salad, relish, and crisps.
8 Prepare the smoothies and serve for dessert.

Chilled Cream of Tomato Soup

6 Servings

Serving Size:
1 cup

Exchanges

1/2 Starch

Ingredients

1/2 lb plum tomatoes, seeded and
      chopped
1 cup low-sodium tomato juice
3 cups low-fat, low-sodium chicken
   broth
1 Tbsp minced basil
1/4 cup minced parsley
1/2 tsp cloves
1 cup evaporated skim milk
Fresh ground pepper
Dash garlic salt (optional)

Preparation—10 minutes

1 Puree the tomatoes in a blender. In a stockpot, combine the pureed tomatoes, tomato juice, broth, basil, parsley, and cloves. Bring to a boil, lower the heat, and simmer for 5 minutes.
2 Refrigerate for several hours. When ready to serve, add the milk and season with pepper and salt.

Calories	60
Calories from Fat	13
Total Fat	1 g
Saturated Fat	0 g
Cholesterol	2 mg
Sodium	111 mg
Carbohydrate	9 g
Dietary Fiber	1 g
Sugars	6 g
Protein	5 g

 ◎ WHY DON'T YOU . . .

*Read your recipe through
before beginning the first step.
This is one rule I always follow.*

California Seafood Salad

6 Servings

Serving Size:
4 oz

Exchanges

1 Starch
4 Very Lean Meat
1 1/2 Monounsat-
    urated Fat

Ingredients

1 Tbsp olive oil
2 Tbsp sherry vinegar
2 cloves garlic, minced
2 Tbsp fresh lemon juice
Fresh ground white or black pepper
    to taste
1 1/2 lb cooked halibut, haddock,
    orange roughy, or bass, flaked
    into large chunks
2 medium tomatoes, diced
1/2 cup diced red onion
1/2 lb cooked baby red
    potatoes, halved
12 thin slices avocado
1/4 cup small capers

Preparation—20 minutes

1 Combine the oil, vinegar, garlic, lemon juice, and pepper in a small bowl.
2 Mix together the fish, tomatoes, onion, and potatoes in a salad bowl. Add the dressing to the salad and toss.
3 Top the salad with avocado and capers and serve.

Calories	286
Calories from Fat	99
Total Fat	11 g
Saturated Fat	2 g
Cholesterol	46 mg
Sodium	330 mg
Carbohydrate	15 g
Dietary Fiber	4 g
Sugars	4 g
Protein	32 g

Cucumber and Fennel Relish

6 Servings

Serving Size:
1/2 cup

Exchanges

1 Vegetable
1/2 Monounsatur-
ated Fat

Ingredients

2 cups thinly sliced cucumber
1 cup thinly sliced fennel bulb
    (remove the core)
1/2 cup very thinly sliced red onion
2 Tbsp chopped black olives
1/2 cup white wine vinegar
1 Tbsp olive oil
2 tsp sugar
Fresh ground pepper

Preparation—15 minutes

1 Mix together the cucumber, fennel, onion, and black olives in a salad bowl.
2 In a small bowl, mix together the vinegar, oil, sugar, and pepper. Pour over the salad and chill for 1 hour before serving.

Calories	42
Calories from Fat	24
Total Fat	3 g
Saturated Fat	0 g
Cholesterol	0 mg
Sodium	34 mg
Carbohydrate	5 g
Dietary Fiber	1 g
Sugars	3 g
Protein	1 g

Herbed Bagel Crisps

6 Servings

Serving Size:
1/2 medium bagel

Exchanges

1 1/2 Starch

Ingredients

3 medium bagels (any variety)
2 tsp olive oil
2 tsp dried basil
1 tsp dried oregano
1/2 tsp paprika
1 tsp garlic powder

Preparation—10 minutes

1 Preheat the oven to 400 degrees. Using a very sharp bread knife, cut each bagel into 6 thin slices. Place the slices on a cookie sheet.
2 Combine the remaining ingredients. Spread the mixture very lightly on each bagel slice.
3 Bake the bagel slices until they are crispy and slightly dry, about 10–12 minutes.

Calories	113
Calories from Fat	19
Total Fat	2 g
Saturated Fat	0 g
Cholesterol	0 mg
Sodium	192 mg
Carbohydrate	19 g
Dietary Fiber	1 g
Sugars	2 g
Protein	4 g

Peach Smoothies

6 Servings

Serving Size:
1/2 cup

Exchanges

1 Fruit

Ingredients

2 cups cubed, peeled peaches
1 cup skim milk
1 Tbsp sugar
1/2 cup fresh blueberries
1 tsp almond extract
Ice cubes

Preparation—5 minutes

Combine all ingredients, using enough ice cubes to make the smoothie cold and thick.

Calories	54
Calories from Fat	1
Total Fat	0 g
Saturated Fat	0 g
Cholesterol	1 mg
Sodium	22 mg
Carbohydrate	12 g
Dietary Fiber	1 g
Sugars	10 g
Protein	2 g

 WHY DON'T YOU . . .

Get a feel for how your menu's organized. Although a balance between taste, color, and texture is important, you'll never get dinner on the table if your recipes are not in sync time wise. Plan on menus that have one recipe chilling while one is baking and another is sauteing.

Far East Flavors

❖ ❖ ❖ ❖

A Taste of Thai 137

Thai Peanut Chicken
Toasted Couscous Asian Style
Cucumber Salad with Fresh Lime
Sesame Spinach
Plum Sorbet

Orange Ginger Salmon 145

Fiery Lime Salad
Orange Ginger Salmon
Five Spice Rice
Vegetables with Cellophane Noodles
Litchis, Kumquats, and Loquats with Watermelon

Asian Sunset Supper 153

Straw Mushroom Soup
Lemongrass Tangerine Tuna
Soba Noodles with Black Sesame Seeds
Daikon and Carrot Salad
Asian Pears with Ginger Syrup

New Year's Feast 161

Asian Salad with Warm Enoki Mushrooms
Lemon Chicken
Jasmine Rice Timbales
Triple Mushroom and Carrot Medley
Sliced Tangerines and Pineapple with
    Pineapple Glaze

Grilled Shanghai Chicken 169

Grilled Chicken with Shallot Ginger Chili Sauce
Fresh Salad with Chinese Vinaigrette
Asian Risotto
Stir-Fried Peppers and Carrots
Tapioca and Pineapple

Spicy Asian Chili 177

Spicy Asian Chili
Cellophane Noodle Salad
Water Chestnuts and Snow Peas
Garlic Rolls
Strawberries and Almonds

❖ ❖ ❖

A Taste of Thai

Thai Peanut Chicken
Toasted Couscous Asian Style
Cucumber Salad with Fresh Lime
Sesame Spinach
Plum Sorbet

MENU TALK

Coconut milk is made of water and fresh or desiccated coconut. The mixture is simmered until foamy, then the liquid is strained through cheesecloth. Coconut is high in saturated fat; however, lite coconut milk is available and is somewhat lower in fat. If you do not want to use coconut milk for this recipe, substitute evaporated skim milk and 1 tsp coconut extract. Reduced-fat peanut butter also is a good product. Just a small amount lends a creamy texture and nutty taste. The marinade for this recipe can be made into a sauce: just thicken with 1 Tbsp cornstarch or arrowroot powder mixed with 2 Tbsp water until smooth, then add to the peanut butter and coconut milk mixture. Toss the sauce with pasta and add fresh steamed vegetables if you like.

Toasted couscous is a relatively new product. Unlike traditional couscous, toasted couscous is made from semolina wheat and looks like little tiny balls of pasta. It is best when sauted with diced onion in a little oil for 5 minutes. Then add 2 cups of broth or water for every 2 cups toasted couscous. Bring the mixture to a boil, lower the heat, cover, and simmer for 15 minutes. Toasted couscous is sold in bags in the grain section of natural food stores. If you cannot find toasted couscous, you can adjust this recipe by omitting it and the broth and using 3 cups of cooked rice or orzo instead.

This cucumber salad is quite spicy. To reduce the spiciness, use fewer chili peppers, or just use 1/4 tsp chili powder. In Asian cultures, a meal is composed of five flavors blended together: bitter, salty, sweet, sour, and

137

pungent. To balance your menu when serving spicy foods, be sure to also serve foods that are cooling, such as the Plum Sorbet.

When sauteing spinach, it is best to wash the leaves (spinach has a tendency to be very gritty) and let the water that clings to the leaves serve as your cooking liquid. Spinach is very delicate and you can drown it with too much liquid. Spinach contains oxalic acid, which inhibits the body's ability to absorb iron. Increase iron absorption by eating foods rich in vitamin C with spinach or meat. I like the fresh spinach packed loose and sold without the cellophane wrapper. Use spinach within three days of purchase.

Fresh plums are available from May to October. Plums should yield to slight pressure. There are many varieties of plums from which to choose, but I like plums with deep red meat. Canned plums packed in water may be substituted for fresh ones. Cherry brandy is made from the distillation of cherry juice and the pits, and may be labeled as kirsch. You may omit this from the recipe if you like.

Pantry List

cherry brandy
sugar
reduced-fat peanut butter
lite soy sauce
garlic
2 cans low-fat, low-sodium chicken
   broth
1 can lite coconut milk
1 small bag toasted unsalted
   peanuts
peanut oil
3 shallots
1 package toasted couscous
oyster sauce
sherry
sesame oil
Asian chili sauce
sesame seeds
rice vinegar
dry white wine

Market List

1 1/2 lb boneless, skinless chicken
   breasts
3 chili peppers
green onions
ginger root
cilantro
1/4 lb shiitake mushrooms
2 medium cucumbers
fresh lime juice
2 1/2 lb fresh spinach
6 plums
fresh lemon juice

Thai Peanut Chicken

6 Servings

Serving Size:
3 oz

Exchanges

4 Very Lean Meat
1 1/2 Fat

Ingredients

2 Tbsp reduced-fat peanut butter
3 Tbsp lite soy sauce
2 chili peppers, minced
2 cloves garlic, minced
1/2 cup low-fat, low-sodium
     chicken broth
1/4 cup lite coconut milk
2 Tbsp minced green onions
2 tsp minced ginger
1 1/2 lb boneless, skinless chicken
     breasts
1/2 cup chopped toasted peanuts
2 Tbsp minced cilantro

Preparation—30 minutes

1 Heat the peanut butter, soy sauce, chili peppers, garlic, and broth in a saucepan over medium heat. Bring to a boil, lower the heat, and simmer for 10 minutes.
2 Add the coconut milk, green onions, and ginger and simmer for 5 minutes. Add the chicken breasts to the marinade and marinate overnight.
3 The next day, broil the chicken with an oven rack set 4–6 inches from the heat source. Broil for 6–7 minutes per side, until no traces of pink remain. Garnish with chopped peanuts and cilantro.

Calories	213
Calories from Fat	82
Total Fat	9 g
Saturated Fat	2 g
Cholesterol	69 mg
Sodium	310 mg
Carbohydrate	4 g
Dietary Fiber	1 g
Sugars	1 g
Protein	28 g

Toasted Couscous Asian Style

6 Servings

Serving Size:
1/2 cup

Exchanges

2 1/2 Starch
1/2 Fat

Ingredients

2 tsp peanut oil
3 shallots, minced
2 tsp minced ginger
2 Tbsp minced green onions
2 cloves garlic, minced
1/2 cup sliced shiitake mushrooms
1 8-oz pkg toasted couscous
2 cups low-fat, low-sodium chicken broth
1 Tbsp oyster sauce
2 Tbsp lite soy sauce
2 Tbsp sherry
1 tsp sesame oil
1/2 tsp Asian chili sauce
2 Tbsp toasted sesame seeds

Preparation—15 minutes

1 Heat the oil in a skillet over medium-high heat. Add the shallots, ginger, green onions, and garlic and saute for 2 minutes.
2 Add the mushrooms and saute for 3 minutes. Add the couscous and the broth. Bring to a boil, lower the heat, cover, and simmer for 15 minutes.
3 Meanwhile, combine the oyster sauce, soy sauce, sherry, sesame oil, and Asian chili sauce in a small bowl. Add to the couscous and simmer for 2 minutes.
4 Garnish with toasted sesame seeds and serve.

Calories	216
Calories from Fat	43
Total Fat	5 g
Saturated Fat	1 g
Cholesterol	0 mg
Sodium	352 mg
Carbohydrate	36 g
Dietary Fiber	3 g
Sugars	4 g
Protein	7 g

Cucumber Salad with Fresh Lime

6 Servings

Serving Size:
1/2 cup

Exchanges

Free Food

Ingredients

3 cups diced cucumbers, seeded
1 red chili pepper, minced (optional)
2 cloves garlic, minced
3 Tbsp fresh lime juice
1/2 tsp sesame oil

Preparation—10 minutes

Combine all ingredients and serve.

Calories	14
Calories from Fat	4
Total Fat	0 g
Saturated Fat	0 g
Cholesterol	0 mg
Sodium	1 mg
Carbohydrate	2 g
Dietary Fiber	0 g
Sugars	2 g
Protein	0 g

 WHY DON'T YOU . . .

*Take inventory of your pots
and pans. Throw out pieces you
never use or that are chipped or
scratched. Purchase what you
need for everyday cooking,
and add a piece or two for
larger-volume cooking, such as
a roasting pan and an 8-quart
pot for soups and stews.*

Sesame Spinach

6 Servings

Serving Size:
1/2 cup

Exchanges

2 Vegetable

Ingredients

2 1/2 lb fresh spinach, washed and
    trimmed
2 Tbsp lite soy sauce
3 tsp rice vinegar
1 tsp white wine
2 tsp sugar
2 Tbsp low-fat, low-sodium chicken
    broth
2 Tbsp toasted sesame seeds

Preparation—5 minutes

1   With the water clinging to the leaves, cook the spinach over medium-high heat in a nonstick skillet until the spinach wilts, about 3 minutes.
2   Combine the soy sauce, vinegar, wine, sugar, and broth. Pour over the spinach and cook for 1 minute.
3   Top with toasted sesame seeds and serve.

Calories	42
Calories from Fat	3
Total Fat	0 g
Saturated Fat	0 g
Cholesterol	0 mg
Sodium	306 mg
Carbohydrate	7 g
Dietary Fiber	4 g
Sugars	2 g
Protein	5 g

Plum Sorbet

6 Servings

Serving Size:
1/3 cup

Exchanges

1 1/2 Carbohydrate

Ingredients

2 1/2 cups peeled and diced plums
1/3 cup fresh lemon juice
1/3 cup sugar
3 Tbsp cherry brandy

Preparation—5 minutes

1 Combine all ingredients in a food processor and blend until smooth.
2 Pour into a container and freeze for several hours. Remove from the freezer, whip, and freeze again for 2 hours.
3 Let the mixture stand for 5 minutes to soften slightly before serving.

Calories	113
Calories from Fat	4
Total Fat	0 g
Saturated Fat	0 g
Cholesterol	0 mg
Sodium	4 mg
Carbohydrate	25 g
Dietary Fiber	1 g
Sugars	21 g
Protein	1 g

Orange Ginger Salmon

Fiery Lime Salad
Orange Ginger Salmon
Five Spice Rice
Vegetables with Cellophane Noodles
Litchis, Kumquats, and Loquats with Watermelon

MENU TALK

You can make your own chili oil for this menu's salad. To do this, brown about 10 small, dried red chilis in about 2 Tbsp sesame oil for 3–5 minutes. Remove from the heat and add an additional 1/4 cup oil. Let stand for about 1–2 weeks. Using highly flavored oils is a great way to cut down on the fat content of your food. A very small amount of oil is needed to flavor the dish. The lime juice in the dressing is another source of flavor without fat. You may also buy already prepared chili oil, but try to make your own at least once. It's fun, easy, inexpensive, and very flavorful!

Salmon, the woodsy, nutty-flavored fish native to both Atlantic and Pacific waters, is one of my favorite fishes to grill, saute, and roast. There are many varieties of salmon, ranging from wild salmon to farm-raised Pacific salmon, which has a milder flavor. You have a little leeway when cooking salmon; it has about 17% fat, so it stands up well to high heat and is hard to dry out unless you really overcook it.

Chinese five spice is a must-have item for your spice rack. In China, there are five elements (fire, water, earth, metal, and wood), five flavors (bitter, salty, sweet, sour, and pungent), and five spices, composed of Szechuan peppercorns, fennel, cloves, cinnamon, and star anise. Star anise may be unfamiliar to American cooks. It is an 8-pointed star of the fruit of native Chinese evergreens, and has a bolder taste than licorice. It can be bought whole, broken, or ground. Whole star anise is used in braised dishes and floated on tea. Broken star anise is used in sauces, and ground is used

See color photo after p. 240.

145

in five spice powder. Chinese five spice produces some of the tastiest dishes you will ever make. You can make your own by grinding 2 Tbsp each of peppercorns, fennel seeds, whole cloves, star anise (ground or broken), and a cinnamon stick until the mixture is powdered.

Cellophane noodles are also known as bean thread noodles. These are fine, dried noodles made from mung bean flour. They are sold in packages and need to be soaked in hot water for 15–20 minutes before using them in recipes. They are clear when they rehydrate. Asian chili sauce is a generic term to cover many sauces that may be labeled as chili paste, chili sauce, or chili paste with garlic. All you need is 1/2 tsp to add flavor. The best Asian chili sauces are found in Asian grocery stores. Use hot pepper sauce if you can't find Asian chili sauce.

Kumquats are tiny orange fruits about the size of large grapes. You eat the skin as well as the fruit. Kumquats are rich in vitamins A and C and contain some calcium. When you cannot find them fresh, use canned kumquats found in Asian grocery stores. Litchis and loquats can also be bought canned and used after rinsing. Litchis, grown in subtropical regions, have a bright red shell encasing a creamy white sweet fruit. Loquats are also called May apples and resemble apricots. They taste sweet, like cherries. Combining these fruits with cold, juicy watermelon is a taste sensation. This recipe was given to me by the merchants at the Sukhothai Food Market in Alexandria, Virginia.

Pantry List

1 red onion
lite soy sauce
sugar
dry white wine
hot chili oil
crushed red pepper
canned litchis
canned loquats
canned kumquats
1 pkg bean thread noodles
1 can low-fat, low-sodium chicken
   broth
garlic
canned straw mushrooms
dry sherry
sesame oil
Asian chili sauce
cornstarch or arrowroot powder
1 box jasmine rice
Chinese five spice

Market List

1 1/2 lb fresh salmon filets
orange juice
lemon juice
ginger root
2 heads green leaf lettuce
2 tomatoes
2 carrots
fresh lime juice
watermelon
1 leek
1 red bell pepper
1 bunch broccoli

1 bunch asparagus
bok choy
1 bag frozen peas
green onions

STEP-BY-STEP COUNTDOWN

1 Marinate the salmon.
2 Prepare the dessert and refrigerate.
3 Prepare the salad and dressing, but do not combine them.
4 Prepare all the ingredients for the vegetables.
5 Prepare the rice and turn off the heat.
6 Cook the vegetables.
7 Grill the salmon.
8 Toss the salad with the dressing and serve.
9 Serve the salmon, rice, and vegetables.
10 Serve the dessert.

Fiery Lime Salad

6 Servings

Serving Size:
1 cup lettuce
1/2 cup vegetables

Exchanges

2 Vegetable
1/2 Fat

Ingredients

6 cups green leaf lettuce, washed
   and torn
2 tomatoes, sliced
1 red onion, thinly sliced
1 carrot, sliced
1/3 cup fresh lime juice
2 tsp hot chili oil
1/2 tsp crushed red pepper
   (optional)
1 Tbsp lite soy sauce
2 tsp sugar

Preparation—15 minutes

1 Mix together the lettuce, tomatoes, red onion, and carrot in a salad bowl.
2 In a small bowl, whisk together the lime juice, hot chili oil, crushed red pepper, soy sauce, and sugar.
3 Toss the salad with the dressing and serve.

Calories	64
Calories from Fat	18
Total Fat	2 g
Saturated Fat	0 g
Cholesterol	0 mg
Sodium	118 mg
Carbohydrate	12 g
Dietary Fiber	3 g
Sugars	7 g
Protein	2 g

❖ ❖ ❖ ❖ ❖ ❖
➥ WHY DON'T YOU . . .

Purchase a beautiful wooden salad bowl. If you did not get one for a wedding, graduation, or first apartment gift, get one now. They look great on every table!

Orange Ginger Salmon

6 Servings

Serving Size:
3 oz

Exchanges

3 Lean
1/2 Monounsatur-
ated Fat

Ingredients

1/2 cup orange juice
1 Tbsp lemon juice
2 Tbsp minced ginger
3 Tbsp lite soy sauce
2 tsp sugar
1 Tbsp white wine
1 1/2 lb fresh salmon filets

Preparation—10 minutes

1 Combine the orange juice, lemon juice, ginger, soy sauce, sugar, and wine in a shallow pan.
2 Add the salmon filets and marinate for 30 minutes or up to 2 hours.
3 Broil or grill the salmon until tender, about 6–7 minutes per side.

Calories	202
Calories from Fat	87
Total Fat	10 g
Saturated Fat	2 g
Cholesterol	77 mg
Sodium	210 mg
Carbohydrate	3 g
Dietary Fiber	0 g
Sugars	3 g
Protein	24 g

Five Spice Rice

6 Servings

Serving Size:
1/2 cup

Exchanges

3 Starch

Ingredients

2 tsp sesame oil
2 cloves garlic, minced
2 tsp minced ginger
2 Tbsp minced green onions
1 1/2 cups rinsed jasmine rice
3 cups low-fat, low-sodium chicken
    broth
2 Tbsp lite soy sauce
1/2 cup frozen peas, thawed
2 tsp Chinese five spice
1/2 cup minced red bell pepper

Preparation—10minutes

1 Heat the oil in a saucepan over medium-high heat. Add the garlic, ginger, and green onions and saute for 2 minutes. Add the rice and saute for 2 minutes.
2 Stir in the broth and bring to a boil. Cover, lower the heat, and cook for 15 minutes.
3 Add the soy sauce, peas, and Chinese five spice. Cook until the rice has absorbed the liquid, about 5 minutes.
4 Garnish with red bell pepper and serve.

Calories	223
Calories from Fat	27
Total Fat	3 g
Saturated Fat	1 g
Cholesterol	0 mg
Sodium	257 mg
Carbohydrate	45 g
Dietary Fiber	2 g
Sugars	2 g
Protein	7 g

Vegetables with Cellophane Noodles

6 Servings

Serving Size:
1/2 cup

Exchanges

1 1/2 Starch
1 Vegetable

Ingredients

6 oz bean thread (cellophane) noodles
1/2 cup low-fat, low-sodium chicken broth
2 cloves garlic, minced
1 leek, white part only, washed and sliced into very thin rings
1/2 cup diced red bell pepper
1/2 cup sliced carrots
1/2 cup broccoli florets
1/2 cup asparagus tips
1/2 cup straw mushrooms or sliced white mushrooms
1/2 cup chopped bok choy
2 Tbsp lite soy sauce
2 Tbsp dry sherry
1/2 tsp sesame oil
1 tsp Asian chili sauce
1/2 cup low-fat, low-sodium chicken broth
1 1/2 Tbsp cornstarch or arrowroot powder

Preparation—25 minutes

1 Add the noodles to a pot of boiling water and cook for 10 minutes. Drain, then set the noodles aside.
2 Heat the broth in a wok or heavy skillet over high heat. Add the garlic and leek and stir-fry for 5 minutes. Add the red bell pepper and carrots and stir-fry for 2 minutes.
3 Add the broccoli and asparagus, cover, and steam for 2 minutes. Add the mushrooms and bok choy and stir-fry for 2 minutes. Stir in the cooked noodles.
4 In a separate bowl, combine the soy sauce, sherry, oil, chili sauce, broth, and cornstarch or arrowroot powder. Add this sauce to the noodle pan and cook until the sauce has thickened, about 1 minute. Serve.

Calories	143
Calories from Fat	9
Total Fat	1 g
Saturated Fat	0 g
Cholesterol	0 mg
Sodium	247 mg
Carbohydrate	33 g
Dietary Fiber	3 g
Sugars	3 g
Protein	2 g

Litchis, Kumquats, and Loquats with Watermelon

6 Servings

Serving Size:
1/2 cup

Exchanges

1 Fruit

Ingredients

1 1/2 cups watermelon cubes
1/2 cup canned litchis, drained
1/2 cup canned kumquats, drained
1/2 cup canned loquats, drained

Preparation—10 minutes

Combine all ingredients. To serve, spoon into individual parfait glasses.

Calories	46
Calories from Fat	3
Total Fat	0 g
Saturated Fat	0 g
Cholesterol	0 mg
Sodium	2 mg
Carbohydrate	11 g
Dietary Fiber	2 g
Sugars	9 g
Protein	1 g

❖ ❖ ❖ ❖ ❖

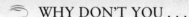 WHY DON'T YOU . . .

Try a new cooking technique each month. If you feel your chopping skills need some work, practice a few minutes every few days. Mastering the basic skills will serve you well in all types of situations.

Asian Sunset Supper

Straw Mushroom Soup
Lemongrass Tangerine Tuna
Soba Noodles with Black Sesame Seeds
Daikon and Carrot Salad
Asian Pears with Ginger Syrup

MENU TALK

The soup for this menu is very versatile. You can add pieces of leftover chicken, shrimp, or tofu; instead of straw mushrooms, you can use sliced white or shiitake mushrooms; and it freezes very well. Straw mushrooms can be found in cans in the grocery store. You do not need to chop them up, just drain and rinse.

Lemongrass is a key seasoning ingredient for Asian cooking. It is better to use fresh lemongrass, because much flavor is lost in the drying process. Lemongrass can be found in most Asian grocery stores and some supermarkets. To use it, cut off the bottom three inches, remove some of the outer leaves, then chop this base like you would chop green onions. If you cannot find lemongrass, the zest (outer peel) of a lemon can be substituted. Lemongrass works very well when combined with garlic and ginger. Buy really fresh tuna, with a rosy red color. Any seafood with an ammonia or fishy smell should be avoided. Use fish within 24 hours of purchase.

Soba noodles are delightful, chewy Asian noodles made from buckwheat flour and wheat flour. You cook soba noodles just like regular pasta. They cook in about 5 minutes. Soba noodles are wonderful stirred into soups and tossed with stir-fried vegetables. Soba noodles are available at all Asian markets, natural food stores, and many supermarkets. Black sesame seeds are used in China to coat meat and fish before cooking to give them an extra crunch. In Japan, they are used to season noodle dishes. Black sesame

153

seeds are available in Asian markets and through mail-order spice houses. Use toasted white sesame seeds if black are unavailable.

Daikon is the Japanese radish. Shaped like a fat carrot, it is white, with a slight bitter taste. Its texture is like a water chestnut's. Daikon is a wonderful vegetable to add for crunchiness. It can be eaten raw, preferably shredded like in this menu's recipe, or it can be sliced and stir-fried along with other vegetables. Often daikon is served pickled.

Asian pears are a cross between an apple and pear. There are more than 100 varieties of Asian pears; most are grown in Japan. They are quite crunchy and sweet. Store ripe pears in the refrigerator. Use another variety of pear or apples in this recipe if Asian pears are unavailable.

Pantry List

rice vinegar
sugar
sesame oil
garlic
crystallized ginger
grenadine
cornstarch or arrowroot powder
4 cans low-fat, low-sodium chicken
      broth
lite soy sauce
dry sherry
1 can straw mushrooms
crushed red pepper
dry white wine
1 pkg soba noodles
black sesame seeds
1 onion

Market List

1 1/2 lb fresh tuna steaks
ginger root
green onions
4 carrots
tangerine juice
1 stalk lemongrass
1 red bell pepper
1 large daikon radish
butter lettuce leaves
3 Asian pears
lemon juice

Straw Mushroom Soup

6 Servings

Serving Size:
1 cup

Exchanges

1/2 Starch

Ingredients

1 tsp sesame oil
1 tsp minced ginger
2 tsp minced garlic
1/2 cup diced carrot
3 Tbsp minced green onions
6 cups low-fat, low-sodium chicken broth
2 Tbsp lite soy sauce
2 Tbsp dry sherry
1 cup canned straw mushrooms, drained, left whole
1/2 cup minced green onions

Preparation—20 minutes

1 Heat the oil in a stockpot over medium-high heat. Add the ginger, garlic, and carrots and saute for 3 minutes. Add 3 Tbsp green onions and saute for 2 minutes.
2 Add the broth, bring to a boil, lower the heat, and simmer for 10 minutes.
3 Add the soy sauce and sherry and simmer for 5 minutes. Add the mushrooms and simmer for 5 minutes.
4 Ladle into individual serving bowls and garnish each serving with the remaining green onions.

Calories	53
Calories from Fat	28
Total Fat	3 g
Saturated Fat	1 g
Cholesterol	0 mg
Sodium	429 mg
Carbohydrate	6 g
Dietary Fiber	1 g
Sugars	3 g
Protein	4 g

Lemongrass Tangerine Tuna

6 Servings

Serving Size:
3 oz

Exchanges

3 Lean Meat

Ingredients

1/2 cup low-fat, low-sodium
      chicken broth
2 Tbsp lite soy sauce
2 Tbsp sesame oil
1/4 cup tangerine juice (or substitute
      orange juice)
1 Tbsp minced fresh lemongrass
1 tsp crushed red pepper
1 1/2 lb fresh tuna steaks

Preparation—10 minutes

1 Combine the broth, soy sauce, oil, juice, lemongrass, and pepper in a shallow pan.
2 Add the tuna and marinate 30 minutes to 2 hours.
3 Broil or grill the tuna on each side for about 4–5 minutes and serve.

Calories	180
Calories from Fat	69
Total Fat	8 g
Saturated Fat	2 g
Cholesterol	42 mg
Sodium	146 mg
Carbohydrate	1 g
Dietary Fiber	0 g
Sugars	1 g
Protein	26 g

Soba Noodles with Black Sesame Seeds

6 Servings

Serving Size:
1/2 cup

Exchanges

1 1/2 Starch
1 Fat

Ingredients

2 Tbsp dry white wine
2 Tbsp low-fat, low-sodium chicken broth
1/2 cup minced onion
2 cloves garlic, minced
1/2 cup sliced carrots
1/2 cup diced red bell pepper
1 cup low-fat, low-sodium chicken broth, divided
2 Tbsp lite soy sauce
1 tsp sesame oil
2 Tbsp dry sherry
1 Tbsp cornstarch or arrowroot powder
3 cups cooked soba (Japanese buckwheat) noodles
1/2 cup black sesame seeds, toasted
1/2 cup minced green onions

Preparation—15 minutes

1 Heat the wine and broth in a wok. Add the onion and garlic and stir-fry for 1 minute.
2 Add the carrots and bell pepper and stir-fry for 2 minutes. Add 1/2 cup of the broth, bring to a boil, lower the heat, cover, and steam for 3 minutes.
3 Combine the remaining 1/2 cup of broth and the soy sauce, oil, sherry, and cornstarch or arrowroot powder in a measuring cup until the cornstarch or arrowroot powder is dissolved. Add the sauce to the vegetables in the wok.
4 Add the soba noodles and cook until the sauce is thickened. Add the black sesame seeds. Garnish with minced green onions to serve.

Calories	171
Calories from Fat	66
Total Fat	7 g
Saturated Fat	1 g
Cholesterol	0 mg
Sodium	268 mg
Carbohydrate	22 g
Dietary Fiber	3 g
Sugars	5 g
Protein	6 g

Daikon and Carrot Salad

6 Servings

Serving Size:
1/2 cup with
lettuce

Exchanges

2 Vegetable

Ingredients

24 butter lettuce leaves
      (4 per person)
1 1/2 cups shredded daikon radish
      (use all carrots if you cannot
      find daikon)
1 1/2 cups shredded carrots
1/2 cup rice vinegar
2 tsp sugar
1 tsp sesame oil
1 clove garlic, minced
Fresh ground white, black, or
      Szechwan pepper

Preparation—5 minutes

1 Line each of 6 salad plates with 4 lettuce leaves.
In a large bowl, combine the daikon and carrots.
2 In a medium bowl, whisk together the
remaining ingredients. Toss the dressing together
with the daikon and carrots.
3 Mound each lettuce-lined plate with the salad
and serve.

Calories	41
Calories from Fat	10
Total Fat	1 g
Saturated Fat	0 g
Cholesterol	0 mg
Sodium	19 mg
Carbohydrate	8 g
Dietary Fiber	2 g
Sugars	6 g
Protein	1 g

Asian Pears with Ginger Syrup

6 Servings

Serving Size:
1/2 pear

Exchanges

1 1/2 Carbohydrate

Ingredients

1 cup water
1/4 cup sugar
2 Tbsp fresh lemon juice
1/4 cup minced crystallized ginger
2 Tbsp grenadine syrup
3 medium Asian pears, sliced, skins on
2 tsp cornstarch or arrowroot powder
1 Tbsp water

Preparation—15 minutes

1   Combine 1 cup water, sugar, and lemon juice in a skillet over medium heat. Cook until the sugar is dissolved. Add the ginger, grenadine, and pears. Cook over low heat for 15 minutes.
2   Mix the cornstarch or arrowroot powder with 1 Tbsp water and add to the skillet. Cook until the sauce is thickened and glazes the pears.

Calories	101
Calories from Fat	0
Total Fat	0 g
Saturated Fat	0 g
Cholesterol	0 mg
Sodium	3 mg
Carbohydrate	26 g
Dietary Fiber	2 g
Sugars	22 g
Protein	0 g

New Year's Feast

Asian Salad with Warm Enoki Mushrooms
Lemon Chicken
Jasmine Rice Timbales
Triple Mushroom and Carrot Medley
Sliced Tangerines and Pineapple with Pineapple Glaze

MENU TALK

Enoki mushrooms are funny little long mushrooms that are sold in most supermarkets and Asian markets. Long, white, and thin, they really do not look like conventional mushrooms at all. They have a crisp, clean taste. They come sold in a package; to use them, cut off the usually dirty base and the mushroom will separate into individual pieces. They are used in soups, salads, and stir-frys. If you cannot find them, use regular mushrooms. The dressing and mushrooms in this salad can also top pasta, chicken, pork, seafood, or rice. I think of the ginger, garlic, green onions, and lemongrass in this dish as seasoning vegetables; without them, this recipe would be a little bland. Whenever you want to prepare Asian food, using some combination of these four seasonings will give you authentic flavor. Using bok choy and spinach will enhance your calcium intake and provide a welcome change from plain lettuce.

When I was living in New York, my favorite Chinese meal was Lemon Chicken. After gaining lots of weight, I developed a version of lemon chicken that is much lower in fat but has the same great taste! My version is less sweet and is not fried; the result is a nice, velvety-tasting chicken with just the right balance of sweet and tart. I retained the traditional method of velveting, where you combine the chicken with egg white and cornstarch or arrowroot powder and let it rest for 15 minutes. This coating protects the chicken when it is sauted and does not allow it to brown. The result is a very tender piece of chicken.

Jasmine rice is the perfumed rice of Thailand. Try to use it when the recipe calls for it—the flavor is worth the effort, although you'll find jasmine rice in most supermarkets. This menu's recipe involves molding the rice, which sounds more complicated than it is. You can have fun with this by buying inexpensive, small molds from any kitchen shop. Spray them lightly with nonstick cooking spray, pack the hot rice into them, and quickly unmold them onto the dinner plates.

Canned straw mushrooms are a favorite of mine. Keep a can of them on the shelf for easy toss-ins to stir-fries and salad. They require no cooking or chopping—just open the can and use them! They are great combined with other mushrooms, as in this recipe.

Use the glaze for this dessert to top low-fat frozen yogurt, fresh fruit, and low-fat cakes. The topping can be made ahead of time and kept in the refrigerator. Use oranges or mandarin oranges if tangerines are not available.

Pantry List

peanut oil
garlic
1 can low-fat, low-sodium
   chicken broth
lite soy sauce
sugar
dry white wine
crushed red pepper
sesame seeds
1 box jasmine rice
dry sherry
honey
chili powder
cornstarch or arrowroot powder
sesame oil
canned straw mushrooms
1 can pineapple chunks
cinnamon
allspice
pineapple extract
nonstick cooking spray

Market List

1 1/2 lb boneless, skinless chicken
   breasts
1 lb fresh spinach
1 bok choy
1 bunch green onions
ginger root
1 stalk lemongrass
1 pkg enoki mushrooms
1 egg white
1 red bell pepper
1/2 lb shiitake mushrooms

lemon juice
1/2 lb white mushrooms
3 tangerines
1 carrot
unsweetened frozen pineapple
   juice concentrate

1 Prepare the dessert and refrigerate.
2 Toss together the spinach, bok choy, and green onions for the salad. Set aside. Prepare all ingredients for the dressing and mushrooms, but do not cook the mushrooms.
3 Prepare step 1 of the chicken recipe. Then combine all ingredients for the sauce except the cornstarch and water. Set aside.
4 Prepare the rice, dice the topping, and set aside.
5 Prepare all the ingredients for the mushrooms and carrots, but do not cook them.
6 Finish preparing the chicken, cover the wok, and turn off the heat.
7 Finish preparing the salad and serve.
8 Cook the mushrooms and carrots.
9 Mold and plate the rice and add the toppings.
10 Reheat the chicken, if necessary, and serve it with the rice and mushrooms and carrots.
11 Serve the dessert.

Asian Salad with Warm Enoki Mushrooms

6 Servings

Serving Size:
1 cup

Exchanges

1 Vegetable
1/2 Fat

Ingredients

5 cups spinach, torn
1 cup sliced bok choy
1/2 cup sliced green onions
2 tsp peanut oil
2 cloves garlic, minced
1 tsp minced ginger
1 Tbsp minced green onions
1 tsp minced lemongrass (optional)
1/2 cup low-fat, low-sodium
    chicken broth
2 Tbsp lite soy sauce
1 tsp sugar
2 Tbsp dry white wine
1/4 tsp crushed red pepper
1 pkg enoki mushrooms (or use 1
    cup sliced white mushrooms)
Toasted sesame seeds

Preparation—15 minutes

1 Toss together the spinach, bok choy, and 1/2 cup green onions. Divide the mixture evenly among 6 salad plates.
2 Heat the oil in a skillet over medium-high heat. Add the garlic, ginger, 1 Tbsp green onions, and lemongrass. Saute for 2 minutes.
3 Add the remaining ingredients except the toasted sesame seeds and cook over medium heat until the mushrooms are cooked, about 3 minutes.
4 Divide the mushrooms among the salad plates and pour some sauce over each salad. Garnish with toasted sesame seeds.

Calories	51
Calories from Fat	24
Total Fat	3 g
Saturated Fat	0 g
Cholesterol	0 mg
Sodium	251 mg
Carbohydrate	5 g
Dietary Fiber	2 g
Sugars	2 g
Protein	3 g

Lemon Chicken

6 Servings

Serving Size:
3 1/2 oz

Exchanges

1/2 Carbohydrate
4 Very Lean Meat

Ingredients

1 1/2 lb boneless, skinless chicken
      breasts, cut into 3-inch strips
1 egg white, beaten
2 Tbsp cornstarch or arrowroot
   powder
2 tsp peanut oil
1 cup low-fat, low-sodium
   chicken broth
4 Tbsp fresh lemon juice
2 tsp dry sherry
1 tsp lite soy sauce
2 Tbsp honey
1/4 tsp chili powder
2 Tbsp cold water
2 Tbsp minced green onions

Preparation—10 minutes

1 In a large bowl, combine the chicken with
the egg white. Add 1 Tbsp cornstarch or arrowroot
powder and mix well until coated. Refrigerate for
15 minutes.
2 Heat the oil in a nonstick wok or skillet. Add
the chicken strips and saute for 10 minutes. Remove
the chicken from the wok or skillet.
3 In a medium bowl, combine the chicken broth,
lemon juice, sherry, soy sauce, honey, and chili
powder. Pour into the wok and bring to a boil,
lower the heat, and simmer for 5 minutes.
4 Mix 1 Tbsp cornstarch or arrowroot powder
with the water and add to the sauce. Cook until the
sauce is thick, about 3–4 minutes. Add the chicken
and cook for 1 minute. Garnish with green onions.

Calories	190
Calories from Fat	43
Total Fat	5 g
Saturated Fat	1 g
Cholesterol	69 mg
Sodium	124 mg
Carbohydrate	10 g
Dietary Fiber	0 g
Sugars	6 g
Protein	26 g

Jasmine Rice Timbales

6 Servings

Serving Size:
1/2 cup

Exchanges

2 1/2 Starch

Ingredients

1 1/2 cups uncooked jasmine rice, rinsed
3 cups low-fat, low-sodium chicken broth
2 Tbsp toasted sesame seeds
Nonstick cooking spray
2 Tbsp finely minced red bell pepper
1 Tbsp finely minced green onions

Preparation—10 minutes

1 Place the rice and broth in a heavy saucepan. Bring to a boil, lower the heat, cover, and simmer until the rice is tender, about 20 minutes. Add the sesame seeds.
2 Lightly spray 6 scalloped custard cups with nonstick cooking spray. Pack the rice into the scalloped custard cups and unmold onto each individual plate.
3 Top the rice timbales evenly with red bell pepper and green onions.

Calories	198
Calories from Fat	27
Total Fat	3 g
Saturated Fat	1 g
Cholesterol	0 mg
Sodium	56 mg
Carbohydrate	39 g
Dietary Fiber	1 g
Sugars	1 g
Protein	5 g

❖ ❖ ❖ ❖ ❖ ❖

VINEGARS

Wine Vinegars

Used primarily in French cooking, the wine vinegars are pleasingly pungent. Red wine vinegar is typically used to make a classic vinaigrette. You can use wine vinegars for general cooking purposes, too. Try the champagne vinegars for a fine, light flavor.

Triple Mushroom and Carrot Medley

6 Servings

Serving Size:
1/2 cup

Exchanges

1 Vegetable
1/2 Fat

Ingredients

1 1/2 tsp sesame oil
1 cup sliced shiitake mushrooms
1 cup sliced white mushrooms
1/2 cup canned whole straw
    mushrooms, drained
1/2 cup sliced carrots
2 Tbsp lite soy sauce
1 Tbsp dry sherry
1 Tbsp honey
1/2 cup low-fat, low-sodium
    chicken broth
1 Tbsp sliced green onions

Preparation—15 minutes

1 Heat the oil in a wok over high heat. Add the mushrooms and saute for 4 minutes. Add the carrots and saute for 3 minutes.
2 Add the remaining ingredients except the green onions. Cover and steam for 5 minutes. Garnish with green onions to serve.

Calories	51
Calories from Fat	14
Total Fat	2 g
Saturated Fat	0 g
Cholesterol	0 mg
Sodium	276 mg
Carbohydrate	9 g
Dietary Fiber	2 g
Sugars	6 g
Protein	2 g

Sliced Tangerines and Pineapple with Pineapple Glaze

6 Servings

Serving Size:
1/2 cup

Exchanges

1 1/2 Fruit

Ingredients

1 1/2 cups sectioned tangerine
1 1/2 cups chunk pineapple
1/2 cup unsweetened frozen
    pineapple juice concentrate,
    thawed
1 tsp cinnamon
Dash allspice
2 tsp cornstarch
1/4 tsp pineapple extract

Preparation—5 minutes

1 Evenly divide a mixture of the tangerine and pineapple among 6 fruit cups.
2 Combine the remaining ingredients in a saucepan and cook over medium heat until thick and of glazing consistency.
3 The fruit cups may be served with the glaze hot or cold. To serve, pour some of the glaze over each fruit serving.

Calories	87
Calories from Fat	2
Total Fat	0 g
Saturated Fat	0 g
Cholesterol	0 mg
Sodium	8 mg
Carbohydrate	21 g
Dietary Fiber	2 g
Sugars	17 g
Protein	1 g

❖ ❖ ❖ ❖ ❖ ❖

 WHY DON'T YOU . . .

Experiment with new foods every month. As long as they are healthy and fit into your meal plan, branch out.

Grilled Shanghai Chicken

Grilled Chicken with Shallot Ginger Chili Sauce
Fresh Salad with Chinese Vinaigrette
Asian Risotto
Stir-Fried Peppers and Carrots
Tapioca and Pineapple

MENU TALK

Instead of commercially prepared barbecue sauces, why not make a simple one at home? This smoky flavored, rich sauce uses an array of Asian ingredients and tastes great on grilled food. Bottled chili sauce is a blend of tomatoes, chilis, garlic, oregano, cumin, coriander, and cloves. It can be found in any supermarket. When the bits of ginger coating this chicken are grilled, they help to form a delicious crust. Brush this sauce on the chicken as it grills and heat the remaining sauce to serve on the side.

Choose your favorite greens for this salad. I like to use spinach and red leaf lettuce. The mandarin oranges add color and sweetness to the greens. Mung bean sprouts are often used for Asian cooking, but feel free to select your favorite variety. Sprouts are best eaten raw, but can be cooked briefly if you're careful to preserve their crispness. Sprouts should be crisp looking, with no mushy or dark spots. Sprouts are very perishable, so they should be refrigerated promptly and used quickly.

The rice represents a fusion of my two favorite cuisines, Italian and Asian. I am again inspired by Hugh Carpenter to create intense flavors. I use arborio rice, the traditional Italian rice found in risotto. It has a fat, short rice kernel with a high starch content. The starchiness imparts a wonderfully creamy texture, rather than the fluffy texture of long-grain rice. Arborio rice can be found at most supermarkets. This is the only rice you do not rinse before using, because, like pasta, rinsing removes some of the starch. The addition of sherry, soy sauce, and hoisin sauce provides the

Asian flavor. This recipe requires a little arm work, so enlist some aid and take turns stirring the rice. Eat this risotto when it's very fresh.

Quickly stir-frying vegetables is a welcome cooking method after the more labor-intensive risotto! Carrots and red bell peppers provide a nice combination of crunch and color. The addition of spicy plum sauce is a plus, but if it is unavailable, omit it.

Enjoy this creamy dessert's tropical pineapple taste. Diced mango and papaya will also work in this recipe. Choose your favorite extract to complement the fruit.

Pantry List

4 shallots
3 cans low-fat, low-sodium
    chicken broth
chili sauce
oyster sauce
hoisin sauce
sugar
garlic
rice vinegar
peanut oil
lite soy sauce
1 small can water-packed
    mandarin oranges
arborio rice
dry sherry
sesame seeds
sesame oil
plum sauce
crushed red pepper
2 cans evaporated skim milk
1 pkg small tapioca
1 can crushed pineapple
almond extract
1 can water chestnuts

Market List

1 1/2 lb boneless, skinless
        chicken breasts
basil
ginger root
6 cups mixed greens of choice
2 red bell peppers
1/2 cup fresh bean sprouts
fresh lemon juice
green onions

1 small leek
2 large carrots
1 egg
1 carton egg substitute

Grilled Chicken with Shallot Ginger Chili Sauce

6 Servings

Serving Size:
3 oz

Exchanges

1/2 Carbohydrate
4 Very Lean Meat

Ingredients

3 shallots, minced
1 cup low-fat, low-sodium
    chicken broth
2 Tbsp chili sauce
1/4 cup water
1/4 cup oyster sauce
2 Tbsp hoisin sauce
1 Tbsp sugar
2 cloves garlic, minced
2 Tbsp minced basil
3 Tbsp minced ginger
1 1/2 lb boneless, skinless
    chicken breasts

Preparation—15 minutes

1 Combine all ingredients except the chicken in a medium bowl.

2 Prepare an outdoor grill with the rack set 6 inches from the heat source or prepare an oven broiler. Grill or broil the chicken 6–7 minutes per side, basting with the sauce.

3 Heat any remaining sauce and serve on the side.

Calories	181	
Calories from Fat	30	
Total Fat	3	g
Saturated Fat	1	g
Cholesterol	69	mg
Sodium	670	mg
Carbohydrate	10	g
Dietary Fiber	1	g
Sugars	6	g
Protein	27	g

Fresh Salad with Chinese Vinaigrette

6 Servings

Serving Size:
1 cup

Exchanges

1 Vegetable
1/2 Fat

Ingredients

6 cups mixed salad greens
1/4 cup sliced red bell pepper
1/2 cup sliced water chestnuts
1/2 cup fresh bean sprouts
1/4 cup water-packed mandarin
    oranges, drained
1/4 cup rice vinegar
2 tsp peanut oil
2 Tbsp lite soy sauce
1 Tbsp lemon juice
2 tsp minced garlic
1 tsp finely minced ginger

Preparation—15 minutes

1 Combine the salad greens, bell pepper, water chestnuts, bean sprouts, and oranges in a large salad bowl.
2 Whisk together the remaining ingredients and refrigerate the dressing for 1/2 hour. Toss the salad with the dressing and serve.

Calories	40
Calories from Fat	15
Total Fat	2 g
Saturated Fat	0 g
Cholesterol	0 mg
Sodium	212 mg
Carbohydrate	6 g
Dietary Fiber	1 g
Sugars	4 g
Protein	1 g

Asian Risotto

6 Servings

Serving Size:
1/2 cup

Exchanges

2 1/2 Starch

Ingredients

3 1/4 cups low-fat, low-sodium chicken broth, divided
4 Tbsp minced green onions
2 Tbsp minced garlic
1/4 cup minced leek
1 1/2 cups arborio rice (do not rinse)
1/2 cup dry sherry
1 Tbsp hoisin sauce
2 tsp lite soy sauce
1 tsp toasted sesame seeds

Preparation—15 minutes

1   Heat 1/4 cup broth in a stockpot over high heat. Add 2 Tbsp green onions, garlic, and leek and saute for 5 minutes. Add the rice and saute for 5 minutes.
2   Add the sherry and cook until the sherry is absorbed. Add the remaining broth 1 cup at a time, until the rice absorbs each cup. The whole process takes about 20 minutes.
3   Add the hoisin and soy sauces. Top the risotto with 2 Tbsp minced green onions and sesame seeds and serve.

Calories	188
Calories from Fat	15
Total Fat	2 g
Saturated Fat	1 g
Cholesterol	0 mg
Sodium	179 mg
Carbohydrate	37 g
Dietary Fiber	2 g
Sugars	3 g
Protein	5 g

Stir-Fried Peppers and Carrots

6 Servings

Serving Size:
1/2 cup

Exchanges

2 Vegetable

Ingredients

1/2 cup low-fat, low-sodium
      chicken broth
1 tsp sesame oil
2 Tbsp minced green onions
1 tsp minced ginger
2 cloves garlic, minced
2 tsp minced shallots
1 1/2 cups julienned red bell pepper
1 1/2 cups julienned carrots
1 Tbsp lemon juice
2 tsp lite soy sauce
1 tsp plum sauce
Pinch crushed red pepper

Preparation—20 minutes

1 Heat the broth and oil in a wok or heavy skillet over medium-high heat. Add the onions, ginger, garlic, and shallots and stir-fry for 2 minutes.
2 Add the bell peppers and carrots and stir-fry for 3 minutes. Add the remaining ingredients, cover, and steam for 1 minute. Serve.

Calories	40
Calories from Fat	9
Total Fat	1 g
Saturated Fat	0 g
Cholesterol	0 mg
Sodium	114 mg
Carbohydrate	8 g
Dietary Fiber	2 g
Sugars	3 g
Protein	1 g

Tapioca and Pineapple

6 Servings

Serving Size:
1/2 cup

Exchanges

2 Carbohydrate

Ingredients

2 cups evaporated skim milk
1/4 cup small tapioca
1/4 cup sugar
1 egg, beaten
Egg substitute to equal 2 eggs
1 cup crushed pineapple, undrained
1 tsp almond extract

Preparation—10 minutes

1 Soak the tapioca in the milk for 1 hour. Place the tapioca and milk in a saucepan and bring to a boil. Lower the heat and cook for about 5 minutes. Add the sugar.
2 Beat the egg. Add the egg substitute and beat well. Add 1/2 cup of the hot tapioca. Add this mixture back to the pot and cook for 2 minutes.
3 Add the pineapple with juice and almond extract and cook for 1 minute. Remove from heat, pour into a bowl, and refrigerate for several hours. Spoon into dessert dishes and serve.

Calories	169
Calories from Fat	10
Total Fat	1 g
Saturated Fat	0 g
Cholesterol	38 mg
Sodium	146 mg
Carbohydrate	31 g
Dietary Fiber	0 g
Sugars	22 g
Protein	10 g

 WHY DON'T YOU . . .

Choose simple ways to entertain. A dinner party is too overwhelming? Just invite people over for appetizers.

Spicy Asian Chili

**Spicy Asian Chili
Cellophane Noodle Salad
Water Chestnuts and Snow Peas
Garlic Rolls
Strawberries and Almonds**

M E N U   T A L K

When you think of chili, images of the Southwest probably enter your mind. Spin the globe, though, and suddenly Asia is associated with this recipe. Asian ingredients such as hoisin sauce, oyster sauce, chili sauce, ginger, and green onions transform this chili into something completely different. This recipe is an adaptation of a chili by California chef Hugh Carpenter.

This menu's salad contains an interesting combination of cool and hot flavors. The cooling rice vinegar complements a dash of hot chili oil. Hot chili oil can be purchased at most supermarkets. Skip this if you want, or make your own (to learn how, see p. 145). The salad dressing is delicious splashed on greens. Cellophane noodles, also known as bean thread noodles, taste best when eaten the same day you prepare them. If cellophane noodles are unavailable, you may use a thin pasta such as angel hair.

A dash of pineapple juice gives water chestnuts and snow peas a sprightly taste. For more intense pineapple flavor, use 1 Tbsp undiluted pineapple juice concentrate. Remember, as with green beans, it is best to cook snow peas just briefly to preserve crispness. To trim snow peas, snip off one end and pull the string attached to the top of the snow pea across to the other end. Snip off the other end of the snow pea. Take your time when selecting snow peas from the market, and always buy fresh—I make it a rule to never buy the dreaded frozen snow pea!

When selecting bread to serve, try to buy whole-grain breads. Whole-grain breads have fiber, vitamins, and minerals that may not be present in products made with refined white flour. Always make sure that there is very little added sweetener. Whole-grain breads are tastier than white and will fill you up faster. Breads made with seeds and crushed nuts are delicious. Keep whole-grain breads refrigerated.

Extracts are concentrated essences of foods that have been evaporated or distilled. Extracts can be stored for a long period if they are properly capped. Look for pure extracts rather than imitation flavors. This menu's dessert is designed as a blueprint for you to use to create your own variations. Choose another berry instead of strawberries; use vanilla, strawberry, or lemon extract; and enjoy hazelnuts, walnuts, or filberts.

Pantry List

peanut oil
2 shallots
garlic
3 cans low-fat, low-sodium
   chicken broth
hoisin sauce
oyster sauce
Asian chili sauce
sesame oil
2 cans black beans
1 pkg bean thread (cellophane)
   noodles
rice vinegar
hot chili oil
lite soy sauce
1 can sliced water chestnuts
pineapple juice
sugar
cornstarch or arrowroot powder
6 small whole-grain rolls
cayenne pepper
almond extract
1 small pkg almond slivers

Market List

ginger root
3 carrots
1 medium cucumber
1 small red bell pepper
cilantro
3/4 lb fresh snow peas
1 pint strawberries

1 container low calorie-whipped
   topping
fresh lemon juice
1 pkg bean sprouts

STEP-BY-STEP COUNTDOWN

1 Prepare the chili and simmer.
2 Prepare the salad and refrigerate.
3 Prepare the dessert and refrigerate.
4 After the chili has simmered and salad has chilled, prepare the water chestnuts and snow peas.
5 Prepare the garlic rolls and bake.
6 Serve the chili, salad, vegetables, and rolls.
7 Serve the dessert.

Spicy Asian Chili

6 Servings

Serving Size:
I cup

Exchanges

I Very Lean Meat
1/2 Fat

Ingredients

2   tsp peanut oil
2   shallots, minced
3   cloves garlic, minced
2   tsp minced ginger
2   tsp minced lemongrass
4   cups low-fat, low-sodium
     chicken broth
2   Tbsp hoisin sauce
1   Tbsp oyster sauce
2   Tbsp lite soy sauce
1–2 tsp Asian chili sauce
1   tsp sesame oil
1   tsp Chinese five spice
3   cups black beans, drained
     and rinsed

Preparation—10 minutes

1   Heat the oil in a stockpot over medium-high heat. Add the shallots, garlic, ginger, and lemongrass and saute for 2 minutes. Add the broth and bring to a boil. Simmer.
2   Combine the remaining ingredients except the beans. Add to the pot. Add the beans and simmer for 1 hour.
3   Serve, or for a thicker, stew-like consistency, take two cups of the chili and puree it, then add the mixture back to the remaining soup.

Calories	172
Calories from Fat	38
Total Fat	4 g
Saturated Fat	I g
Cholesterol	0 mg
Sodium	644 mg
Carbohydrate	26 g
Dietary Fiber	8 g
Sugars	6 g
Protein	II g

Cellophane Noodle Salad

6 Servings

Serving Size:
1/2 cup

Exchanges

1 1/2 Starch
1 Vegetable

Ingredients

6 oz dried bean thread (cellophane) noodles
3 medium carrots, julienned
1 medium cucumber, seeded and diced
1 small red bell pepper, julienned
1/2 cup rice vinegar
1 tsp hot chili oil
1 Tbsp minced cilantro
1 tsp lite soy sauce
1 garlic cloves, minced

Preparation—15 minutes

1 Add the noodles to a pot of boiling water. Cook for 8 minutes and drain. Set aside in the refrigerator.
2 Toss the vegetables with the noodles.
3 Whisk together the vinegar, chili oil, cilantro, soy sauce, and garlic. Toss with the noodles and vegetables. Refrigerate for 1 hour before serving.

Calories	138
Calories from Fat	8
Total Fat	1 g
Saturated Fat	0 g
Cholesterol	0 mg
Sodium	56 mg
Carbohydrate	33 g
Dietary Fiber	3 g
Sugars	6 g
Protein	1 g

Water Chestnuts and Snow Peas

6 Servings

Serving Size:
1/2 cup

Exchanges

2 Vegetable

Ingredients

1 tsp sesame oil
3 garlic cloves, minced
2 cups fresh snow peas
1 cup sliced water chestnuts
1/4 cup fresh bean sprouts
1/2 cup low-fat, low-sodium
    chicken broth
1 Tbsp lite soy sauce
2 Tbsp pineapple juice
1 tsp sugar
2 tsp grated ginger
2 tsp cornstarch or arrowroot
    powder

Preparation—10 minutes

1 Heat the oil in a wok or skillet over medium-high heat. Add the garlic and saute for 30 seconds. Add the snow peas, water chestnuts, and bean sprouts and saute for 1 minute.
2 In a measuring cup, mix together the remaining ingredients. Add to the pan and cook until the sauce is thickened, about 1 minute. Serve immediately.

Calories	55	
Calories from Fat	10	
Total Fat	1	g
Saturated Fat	0	g
Cholesterol	0	mg
Sodium	114	mg
Carbohydrate	10	g
Dietary Fiber	2	g
Sugars	5	g
Protein	2	g

Garlic Rolls

6 Servings

Serving Size:
1 roll

Exchanges

1 Starch

Ingredients

6 small whole-grain rolls (1 oz each)
1 Tbsp very finely minced garlic
1 tsp sesame oil
Dash cayenne pepper
1/4 tsp salt

Preparation—5 minutes

Preheat the oven to 350 degrees. Split open each roll. Combine the remaining ingredients. Spread the mixture over each roll and put the two halves back together. Wrap each roll in foil and bake for 5 minutes.

Calories	79	
Calories from Fat	18	
Total Fat	2	g
Saturated Fat	0	g
Cholesterol	0	mg
Sodium	247	mg
Carbohydrate	14	g
Dietary Fiber	2	g
Sugars	2	g
Protein	3	g

 WHY DON'T YOU . . .

Try a fresh fish market instead of the supermarket. You will find the staff extremely knowledgeable, and you'll love the great selection.

Strawberries and Almonds

6 Servings

Serving Size:
1/2 cup

Exchanges

1/2 Carbohydrate
1 Fat

Ingredients

2 cups sliced fresh strawberries
1/2 tsp almond extract
2 tsp sugar
2 tsp lemon juice
1 cup low-calorie whipped topping
1/4 cup toasted almond slivers

Preparation—10 minutes

1. Combine the berries with the extract, sugar, and lemon juice. Let the mixture stand for 20 minutes.
2. In parfait glasses, layer the whipped topping and strawberries. Top each serving with almonds.

Calories	75
Calories from Fat	35
Total Fat	4 g
Saturated Fat	2 g
Cholesterol	0 mg
Sodium	4 mg
Carbohydrate	9 g
Dietary Fiber	2 g
Sugars	5 g
Protein	1 g

A Passion for Poultry

❖ ❖ ❖ ❖

Chicken Romano

Vegetable Soup with Pesto
Chicken Romano
Romaine with Artichoke Bottoms
Barley Primavera
Caramel Pears

MENU TALK

Pesto, a familiar Italian sauce, made a splash in American cooking during the 1980s. Composed of fresh basil leaves, garlic, pine nuts, Parmesan cheese, and olive oil, the traditional rendition of this creamy sauce is way too high in fat. I have always loved pesto; its intense flavors are so good with pasta. Here I substitute low-fat chicken broth for most of the oil, use fewer pine nuts, and include plenty of perfumed fresh basil. Pesto is delicious stirred into soup. Try making broccoli pesto with 1/2 cup of very thinly sliced broccoli stems and half as much basil, or sun-dried tomato pesto with 1/2 cup of diced, rehydrated sun-dried tomatoes and half as much basil. The soup and pesto can be frozen for up to six months.

Romano cheese is a very strong, hard cheese that has a sharper flavor than Parmesan. The most well known is pecorino Romano, made from sheep's milk. Although Romano is certainly easier to buy already grated, try buying it in wedges—you may find it easier to use less when you have to grate it yourself! The tomato must be finely minced and seeded in this recipe to avoid excess water in the sauce. Try this sauce over pasta as well.

Artichoke bottoms are the delicious, soft, meaty part of the artichoke that is available canned. Artichoke hearts can be used instead. Rosemary is one of the oldest herbs in use, dating back hundreds of years before Christ. Rosemary has a slight taste of lemon and scent of pine. I like to use rosemary in salad dressing, as in this recipe, and it is delicious paired with chicken. In the summer when I'm grilling outside, I like to use rosemary as a basting brush for meats, poultry, and seafood. Rosemary is strong—a little goes a long way.

There are several types of barley available. Hulled barley has only its outer layer removed and is the most nutritious, but takes the longest to cook. Pearled barley has the outer layer and the bran removed and has been steamed and polished. Although less nutritious, it is quicker-cooking than hulled barley. If you use pearled barley, be sure to pair it with more nutritious foods. You can use brown rice instead of barley in this recipe if you wish.

Eating these caramel pears will remind you of caramel apples without all the excess sugar. These pears are good warm or cold. This recipe is adapted from a similar one by Nikki and David Goldbeck.

Pantry List

olive oil
garlic
6 cans low-fat, low-sodium chicken
   broth
white pepper
pine nuts
1 yellow onion
1 red onion
unbleached white flour
red wine vinegar
Dijon mustard
1 can evaporated skim milk
cornstarch or arrowroot powder
crushed red pepper
pearled barley
maple syrup
1 can artichoke bottoms

Market List

1 1/2 lb boneless, skinless
   chicken breasts
1 medium leek
2 carrots
1 yellow squash
1/4 lb green beans
2 medium tomatoes
1 bunch basil
Parmesan cheese
2 heads romaine lettuce
1 red bell pepper
1 small head radicchio
fresh lemon juice
Romano cheese
Italian parsley

1 zucchini
3 medium pears
rosemary

Vegetable Soup with Pesto

6 Servings

Serving Size:
1 cup

Exchanges

1/2 Starch
1 Monounsaturated
　Fat

Ingredients

4　tsp olive oil
1/2　cup thinly sliced leeks
1/2　cup diced carrot
1/2　cup diced yellow squash
1/2　cup trimmed green beans
1　cup diced tomatoes
2　Tbsp minced garlic
5 1/2　cups low-fat, low-sodium
　　chicken broth
Fresh ground white pepper
1/2　cup tightly packed basil leaves
1　Tbsp toasted pine nuts
1　Tbsp Parmesan cheese
4　cloves garlic, minced

Preparation—30 minutes

1　Heat 1 tsp oil in a stockpot over medium-high heat. Add the leeks and saute for 3 minutes. Add the carrots and saute for 5 minutes. Add the yellow squash and saute for 4 minutes.
2　Add the green beans, tomatoes, garlic, 5 cups broth, and pepper. Bring to a boil, lower the heat, cover, and simmer for 20–25 minutes.
3　In a blender, combine 1/2 cup broth, 3 tsp oil, the basil, pine nuts, cheese, and garlic. Serve a spoonful of pesto over each serving of hot soup.

Calories	86
Calories from Fat	57
Total Fat	6 g
Saturated Fat	1 g
Cholesterol	2 mg
Sodium	124 mg
Carbohydrate	7 g
Dietary Fiber	2 g
Sugars	4 g
Protein	5 g

Chicken Romano

6 Servings

Serving Size:
4 oz

Exchanges

1/2 Starch
1/2 Skim Milk
4 Very Lean Meat

Ingredients

2 Tbsp unbleached white flour
Fresh ground pepper
1 1/2 lb boneless, skinless
    chicken breasts, pounded to
    1/4-inch thickness
2 tsp olive oil
1/2 cup chopped onion
2 cloves garlic, minced
1 small tomato, seeded and finely
    chopped
1 12-oz can evaporated skim milk
2 Tbsp strong Romano cheese
1 Tbsp Parmesan cheese
2 tsp cornstarch or arrowroot
    powder
4 tsp water
2 Tbsp minced Italian parsley
Dash crushed red pepper
Dash salt (optional)

Preparation—10 minutes

1 Combine the flour and pepper in a zippered plastic bag. Add the chicken breasts and shake to coat.
2 Heat the oil in a skillet over medium-high heat. Add the chicken breasts and saute about 3 minutes per side. Remove from the skillet.
3 Saute the onion for 4 minutes in the pan drippings. Add the garlic and saute for 2 minutes. Add the tomato, milk, and cheeses and simmer for 4 minutes.
4 Mix together the cornstarch or arrowroot powder with the water and add to the skillet. Cook until the sauce thickens, about 1–2 minutes. Add the parsley, red pepper, and salt. Add the chicken and simmer for 1 minute.

Calories	233
Calories from Fat	49
Total Fat	5 g
Saturated Fat	2 g
Cholesterol	73 mg
Sodium	183 mg
Carbohydrate	13 g
Dietary Fiber	1 g
Sugars	7 g
Protein	32 g

Romaine with Artichoke Bottoms

6 Servings

Serving Size:
I cup

Exchanges

I Vegetable
I/2 Monounsatur-
ated Fat

Ingredients

5 cups romaine lettuce, washed and
   torn
1/2 cup julienned red bell pepper
1/2 cup radicchio, washed and torn
1 cup canned artichoke bottoms,
   drained
1/3 cup red wine vinegar
1 1/2 Tbsp olive oil
2 tsp lemon juice
1 tsp minced rosemary
1 tsp sugar
1 Tbsp Dijon mustard
Fresh ground pepper
Dash salt (optional)

Preparation—10 minutes

1 Combine the lettuce, bell pepper, radicchio, and artichoke in a salad bowl.
2 Whisk together the remaining ingredients, toss with the salad, and serve.

Calories	55
Calories from Fat	35
Total Fat	4 g
Saturated Fat	I g
Cholesterol	0 mg
Sodium	179 mg
Carbohydrate	5 g
Dietary Fiber	2 g
Sugars	2 g
Protein	2 g

❖ ❖ ❖ ❖ ❖ ❖

🦅 WHY DON'T YOU . . .

*Have breakfast for dinner.
As long as the foods are
appropriate for your meal plan,
enjoy a frittata or French toast
for dinner.*

Barley Primavera

6 Servings

Serving Size:
1/2 cup

Exchanges

2 Starch

Ingredients

4 cups low-fat, low-sodium chicken
   broth, divided
2 cloves garlic, minced
1/2 cup minced red onion
1/2 cup diced carrot
1 cup pearled barley
1/2 cup diced zucchini
2 Tbsp minced Italian parsley
1 tsp olive oil
1 Tbsp fresh lemon juice
Fresh ground pepper
Dash salt (optional)

Preparation—15 minutes

1 Heat 1/4 cup broth in a saucepan over medium-high heat. Add the garlic and onion and saute for 5 minutes. Add the carrots and saute for 5 minutes.
2 Add the rest of the broth and bring to a boil. Add the barley, lower the heat, cover, and simmer until the liquid is almost absorbed, about 50 minutes.
3 Add the zucchini, parsley, oil, and lemon juice. Simmer for 5 more minutes. Season with pepper and salt.

Calories	155
Calories from Fat	24
Total Fat	3 g
Saturated Fat	1 g
Cholesterol	0 mg
Sodium	79 mg
Carbohydrate	31 g
Dietary Fiber	6 g
Sugars	3 g
Protein	6 g

Caramel Pears

6 Servings

Serving Size:
1/2 pear

Exchanges

2 1/2 Carbohydrate

Ingredients

3 medium pears
1 cup water
2/3 cup pure maple syrup

Preparation—5 minutes

1   Peel, halve, and core each pear. Combine the water and syrup in a 2-quart saucepan and bring to a boil. Add the pears and simmer, partially covered, for 20 minutes.
2   Turn the pears and cook until the pears are thickly coated with syrup, about 15–20 minutes. If you need additional water to prevent the pears from drying out, add 1/4 cup more during cooking. Serve hot or cold.

Calories	139
Calories from Fat	3
Total Fat	0 g
Saturated Fat	0 g
Cholesterol	0 mg
Sodium	3 mg
Carbohydrate	36 g
Dietary Fiber	2 g
Sugars	32 g
Protein	0 g

❖ ❖ ❖

Moroccan Buffet

Date and Cashew-Stuffed Chicken
Tangy Carrot Salad
Cumin Couscous
Green Beans with Lemon and Garlic
Moroccan Oranges

MENU TALK

Dates really are dated! They've been used in foods for over 5,000 years. Native to the Middle East, dates also grow in the dry heat of California and Arizona. They are delicious to eat but can be high in calories. Avoid very shriveled dates or ones that show visible signs of sugar crystallization. Dates are a good source of iron. Nuts and dates are a natural combination, and because they are so rich, you will feel satisfied with a smaller portion of this stuffing. Try it with pork, beef, or turkey.

Cumin seeds are used frequently in Middle Eastern cuisine and can be purchased in specialty markets. For best results, grind the seeds yourself in a spice or coffee grinder. Thirty seconds later, you'll have rich, flavorful ground cumin.

Couscous is also called Moroccan pasta and is a staple in the Moroccan diet. Many people confuse bulgur wheat and couscous. Bulgur wheat has more of the wheat bran and germ left in, so it has a heavier taste. Couscous is one of the fastest grains to prepare. Simply pour boiling liquid over the couscous, the liquid is absorbed in about 5–10 minutes, and the couscous is ready to eat. Couscous is easy to find in supermarkets today.

Use the dressing for these green beans over any other cooked vegetables, such as tomatoes or zucchini. For best results, squeeze your own fresh lemon juice—most of the bottled varieties taste like the bottle! Enjoy this side dish hot, at room temperature, or chilled.

Orange blossom or orange flower water is a distillation of bitter orange blossoms. It is used as a flavoring in sweet dishes as well as in cocktails. Sprinkled over oranges paired with cinnamon, it makes this dessert a refreshing counterpoint to the heavy spices of a Moroccan meal.

Pantry List

orange blossom water
cinnamon
dates
cashews
honey
canola oil
5 cans low-fat, low-sodium chicken
    broth
dry white wine
1 yellow onion
garlic
white wine vinegar
olive oil
cumin
turmeric
paprika
cumin seeds
coriander seeds
ground ginger
1 pkg couscous

Market List

1 1/2 lb boneless, skinless chicken
    breasts
fresh lemon juice
parsley
3 oranges
3 carrots
1/2 lb green beans

1 Prepare step 1 of the chicken recipe.
2 Prepare the carrot salad and dressing but do not combine them.
3 Prepare the dessert and refrigerate.
4 Prepare the green beans and set aside.
5 Finish preparing the chicken.
6 While the chicken bakes, prepare the cumin couscous.
7 Toss the carrots with the dressing and serve.
8 Serve the chicken, couscous, and green beans (choose to serve the green beans chilled or at room temperature).
9 Serve the dessert.

Date and Cashew-Stuffed Chicken

6 Servings

Serving Size:
3 oz

Exchanges

1 Fruit
4 Very Lean Meat
1 Monounsaturated
    Fat

Ingredients

1/2 cup chopped dates
1/4 cup toasted cashew pieces
1 Tbsp honey
1 Tbsp canola oil
2 Tbsp lemon juice
1 1/2 lb chicken breasts, at least
        1 1/2 inch thick
1 cup low-fat, low-sodium
    chicken broth
1/2 cup dry white wine

Preparation—35 minutes

1 Preheat the oven to 350 degrees. In a blender or food processor, combine the dates, cashews, honey, oil, and lemon juice until well mixed.
2 Cut a pocket in each chicken breast without cutting all the way through. Spoon some of the stuffing into each breast.
3 Place the chicken breasts into a casserole dish. Add the broth and wine to cover the chicken.
4 Cover the dish and bake for 20 minutes. Uncover and bake until the chicken is brown, about 10 minutes.

Calories	249
Calories from Fat	76
Total Fat	8 g
Saturated Fat	2 g
Cholesterol	69 mg
Sodium	79 mg
Carbohydrate	16 g
Dietary Fiber	1 g
Sugars	13 g
Protein	27 g

Tangy Carrot Salad

6 Servings

Serving Size:
1/2 cup

Exchanges

2 Vegetable
1/2 Monounsatur-
ated Fat

Ingredients

3 cups diagonally sliced carrots
1/4 cup minced parsley
1/2 cup minced onion
2 cloves garlic, minced
1/4 cup white wine vinegar
1 1/2 Tbsp olive oil
1 1/2 tsp cumin
1/2 tsp turmeric
1/2 tsp paprika

Preparation—15 minutes

1 Blanch the carrots for 2 minutes in a pot of boiling water. Drain, then plunge the carrots into ice water and drain again. Place the carrots in a salad bowl and toss with the parsley, onion, and garlic.
2 In a small bowl, whisk together the remaining ingredients. Pour over the salad and let chill for 1 hour before serving.

Calories	73
Calories from Fat	32
Total Fat	4 g
Saturated Fat	0 g
Cholesterol	0 mg
Sodium	50 mg
Carbohydrate	3 g
Dietary Fiber	5 g
Sugars	1 g
Protein	0 g

Cumin Couscous

6 Servings

Serving Size:
1/2 cup

Exchanges

2 1/2 Starch

Ingredients

1 tsp olive oil
2 Tbsp minced onion
1 tsp cumin seeds
1/2 tsp coriander seeds
1/4 tsp ground ginger
3 cups low-fat, low-sodium chicken
    broth
1 1/2 cups dry couscous
1 Tbsp lemon juice
Fresh ground pepper
Dash salt (optional)
2 Tbsp minced parsley

Preparation—15 minutes

1 Heat the oil in a skillet over medium-high heat. Add the onion, cumin seeds, coriander seeds, and ginger and saute for 2 minutes.
2 Add the broth and bring to a boil. Add the couscous and stir well. Add the lemon juice. Cover, remove from heat, and let stand until the couscous has absorbed the broth, about 5–7 minutes.
3 Season with pepper and salt, garnish with parsley, and serve.

Calories	194
Calories from Fat	20
Total Fat	2 g
Saturated Fat	1 g
Cholesterol	0 mg
Sodium	59 mg
Carbohydrate	37 g
Dietary Fiber	2 g
Sugars	2 g
Protein	7 g

Green Beans with Lemon and Garlic

Serving Size:
1/2 cup

Exchanges

1 Vegetable

Ingredients

1/2 lb fresh green beans, trimmed
2 cloves garlic, minced
3 Tbsp fresh lemon juice
1 tsp olive oil
1/2 tsp paprika
1/4 tsp cumin
Fresh ground pepper

Preparation—15 minutes

1 Blanch the green beans in a pot of boiling water for 2 minutes and drain.
2 Whisk together the remaining ingredients and sprinkle over the green beans.
3 Serve at room temperature or refrigerate and serve chilled.

Calories	20
Calories from Fat	8
Total Fat	1 g
Saturated Fat	0 g
Cholesterol	0 mg
Sodium	1 mg
Carbohydrate	3 g
Dietary Fiber	1 g
Sugars	1 g
Protein	1 g

Moroccan Oranges

6 Servings

Serving Size:
1/2 cup

Exchanges

1 Fruit

Ingredients

3 cups sectioned oranges, peeled and white pith removed
2 Tbsp orange blossom water
1 tsp cinnamon

Preparation—10 minutes

Distribute the orange sections among 6 individual serving dishes. Sprinkle each serving with the orange blossom water and cinnamon. Refrigerate for 1/2 hour before serving.

Calories	49
Calories from Fat	1
Total Fat	0 g
Saturated Fat	0 g
Cholesterol	0 mg
Sodium	0 mg
Carbohydrate	12 g
Dietary Fiber	2 g
Sugars	9 g
Protein	1 g

❖ WHY DON'T YOU . . .

Try turning off the TV when you eat. Rediscover the art of conversation, or if you are alone, enjoy some quiet time with your personal thoughts.

❖   ❖   ❖

Southern-Style Supper

Honey-Mustard Chicken
Peppered Rice
Down-Home Green Beans
Chilled Broccoli Salad with Garlic and Lemon
Apple Cheese Tartlets

MENU   TALK

Dijon mustard is known for its clean, sharp taste. It is made from brown or black mustard seeds, white wine, unfermented grape juice, and seasonings. I prefer the coarse Dijon mustard, because the visible mustard seeds provide a pleasing and interesting texture. Try to avoid plain yellow mustard—it is a pale cousin to true Dijon. Because mustard is acidic, it makes a great marinade ingredient for tough protein fibers in chicken or beef. Try this marinade as a salad dressing, too.

Fragrant basmati rice has grown in the Himalayas for thousands of years; after a quick trip to the supermarket, you can enjoy it every day! "Basmati" means "queen of fragrance." The rice grain is aged so the moisture content is decreased, yielding a unique aroma and taste. Peppers are an excellent source of vitamin C, contain a fair amount of vitamin A, and a small amount of calcium, iron, and niacin.

Canadian bacon is a lean, smoked meat more similar to ham than sliced bacon. It comes from the lean eye of the pork loin and is leaner than bacon. It is a good flavoring to use instead of regular bacon. Green beans are available all year. Choose beans that are free from blemishes and look crisp. They can be stored in a tightly covered bag in the refrigerator for up to five days.

Broccoli's name comes from the Italian word for cabbage sprout. Broccoli is a member of the cruciferous, or cancer-fighting, vegetable family. Other vegetables from the cruciferous family include Brussels sprouts and cauliflower. Broccoli is a good source of vitamin C, calcium, and iron.

See color photo after p. 240.

When you omit the crusts from pies and tarts, you also say farewell to those unwanted calories and excess fat. These tarts are just as delicious with a tasty crumb topping instead of a crust. Granny Smith apples are a good choice for baking. Cheese and apples are natural flavor pairs; you can still enjoy this winning combination when the cheese is low in fat! These tarts are easy to eat outside, so serve them at picnics and patio parties.

Pantry List

Dijon mustard
honey
olive oil
nutmeg
garlic
basmati rice
3 cans low-fat, low-sodium chicken
  broth
1 yellow onion
1 red onion
red wine vinegar
brown sugar
unbleached white flour
cinnamon
sugar

Market List

1 1/2 lb boneless, skinless chicken
  breasts
1 red bell pepper
1 yellow bell pepper
lemon juice
2 oz Canadian bacon
1 lb green beans
green onions
1 1/2 lb broccoli
2 Granny Smith apples
low-fat cheddar cheese
low-calorie margarine

1 Marinate the chicken.
2 Prepare the salad and refrigerate. This can be done the day before.
3 Prepare the dessert.
4 Prepare the rice and turn off the heat.
5 Prepare the green beans.
6 Grill the chicken.
7 Serve the salad.
8 Serve the chicken, rice, and green beans.
9 Serve the dessert.

Honey-Mustard Chicken

6 Servings

Serving Size:
3 oz

Exchanges

4 Very Lean Meat
1/2 Monounsaturated Fat

Ingredients

1/2 cup Dijon mustard
2 Tbsp honey
2 Tbsp olive oil
Pinch nutmeg
1 1/2 lb boneless, skinless chicken
   breasts

Preparation—10 minutes

1 Mix together the mustard, honey, oil, and nutmeg in a shallow glass baking dish. Add the chicken and marinate for at least 2 hours.
2 Prepare an outdoor grill with the rack set 6 inches from the heat source or prepare an oven broiler. Grill the chicken until it is tender and opaque throughout, about 6–7 minutes per side.

Calories	172	
Calories from Fat	50	
Total Fat	6	g
Saturated Fat	1	g
Cholesterol	69	mg
Sodium	186	mg
Carbohydrate	3	g
Dietary Fiber	0	g
Sugars	3	g
Protein	25	g

Peppered Rice

6 Servings

Serving Size:
1/2 cup

Exchanges

2 1/2 Starch
1 Vegetable

Ingredients

2 tsp olive oil
2 cloves garlic, minced
1/2 cup each diced red and yellow
    bell peppers
1 1/2 cups basmati rice, rinsed
3 cups low-fat, low-sodium chicken
    broth
1 Tbsp lemon juice
Fresh ground pepper
Dash salt (optional)

Preparation—10 minutes

1 Heat the oil in a saucepan over medium-high heat. Add the garlic and saute for 30 seconds. Add the bell peppers and saute for 4 minutes.
2 Add the rice and saute for 2 minutes.
3 Add the broth, bring to a boil, lower the heat, and cover. Simmer until broth is absorbed, about 20 minutes.
4 Season with lemon juice, pepper, and salt to serve.

Calories	212
Calories from Fat	27
Total Fat	3 g
Saturated Fat	1 g
Cholesterol	0 mg
Sodium	55 mg
Carbohydrate	44 g
Dietary Fiber	2 g
Sugars	1 g
Protein	6 g

Down-Home Green Beans

6 Servings

Serving Size:
1/2 cup

Exchanges

1 Vegetable
1/2 Monounsatur-
ated Fat

Ingredients

1 tsp olive oil
1/4 cup minced onion
2 oz Canadian bacon, minced
3 cups green beans, cut into 3-inch
    lengths
1/2 cup low-fat, low-sodium
    chicken broth
Fresh ground pepper

Preparation—10 minutes

1 Heat the oil in a skillet over medium heat. Add the onion and saute for 3 minutes.
2 Add the bacon and cook until crispy, about 5 minutes. Remove the bacon mixture from the skillet.
3 Add the green beans and broth to the skillet. Cover and steam for 3 minutes. Return the bacon mixture to the skillet and mix well.
4 Season with pepper and serve.

Calories	47
Calories from Fat	16
Total Fat	2 g
Saturated Fat	0 g
Cholesterol	5 mg
Sodium	131 mg
Carbohydrate	6 g
Dietary Fiber	2 g
Sugars	2 g
Protein	3 g

Chilled Broccoli Salad with Garlic and Lemon

6 Servings

Serving Size:
1/2 cup

Exchanges

1 Vegetable
1/2 Monounsatur-
ated Fat

Ingredients

3 cups broccoli florets
3 cloves garlic, finely minced
2 Tbsp finely minced red onion
2 Tbsp minced green onion
3 Tbsp lemon juice
1 Tbsp red wine vinegar
1 Tbsp olive oil

Preparation—20 minutes

1 Blanch the broccoli for 3 minutes in a pot of boiling water. Drain, plunge the broccoli into ice water, and drain again.
2 In a medium bowl, whisk together the remaining ingredients.
3 Pour the mixture over the broccoli and refrigerate for at least 1/2 hour.

Calories	36
Calories from Fat	22
Total Fat	2 g
Saturated Fat	0 g
Cholesterol	0 mg
Sodium	12 mg
Carbohydrate	3 g
Dietary Fiber	1 g
Sugars	2 g
Protein	1 g

 WHY DON'T YOU . . .

Bring home flowers for the dining table, even when there are no guests coming.

Apple Cheese Tartlets

6 Servings

Serving Size:
1/2 cup

Exchanges

2 Carbohydrate
1/2 Fat

Ingredients

2 large Granny Smith apples, thinly
   sliced, skins on
1 Tbsp brown sugar
1 Tbsp honey
1 Tbsp unbleached white flour
2 tsp cinnamon
1 cup shredded low-fat cheddar
   cheese
1/2 cup unbleached white flour
1 Tbsp sugar
2 Tbsp low-calorie margarine
1 tsp cinnamon
1/4 tsp nutmeg
Water

Preparation—15 minutes

1 Preheat the oven to 350 degrees. Combine the apples with the brown sugar, honey, 1 Tbsp flour, and cinnamon. Toss well.
2 Divide the apple mixture among 6 custard cups. Sprinkle each tart with some cheese.
3 Combine 1/2 cup flour, sugar, margarine, cinnamon, and nutmeg. Sprinkle evenly over the tarts. Sprinkle with a little water to moisten.
4 Bake until the apples are cooked and the topping is browned, about 20 minutes.

Calories	161
Calories from Fat	32
Total Fat	4 g
Saturated Fat	1 g
Cholesterol	4 mg
Sodium	147 mg
Carbohydrate	27 g
Dietary Fiber	2 g
Sugars	16 g
Protein	6 g

Aegean Turkey

Leek, Shallot, and Garlic Soup
Artichoke and Romaine Salad
Turkey Stuffed with Goat Cheese and Sun-Dried Tomatoes
Saffron Orzo
Phyllo Fruit Pie

MENU TALK

The giant scallion, the leek, is related to both onion and garlic, but it has a much milder flavor. The leek stalk is used to create delicious soups, stews, and stir-fries. Generally smaller leeks yield more delicate flavors. You will have to wash the inside of the leek stalk very carefully, because leeks are notoriously dirty. To do this, slit open the stalk and wash between the layers. Leeks can be kept in the refrigerator for five days. Leek leaves are generally used to flavor soups and then discarded because they have a tough texture. This soup is a light, refreshing version of the traditionally heavy onion soup. Try adding shredded low-fat cheese to melt on top of individual servings.

Use these marinated artichokes as an appetizer, a topping for pasta, or mixed into rice. As prepared in this recipe, they make a light salad. To prepare a more substantial salad, add canned beans or tuna. The longer the artichokes marinate, the more flavor will develop. When you want crunchy texture, choose romaine. Red romaine lettuce is now available in most supermarkets and is pretty in salads.

Goat or chevre cheese is pure goat's milk cheese. It has a sharp taste, so a little goes a long way, making it ideal for adding flavor to a low-fat meal plan. You can find many varieties of goat cheese, including the popular bucheron or montrachet. If you can't find goat cheese, use nonfat cream cheese in this recipe instead. Walnuts are the fruit of the walnut tree and come in two varieties, English and black. English is the most familiar and easily available. Freezing nuts is a good way to keep them fresh. Use nuts sparingly to add texture and flavor. You may also use flattened chicken breasts or pounded pork tenderloin instead of turkey in this recipe.

Orzo is a delightful pasta the size of a rice kernel and is a great substitute for rice. Orzo is delicious in soups and is easy for children to eat. Because the pasta is so small, it is easy to overwhelm it with too many flavors. Just a sprinkling of herbs will enliven orzo. Coloring orzo with saffron adds a lot of eye appeal. Try adding saffron to other types of pasta, too.

Phyllo dough consists of tissue-thin layers of pastry dough used extensively in Middle Eastern and Greek cuisines. Phyllo is fun to work with. You can buy frozen phyllo in supermarkets and fresh phyllo in Greek grocery stores. Because phyllo dough is so thin, it dries out very quickly. When preparing the crust for this menu's dessert, be sure to keep the phyllo covered with a towel. Only remove one layer at a time and keep the rest covered. Do not thaw and refreeze frozen phyllo, or it will become brittle. Phyllo is an ideal dough to use when making low-fat crusts. Just melt a little low-calorie margarine or spray butter-flavored nonstick cooking spray between each layer. It will take you a little time to feel comfortable working with phyllo dough, but you'll find it a great alternative to fat-laden pie crusts.

Pantry List

olive oil
4 large shallots
garlic
dry white wine
3 cans low-fat, low-sodium beef or
chicken broth
bay leaf
dried basil
1 can artichoke hearts
1 red onion
balsamic vinegar
1 jar roasted red peppers
1 pkg sun-dried tomatoes
walnuts
1 pkg orzo
saffron threads
brown sugar
honey
cinnamon
butter-flavored nonstick cooking spray
cornstarch or arrowroot powder
1 4-oz pkg fat-free, sugar-free
instant vanilla pudding
Grand Marnier

Market List

1 1/2 lb turkey breasts
2 large leeks
basil
2 large heads romaine lettuce
oregano
1 carrot
parsley
mint
phyllo dough

low-calorie margarine
blueberries, apples, pears, peaches,
or raspberries
fresh lemon juice
mint sprigs
goat cheese
nonfat milk
1 carton strawberries

Leek, Shallot, and Garlic Soup

6 Servings

Serving Size:
I cup

Exchanges

1/2 Starch
1/2 Fat

Ingredients

2 tsp olive oil
2 large leeks, white part only, rinsed
    and sliced into very thin rings
4 large shallots, minced
4 cloves garlic, minced
1 cup dry white wine
5 cups low-sodium low-fat beef or
    chicken broth
1 bay leaf
1 tsp dried basil
Fresh ground pepper
Dash salt (optional)

Preparation—15 minutes

1 Heat the oil in a stockpot over medium-high heat. Add the leeks, shallots, and garlic and saute for 5 minutes. Add the wine, broth, bay leaf, and basil and bring to a boil.
2 Lower the heat and simmer for 20 minutes. Remove the bay leaf, season with pepper and salt, and serve.

Calories	71
Calories from Fat	31
Total Fat	3 g
Saturated Fat	I g
Cholesterol	0 mg
Sodium	96 mg
Carbohydrate	8 g
Dietary Fiber	2 g
Sugars	2 g
Protein	4 g

Artichoke and Romaine Salad

6 Servings

Serving Size:
1 cup

Exchanges

1 Vegetable

Ingredients

1 can artichoke hearts, rinsed and
   halved
1/4 cup minced red onion
2 cloves garlic, minced
3 Tbsp balsamic vinegar
1 Tbsp minced basil
1 tsp olive oil
6 cups romaine lettuce, washed
   and torn
Strips of roasted red peppers
   (from a jar)

Preparation—15 minutes

1 Combine the artichokes, onion, garlic, vinegar, basil, and oil. Marinate for 2 hours.
2 When ready to serve, arrange lettuce on individual plates. Top with the artichoke mixture and garnish with red pepper strips.

Calories	36
Calories from Fat	10
Total Fat	1 g
Saturated Fat	0 g
Cholesterol	0 mg
Sodium	132 mg
Carbohydrate	6 g
Dietary Fiber	2 g
Sugars	2 g
Protein	2 g

 WHY DON'T YOU . . .

Make your own flavored vinegar and oil by adding 2 sprigs fresh rosemary, 2 sprigs fresh oregano, 2 sprigs fresh basil, and 1 Tbsp black peppercorns to 1 pint red wine vinegar or olive oil. Let the mixture stand 2 weeks. Just a bit adds great flavor to foods.

Turkey Stuffed with Goat Cheese and Sun-Dried Tomatoes

6 Servings

Serving Size:
3 oz

Exchanges

5 Very Lean Meat
1 1/2 Fat

Ingredients

1   cup goat cheese, softened
1/2 cup rehydrated sun-dried
     tomatoes, diced
2   Tbsp toasted chopped walnuts
2   tsp minced basil
1   tsp minced oregano
3   tsp olive oil
1 1/2 lb turkey breasts, pounded to
     1/4-inch thickness
1   cup low-fat, low-sodium chicken
     broth
1/2 cup dry white wine

Preparation—15 minutes

1 Preheat the oven to 350 degrees. Combine the cheese, tomatoes, walnuts, basil, oregano, and oil in a food processor until smooth.
2 Place 2 tablespoons of stuffing on each turkey breast, fold the sides over, and roll up. Secure with toothpicks.
3 Place the turkey breasts in a casserole dish and add the broth and wine. Bake, covered, for 35–40 minutes. Uncover and bake until the turkey is browned, about 5 minutes.

Calories	241
Calories from Fat	92
Total Fat	10 g
Saturated Fat	4 g
Cholesterol	93 mg
Sodium	182 mg
Carbohydrate	2 g
Dietary Fiber	0 g
Sugars	0 g
Protein	33 g

Saffron Orzo

6 Servings

Serving Size:
1/2 cup

Exchanges

2 Starch

Ingredients

1 1/2 cups dry orzo
Pinch saffron threads
1/4 cup dry white wine
2 cloves garlic, minced
1/4 cup diced onion
1/3 cup diced carrot
2 Tbsp minced parsley
2 tsp minced mint
Fresh ground pepper
Dash salt (optional)

Preparation—15 minutes

1 Add the orzo and saffron to a pot of boiling water and cook according to package directions.
2 Meanwhile, heat the wine in a skillet over medium heat. Add the garlic and onion and saute for 2 minutes. Add the carrots and saute for 3 minutes, adding broth or water if necessary.
3 Drain the orzo. Toss the orzo with the vegetables. Add the herbs, pepper, and salt and serve.

Calories	172
Calories from Fat	6
Total Fat	1 g
Saturated Fat	0 g
Cholesterol	0 mg
Sodium	7 mg
Carbohydrate	35 g
Dietary Fiber	1 g
Sugars	3 g
Protein	6 g

Phyllo Fruit Pie

6 Servings

Serving Size:
1 tart

Exchanges

3 Carbohydrate

Ingredients

4 sheets phyllo dough
2 Tbsp low-calorie margarine, melted
Butter-flavored nonstick cooking spray
3 tsp brown sugar
3 cups of a mixture of fresh blueberries, diced apples, diced pears, diced peaches, or fresh raspberries
1/2 cup water
1/4 cup honey
1 tsp cinnamon
1 Tbsp fresh lemon juice
1 1/2 Tbsp cornstarch or arrowroot powder
1 pkg fat-free, sugar-free, instant vanilla pudding, prepared according to package directions (use skim milk)
1 Tbsp Grand Marnier
Sliced strawberries
Mint sprigs

Preparation—35 minutes

1 Preheat the oven to 350 degrees. Spread a sheet of phyllo dough on a flat surface.
2 Brush the phyllo sheet with a combination of melted margarine and butter spray. Sprinkle with brown sugar. Continue with the remaining sheets, layering the sheets on each other. Cut the stack vertically into two sections. Cut each section into three horizontal squares.
3 In nonstick custard cups, press each stack of phyllo squares into the cup, fitting it in while pressing the corners back. Bake until browned, about 8–9 minutes. Remove the tart shells from the oven and let them cool for 10 minutes in the pan, then remove them from the cups and set them aside.
4 Combine the fruit with the water, honey, cinnamon, lemon juice, and cornstarch or arrowroot powder in a medium saucepan and bring to a boil. Reduce the heat to medium and continue cooking until the filling has thickened.
5 Add the Grand Marnier to the prepared pudding. To serve, place some of the pudding into each crust and top with fruit filling. Decorate with sliced strawberries and a mint sprig.

Calories	220
Calories from Fat	23
Total Fat	3 g
Saturated Fat	0 g
Cholesterol	1 mg
Sodium	376 mg
Carbohydrate	44 g
Dietary Fiber	3 g
Sugars	25 g
Protein	5 g

Tamarind Game Hens

Tamarind Game Hens
Cauliflower and Carrot Saute
Basmati Rice with Toasted Cashews
Spinach with Ginger
Sliced Pineapple and Mangoes with Lime

MENU TALK

The tamarind is the Indian date, the fruit of a tall shade tree in Asia, northern Africa, and India. It grows in a long pod that contains small seeds with a sweet-and-sour pulp. Tamarind pulp is used to season curry dishes and chutneys. Tamarind can be found in various forms in Indian and Asian grocery stores, including the tamarind chutney used in this recipe. Try tamarind chutney as a condiment with grilled fish and chicken. You can use the tamarind glaze to brush on skewers of shrimp as they grill, or brush over vegetable kabobs made with peppers, zucchini, yellow squash, eggplant, and red onion wedges.

The turmeric added to this menu's vegetables produces a bright orange-yellow hue that is beautiful served with the main course. Add cooked, cubed potatoes and cooked green beans for a typical Indian side dish.

You may use brown basmati rice instead of white basmati rice in this rice recipe. Brown basmati rice takes about 40–45 minutes to cook. The nutty brown rice is a welcome change from the more bland white rice. Cashews grow on the cashew apple tree, native to the West Indies and India. The nut grows on the outside base of the apple. As with all nuts, toast cashews to bring out the best flavor.

Spinach, with its naturally slight peppery flavor, is best with warm spices, such as ginger and cumin. Ginger and cumin help foods taste spicy without the intense heat of chilis. Use any other green such as chard, kale, mustard greens, bok choy, or Chinese cabbage instead of spinach.

Allspice is also called the Jamaica pepper, because it is used extensively in Caribbean cuisine. Allspice is the berry of a West Indian tree in the myrtle family. It tastes like a combination of cinnamon, cloves, and nutmeg. Use a papaya in this recipe if mangoes are not available. You can also use canned, sliced pineapple instead of fresh.

Pantry List

1 jar tamarind chutney
3 cans low-fat, low-sodium chicken broth
sugar
nutmeg
turmeric
raisins
basmati rice
cloves
unsalted cashews
canola oil
garlic
1 yellow onion
cumin
chili powder
paprika
mustard seeds
corn oil
sugar
cinnamon
allspice

Market List

3 Cornish game hens
ginger root
1 stalk lemongrass
3 lb spinach
2 large carrots
1 head cauliflower
1 pineapple (you may use canned pineapple rings in their own juice)
1 small mango
fresh lime juice

Tamarind Game Hens

6 Servings

Serving Size:
1/2 hen

Exchanges

1 Carbohydrate
3 Very Lean Meat

Ingredients

1 cup tamarind chutney
1/2 cup low-fat, low-sodium
   chicken broth
1 tsp sugar
2 tsp minced ginger
2 tsp minced lemongrass
Pinch nutmeg
2 Tbsp minced onion
Fresh ground pepper
Dash salt (optional)
3 Cornish game hens, washed,
   giblets removed, split, and
   skinned

Preparation—15 minutes

1 Preheat the oven to 375 degrees. Combine all ingredients except the game hens in a saucepan and cook over medium heat for 5 minutes.
2 Place all the hens on a roasting rack and brush each with some of the glaze. Roast for 45 minutes to 1 hour, basting with the remaining glaze until the juices run clear.

Calories	178	
Calories from Fat	32	
Total Fat	4	g
Saturated Fat	1	g
Cholesterol	94	mg
Sodium	106	mg
Carbohydrate	15	g
Dietary Fiber	0	g
Sugars	15	g
Protein	21	g

Cauliflower and Carrot Saute

6 Servings

Serving Size:
1/2 cup

Exchanges

1 Vegetable
1/2 Polyunsaturated
   Fat

Ingredients

1 1/2 cups sliced carrots
1 1/2 cups cauliflower florets
2 tsp corn oil
1/2 tsp turmeric
2 Tbsp minced ginger
2 tsp minced garlic
1/2 cup low-fat, low-sodium
    chicken broth

Preparation—10 minutes

1   Add the carrots and cauliflower to a pot of boiling water and blanch for 3 minutes. Drain, splash with cold water, and set aside.
2   Heat the oil in a skillet over medium heat. Add the turmeric and ginger and saute for 2 minutes. Add the garlic and saute for 1 minute.
3   Add the cauliflower, carrots, and broth. Lower the heat, cover, and simmer for 5 minutes.

Calories	42
Calories from Fat	19
Total Fat	2 g
Saturated Fat	0 g
Cholesterol	0 mg
Sodium	37 mg
Carbohydrate	6 g
Dietary Fiber	2 g
Sugars	3 g
Protein	1 g

 WHY DON'T YOU . . .

Invest in a really nice silk flower arrangement. You won't have to worry about watering it!

Basmati Rice with Toasted Cashews

6 Servings

Serving Size:
1/2 cup

Exchanges

3 Starch

Ingredients

3 cups low-fat, low-sodium chicken
broth
1 1/2 cups rinsed basmati rice
1/2 tsp turmeric
2 Tbsp plumped raisins (soak in 1/4
cup boiling water and drain)
2 tsp sugar
Pinch cloves
2 Tbsp toasted unsalted cashews

Preparation—10 minutes

1 Heat the broth to boiling in a saucepan. Add the rice and turmeric and bring to a boil again. Lower the heat, cover, and simmer until the water is absorbed, about 15–20 minutes.
2 Add the remaining ingredients and serve.

Calories	223
Calories from Fat	26
Total Fat	3 g
Saturated Fat	1 g
Cholesterol	0 mg
Sodium	55 mg
Carbohydrate	47 g
Dietary Fiber	2 g
Sugars	4 g
Protein	6 g

Spinach and Ginger

6 Servings

Serving Size:
1/2 cup

Exchanges

1 Vegetable
1/2 Monounsatur-
ated Fat

Ingredients

2 tsp canola oil
2 cloves garlic, minced
1/4 cup minced onion
2 Tbsp minced ginger
1 tsp ground cumin
1/4 tsp chili powder
1/8 tsp paprika
1 tsp mustard seeds
3 lb spinach leaves, stems removed,
    washed, but not dried
Fresh ground pepper
Dash salt (optional)

Preparation—15 minutes

1 Heat the oil in a skillet over high heat. Add the garlic, onion, and ginger and saute for 2 minutes. Add the cumin, chili powder, paprika, and mustard seeds and saute until the seeds pop.
2 Add the spinach, cover, and steam until the spinach wilts, about 2–3 minutes. Season with pepper and salt and serve.

Calories	55
Calories from Fat	21
Total Fat	2 g
Saturated Fat	0 g
Cholesterol	0 mg
Sodium	120 mg
Carbohydrate	7 g
Dietary Fiber	4 g
Sugars	2 g
Protein	5 g

Sliced Pineapple and Mango with Lime

6 Servings

Serving Size:
1/2 cup

Exchanges

1 Fruit

Ingredients

1 1/2 cups sliced fresh pineapple
1 1/2 cups sliced fresh mango
2 Tbsp fresh lime juice
2 tsp sugar
Pinch cinnamon
Pinch allspice

Preparation—15 minutes

Combine all ingredients and serve chilled.

Calories	53
Calories from Fat	3
Total Fat	0 g
Saturated Fat	0 g
Cholesterol	0 mg
Sodium	1 mg
Carbohydrate	14 g
Dietary Fiber	1 g
Sugars	12 g
Protein	0 g

SPEAKING OF SPICES

Ginger

Ginger is one of the world's most widely used spices. It is essential in Asian and Indian dishes. When recipes call for fresh ginger, do use it—you won't be sorry! First peel the ginger, then make three thin slices, stack the slices, and make vertical cuts. Turn the ginger slices and chop downward. Ginger is great as a replacement for some of the salt in a recipe. Crystallized ginger, found in the spice section of supermarkets, is nice to use on top of desserts; it contains a small amount of sugar and adds unique flavor to most sauces and marinades.

Bombay Palace Dinner

Curried Apple Soup
Barbecued Chicken Breasts with Mango Chutney
Pan-Roasted Potatoes with Whole Mustard Seeds
Carrots with Green Beans and Cloves
Pomegranate Dessert

MENU TALK

Indians never use the commercially prepared curry powders found in American supermarkets. In India, curry powder is ground fresh each day from about 20 different spices and herbs. Curry powder can be made from cardamom, chilis, cinnamon, cloves, coriander, cumin, fennel, nutmeg, pepper, sesame seeds, saffron, tamarind, and turmeric. Commercially prepared curry only uses some of these spices and herbs and is a pale substitute for the real thing. When you do have time, consider grinding your own curry powder. Madras curry powder is hotter than the standard supermarket curry powder. This soup is a favorite with children, so you may want to use less curry for them. Use Granny Smith apples in this recipe.

Chutney is a somewhat spicy condiment composed of fruit, vinegar, and spices. It ranges from mild to very spicy. Bottled chutneys are now available in most grocery stores. Because they are so dense in flavor, you only need a little to add flavor to foods. Chutneys make a great base for sauces, as in this recipe. This sauce can double as a marinade, or it can be brushed on grilled shrimp or pork.

Mustard seeds lend flavor and aroma to foods. Typically used whole in Indian cuisine, they are black rather than yellow. They look similar to poppy seeds and are sold at Indian grocery stores. Bay leaf is the leaf of the bay tree native to Asia and the Mediterranean. The bay leaf used in Indian cooking is sweeter than the bay leaf most Americans stock in their spice cabinets. Either one will work for this dish. The mustard seeds and bay leaf are cooked to extract their flavors.

Pan roasting the potatoes increases their crispiness, a texture I really enjoy. New potatoes, since they retain their shape well after briefly cooking, would be ideal in this recipe.

The carrots and green beans provide the color for this meal. The addition of sweet spices is an interesting twist to this side dish. Add half mace and half cloves instead of all cloves to these vegetables, or substitute cinnamon for the nutmeg.

A pomegranate is about the size of a large orange. The skin is inedible, but inside a pomegranate are dozens of jewel-like seeds that are sweet and tart. To use a pomegranate, cut it in half and scoop out the seeds, removing any membrane. In this recipe, they are slightly mashed and combined with the traditional Indian rose water. Rose water comes from rose petals that have been distilled, resulting in a heady perfume. If you can't find rose water, omit it.

Pantry List

canola oil
1 yellow onion
garlic
mango chutney
unbleached white flour
curry powder
3 cans low-fat, low-sodium chicken
   broth
1 can tomatoes
whole cloves
sugar
mace
rose water
ground cloves (try grinding whole
   cloves in an electric coffee
   grinder)
cinnamon
1 1/2 lb red or russet potatoes
bay leaf
black (or yellow) mustard seeds
paprika
cumin

Market List

1 1/2 lb boneless, skinless chicken
   breasts
ginger root
fresh lemon juice
1 bunch celery
3 carrots
2 tart apples
parsley
1 large pomegranate
1 lb green beans
low-calorie margarine

STEP-BY-STEP COUNTDOWN

1 Prepare the dessert and refrigerate. This can be done the day before.
2 Prepare the soup and turn off the heat.
3 Prepare steps 1 and 2 of the chicken recipe.
4 Prepare the potatoes. While the potatoes are cooking, prepare the ingredients for the carrots and green beans, but do not cook them.
5 Grill the chicken. While it is grilling, finish preparing the green beans and carrots.
6 Reheat the soup and serve.
7 Serve the chicken, potatoes, green beans, and carrots.
8 Serve the dessert.

Curried Apple Soup

6 Servings

Serving Size:
1 cup

Exchanges

1 Starch

Ingredients

2 tsp canola oil
1/4 cup chopped onion
1/4 cup chopped celery
1/4 cup diced carrots
2 tart apples, peeled, cored, and
     thinly sliced
1/4 cup unbleached white flour
1 tsp curry powder
5 cups low-fat, low-sodium chicken
     broth
1 cup canned tomatoes, drained and
     cut into pieces
1 tsp minced parsley
2 whole cloves
1 tsp sugar
1/2 tsp mace
Fresh ground pepper
Dash salt (optional)

Preparation—25 minutes

1 Heat the oil in a stockpot over medium-high heat. Add the onion, celery, carrots, and apples and saute for 5 minutes.
2 Mix together the flour and curry powder. Sprinkle over the mixture in the pot.
3 Add the broth and cook for 2 minutes. Add the tomatoes, parsley, and cloves.
4 Add the sugar, mace, pepper, and salt. Cook, covered, for 20 minutes. Discard the cloves and serve.

Calories	94
Calories from Fat	30
Total Fat	3 g
Saturated Fat	1 g
Cholesterol	0 mg
Sodium	140 mg
Carbohydrate	17 g
Dietary Fiber	2 g
Sugars	10 g
Protein	3 g

Barbecued Chicken Breasts with Mango Chutney

6 Servings

Serving Size:
3 oz

Exchanges

2 Carbohydrate
4 Very Lean Meat

Ingredients

1 Tbsp canola oil
1/2 cup minced onion
1 clove garlic, minced
2 tsp minced ginger
1 cup mango chutney
2 Tbsp lemon juice
1/2 cup water
1 1/2 lb boneless, skinless chicken breasts

Preparation—10 minutes

1 Heat the oil in a saucepan over medium-high heat. Add the onion and garlic and saute for 4 minutes. Add the ginger and saute for 3 minutes.
2 Add the chutney and bring to a boil. Lower the heat and simmer for 5 minutes. Add the lemon juice and water.
3 Prepare an outdoor grill with the rack set 4–6 inches from the heat source, or prepare an indoor broiler. Grill or broil the chicken on each side until it is opaque, about 12 minutes total, basting constantly with mango barbecue sauce.

Calories	272
Calories from Fat	47
Total Fat	5 g
Saturated Fat	1 g
Cholesterol	69 mg
Sodium	152 mg
Carbohydrate	30 g
Dietary Fiber	0 g
Sugars	29 g
Protein	26 g

Pan-Roasted Potatoes with Whole Mustard Seeds

6 Servings

Serving Size:
1/2 cup

Exchanges

1 Starch
1/2 Monounsaturated Fat

Ingredients

3 cups potato chunks (use russet or red), unpeeled
2 tsp canola oil
1 bay leaf
1 Tbsp black (or yellow) mustard seeds
1/4 cup minced onion
2 tsp paprika
Dash cumin
Dash cloves
Fresh ground pepper
Dash salt (optional)

Preparation—10 minutes

1 Parboil the potatoes for 5–6 minutes in a pot of boiling water and drain. They should be firm, yet a little tender.
2 Heat the oil in a large nonstick skillet over high heat. Add the bay leaf and mustard seeds and saute until the seeds begin to pop. Add the onion and lower the heat to medium-high.
3 Add the potatoes and saute, turning constantly, until the potatoes begin to turn crispy. Add the paprika and saute for a few more minutes.
4 Add the additional seasonings and toss to coat the potatoes. Cook for a few more minutes. Remove the bay leaf and serve.

Calories	98
Calories from Fat	21
Total Fat	2 g
Saturated Fat	0 g
Cholesterol	0 mg
Sodium	7 mg
Carbohydrate	18 g
Dietary Fiber	3 g
Sugars	2 g
Protein	3 g

Carrots and Green Beans with Cloves

6 Servings

Serving Size:
1/2 cup

Exchanges

1 Vegetable
1/2 Polyunsaturated
Fat

Ingredients

1 1/2 cups thinly sliced carrots
1 1/2 cups cut green beans
1/2 cup low-fat, low-sodium
   chicken broth
2 Tbsp low-calorie margarine
1 tsp ground cloves
1/2 tsp cinnamon
Fresh ground pepper

Preparation—10 minutes

1 Place the carrots and green beans in a skillet over medium heat. Add the broth, cover, and cook for about 5 minutes. The carrots should look bright orange and the green beans should be crisp.
2 Melt the margarine and add the cloves and cinnamon. Pour this mixture over the cooked vegetables. Toss well, season with pepper, and serve.

Calories	41
Calories from Fat	17
Total Fat	2 g
Saturated Fat	0 g
Cholesterol	2 mg
Sodium	49 mg
Carbohydrate	6 g
Dietary Fiber	2 g
Sugars	3 g
Protein	1 g

⌁ OILS

Canola Oil

Although relatively bland, canola oil is the oil of choice for many cooks today. Pressed from rapeseeds, canola oil became popular in Canada; its use is widespread here because it has a lower saturated fat content than any other oil. Next to olive oil, is has more monounsaturated fat than any other oil. Canola oil can be used for cooking and for salad dressings.

Pomegranate Dessert

6 Servings

Serving Size:
1/2 cup

Exchanges

1 Carbohydrate

Ingredients

3 cups mashed pomegranate pulp
   (remove the light-colored
   membrane)
1 Tbsp rose water
1 Tbsp lemon juice
2 Tbsp sugar

Preparation—10 minutes

Combine all ingredients and refrigerate for several hours. Serve chilled in dessert dishes.

Calories	69
Calories from Fat	2
Total Fat	0 g
Saturated Fat	0 g
Cholesterol	0 mg
Sodium	3 mg
Carbohydrate	18 g
Dietary Fiber	1 g
Sugars	11 g
Protein	1 g

❖ ❖ ❖ ❖ ❖ ❖ ❖

 WHY DON'T YOU . . .

*Learn to make interesting
napkin folds. Buy a book on
the subject. You'd be surprised
how many guests will comment
on your work!*

Island Breezes

❖ ❖ ❖ ❖ ❖

Spicy Sea Bass 237

Spicy Sea Bass
Cool Pineapple Salsa
Black Beans with Caramelized Red Onion
  and Peppers
Zucchini in Sofrito
Key Lime Parfait

Rum and Lime Pork 245

Run and Lime Pork
Banana Salsa
Butter Lettuce with Toasted Pumpkin Seeds
Mexican Cornbread
Mango Whip

Tropical Meatballs 253

Japanese Eggplant Appetizer
Ginger Pineapple Meatballs
Water Chestnut Rice
Sweet and Sour Vegetables
Almond Cookies

Caribbean Chicken 261

Caribbean Black Bean Soup
Warm Jerk Chicken Salad
Zucchini with Lime Dressing
Sweet Potato Fries
Ugli Fruit, Guava, and Cherimoya Dessert

Colorful Crabmeat Salad 269

Avocados with Cilantro Lime Salsa
Spicy Crabmeat Salad with Orange
  Cumin Vinaigrette
Chilled Asparagus with Lemon and Parsley
Chili Crisp Toasts
Kiwi and Peaches in Rum

Spicy Sea Bass

Spicy Sea Bass
Cool Pineapple Salsa
Black Beans with Caramelized Red Onion and Peppers
Zucchini in Sofrito
Key Lime Parfait

MENU TALK

If you haven't tried Chilean sea bass, you are in for a treat. Chilean sea bass is a thick, white fish with a texture like butter. It grills beautifully and is best prepared in some kind of marinade. Even if slightly overcooked, Chilean sea bass remains nice and moist. If Chilean sea bass is unavailable, another bass such as rockfish or striped bass will do. Orange roughy is also a good choice for this recipe.

This menu's salsa is a good example of a successful departure from the traditional tomato salsa. The cool, sweet pineapple and citrusy oranges blend well with the warmth of ginger, the heat of jalapenos, and the tartness of lime juice. Do allow a full hour for chilling so these wonderful flavors can marry. Use this salsa to accompany grilled chicken and pork, too.

Sofrito is a sauted mixture of garlic, peppers, onions, and cilantro. In this recipe, sofrito tops fresh steamed zucchini, but it's also great with cauliflower, corn, or mixed vegetables. If you're stuck with frozen vegetables one night, enliven them with this tasty topping.

Black beans are a staple food of the islands. Here, the bright colors of red onion and red bell peppers are set against the black of the beans. Black beans are also known as turtle beans. They have a sweet flavor the islanders like. In this recipe, the sweetness is enhanced by caramelizing the vegetables. The result is a colorful, delicately flavored bean dish that everyone will enjoy.

The key lime originates from Florida. Key limes are smaller and more yellow than green. Outside of Florida, key limes can be found in specialty food stores. Key lime juice can be found in natural food stores. Key lime juice is sweeter than that of regular limes. If you can obtain a key lime, use that to zest; otherwise, just use a regular lime. Zesting is easier with a zester, but you can use a vegetable peeler. When you zest, you want to scrape off only the outermost skin of the fruit; be sure not to include the white pith underneath. The zest of the fruit contains the aromatic oils that are so highly prized for adding flavor to foods.

Pantry List

1 can low-fat, low-sodium chicken
   broth
sesame oil
lite soy sauce
1 can crushed pineapple
1 can mandarin oranges, packed in
   their own juice
tequila
1 red onion
dry white wine
2 cans black beans
sugar
1 onion
1 can evaporated skim milk
olive oil
garlic
cornstarch or arrowroot powder

Market List

1 1/2 lb Chilean sea bass
ginger root
2 red bell peppers
1 yellow bell pepper
1 jalapeno pepper
red chili peppers
1 large zucchini
fresh lime juice
2 limes
key lime juice
low-calorie margarine
cilantro
2 eggs
low-calorie whipped topping
pineapple juice concentrate

STEP-BY-STEP COUNTDOWN

1 Prepare the dessert and refrigerate.
2 Prepare the salsa and refrigerate.
3 Prepare step 1 of the sea bass recipe.
4 Prepare the black beans and keep them
   in the skillet. Turn off the heat when they
   have cooked.
5 Prepare the zucchini, and leave this in the
   skillet with the heat off.
6 Grill the fish.
7 Serve the fish, salsa, zucchini, and black beans.
8 Serve the dessert.

Spicy Sea Bass

6 Servings

Serving Size:
3 oz

Exchanges

3 Very Lean Meat

Ingredients

1/4 cup pineapple juice concentrate,
    thawed
1/4 cup low-fat, low-sodium
    chicken broth
1   tsp sesame oil
2   tsp minced red chili peppers
2   tsp minced ginger
1   Tbsp lite soy sauce
1 1/2 lb Chilean sea bass

Preparation—15 minutes

1 Combine all ingredients except the sea bass, then add the sea bass and allow it to marinate for 1 hour in the refrigerator.
2 Prepare an outdoor grill with a rack set 6 inches from the heat source, or prepare an oven broiler. Grill or broil the sea bass on each side until the fish turns opaque, about 4-5 minutes per side, basting with excess marinade.

Calories	133
Calories from Fat	25
Total Fat	3 g
Saturated Fat	1 g
Cholesterol	47 mg
Sodium	158 mg
Carbohydrate	4 g
Dietary Fiber	0 g
Sugars	3 g
Protein	21 g

Cool Pineapple Salsa

6 Servings

Serving Size:
1/4 cup

Exchanges

1/2 Fruit

Ingredients

1 cup crushed pineapple, drained
1/2 cup mandarin oranges, drained
2 Tbsp minced red bell pepper
2 tsp minced jalapeno pepper
1 Tbsp tequila
2 Tbsp lime juice
1 tsp minced ginger
2 Tbsp minced red onion

Preparation—10 minutes

Combine all ingredients. Refrigerate for 1 hour before serving.

Calories	30
Calories from Fat	1
Total Fat	0 g
Saturated Fat	0 g
Cholesterol	0 mg
Sodium	2 mg
Carbohydrate	6 g
Dietary Fiber	1 g
Sugars	5 g
Protein	0 g

 WHY DON'T YOU . . .

Buy some really nice paper plates. Use them on busy nights to add a festive touch while reducing clean-up time!

Black Beans with Caramelized Red Onion and Peppers

6 Servings

Serving Size:
1/2 cup

Exchanges

2 Starch

Ingredients

1/4 cup dry white wine
2 cloves garlic, minced
3 cups black beans, drained and
    rinsed
1/4 cup low-fat, low-sodium
    chicken broth
2 Tbsp low-calorie margarine
1/2 cup very thinly sliced red onion
1/2 each red and yellow bell pepper,
    diced
1 Tbsp sugar
1/4 cup minced cilantro
Dash salt (optional)

Preparation—20 minutes

1 Heat the wine in a skillet over medium-high heat. Add the garlic and saute for 1 minute. Add the beans and the broth.
2 Bring to a boil, cover, lower the heat, and simmer for 15 minutes. Add additional liquid to prevent burning if necessary. The liquid should be absorbed by the end of the cooking time.
3 Meanwhile, melt the margarine in a small skillet. Add the red onion and bell peppers and saute until soft, about 5 minutes.
4 Add the sugar and stir constantly until the red onions and peppers are coated and caramelized. Add to the beans, garnish with cilantro, season with salt, and serve.

Calories	165
Calories from Fat	23
Total Fat	3 g
Saturated Fat	1 g
Cholesterol	0 mg
Sodium	188 mg
Carbohydrate	28 g
Dietary Fiber	8 g
Sugars	7 g
Protein	8 g

Zucchini in Sofrito

6 Servings

Serving Size:
1/2 cup

Exchanges

1 Vegetable

Ingredients

2 tsp olive oil
1/2 cup minced onion
1/2 cup minced red bell pepper
1 clove garlic, minced
1 1/2 Tbsp minced cilantro
3 cups sliced zucchini
Fresh ground pepper
Dash salt (optional)

Preparation—15 minutes

1 Heat the oil in a skillet over medium-high heat. Add the onions and bell pepper and saute for 10 minutes. Add the garlic and cilantro and cook for 2 minutes.
2 Steam the zucchini over boiling water for 5 minutes and drain. Toss the sofrito with the cooked zucchini. Season with pepper and salt and serve.

Calories	36
Calories from Fat	14
Total Fat	2 g
Saturated Fat	0 g
Cholesterol	0 mg
Sodium	3 mg
Carbohydrate	6 g
Dietary Fiber	1 g
Sugars	3 g
Protein	1 g

Key Lime Parfait

6 Servings

Serving Size:
1/3 cup

Exchanges

1 1/2 Carbohydrate
1/2 Saturated Fat

Ingredients

2 egg yolks
1 12-oz can evaporated skim milk
1 Tbsp cornstarch or arrowroot
    powder
1/3 cup sugar
1/3 cup key lime juice
Zest of 1/2 lime
1 cup low-calorie whipped topping
Lime twists

Preparation—10 minutes

1 Combine the egg yolks, milk, cornstarch or arrowroot powder, and sugar in a medium saucepan. Cook over medium heat until the mixture comes to a boil.
2 Remove from heat and stir in the lime juice and zest. Pour into a bowl and refrigerate for 2 hours.
3 Mix the filling with the whipped topping. Spoon into dessert glasses and serve with a twist of lime on top.

Calories	149
Calories from Fat	29
Total Fat	3 g
Saturated Fat	2 g
Cholesterol	73 mg
Sodium	79 mg
Carbohydrate	24 g
Dietary Fiber	0 g
Sugars	18 g
Protein	6 g

Rum and Lime Pork

Rum and Lime Pork
Banana Salsa
Butter Lettuce with Toasted Pumpkin Seeds
Mexican Cornbread
Mango Whip

MENU TALK

*L*imes, rich in vitamin C, grow best in tropical climates. British sailors ate them to prevent scurvy aboard ship; hence the nickname "Limey." Look for limes with smooth skins and no shriveling. Limes are available all year, with a peak season from May through August. When you have the time, squeeze your own lime juice. One lime generally yields 3 Tbsp of juice. To extract the juice, first warm the lime in the microwave for 60 seconds. Remove the lime from the microwave and allow it to cool for 10 minutes. Cut the lime in half and squeeze. This process warms the membrane of the lime and causes the juice to collect in the center of the fruit, making it easier to extract all the juice. Bottled lime juice will do, but look for small bottles—the flavor is better. White rum is lighter than dark and needs to be used in this recipe—dark rum will give the pork too heavy a taste. If you wish, omit the rum completely.

Bananas grow in warm, humid climates. There are hundreds of banana species, but the common yellow banana is the most popular. Try this salsa on chicken or fish—or even chilled for a light dessert!

Butter lettuce has soft, buttery, textured leaves with a sweet flavor. Gently wash the butter lettuce leaves because they are quite delicate. Boston and Bibb are the most well known of the butter lettuces. Store the lettuce in ventilated plastic bags in the refrigerator, and use within two days. Pumpkin seeds or pepitas are a popular ingredient in Mexican cooking. Pepitas can be found at natural food stores and speciality shops. For the best flavor, buy

See color photo after p. 240.

245

unsalted, raw pepitas, and roast them yourself by placing them in a dry skillet. Toast the nuts over medium heat for about 5–6 minutes, shaking the pan constantly. Store them in bags or jars.

Cornmeal consists of dried corn kernels that have been ground to be fine, medium, or coarse. Stone-ground cornmeal is the best to use because this process retains most of the corn's germ and bran. Stone-ground cornmeal must be refrigerated. Blue cornmeal makes wonderful pancakes, and muffins made with white cornmeal are deliciously sweet. There are as many variations of cornbread as there are cooks. This version is somewhat spicy and savory, with the addition of peppers and cheese. I prefer to use some flour in cornbread recipes. If you use only cornmeal, you'll bake a coarser and grainier cornbread.

The mango first originated in India. Today it grows in temperate climates all over the world. If you have never had a mango, you will love its exotic, succulent flavor. Just peel the fruit, cut it in half, and slice around the pit that runs the length of the mango. Fruit will be easily cut from the mango if it is ripe and not overly mushy. Look for mangoes with yellow to red mottling that yield to pressure. Mangoes are rich in vitamins A and C.

Pantry List

white rum
olive oil
garlic
sugar
sherry vinegar
cumin
1 yellow onion
1 red onion
pumpkin seeds
pecans
yellow cornmeal
unbleached white flour
baking powder
baking soda
evaporated skim milk
canola oil

Market List

1 1/2 lb pork tenderloin
fresh lime juice
green onions
2 bananas
4 mangoes
3 jalapeno peppers
1 red bell pepper
cilantro
3 heads butter lettuce
1 avocado
1 small bag frozen corn or 2 ears
    corn
1/2 pint cherry tomatoes
orange juice
1 papaya

low-calorie whipped topping
low-fat cheddar cheese
2 eggs

Rum and Lime Pork

6 Servings

Serving Size:
3 oz

Exchanges

4 Very Lean Meat
1 Monounsaturated
   Fat

Ingredients

1/2 cup white rum
1/4 cup fresh lime juice
2 Tbsp olive oil
3 cloves garlic, minced
3 green onions, minced
1 1/2 lb lean pork tenderloin

Preparation—5 minutes

1 Preheat the oven to 350 degrees. Combine rum, lime juice, oil, garlic, and onions in a shallow dish. Add the pork tenderloin and marinate in the refrigerator for 24 hours.
2 Roast the tenderloin until it reaches an internal temperature of 155–160 degrees, about 40–45 minutes.

Calories	192
Calories from Fat	67
Total Fat	7 g
Saturated Fat	2 g
Cholesterol	71 mg
Sodium	51 mg
Carbohydrate	1 g
Dietary Fiber	0 g
Sugars	1 g
Protein	25 g

Banana Salsa

6 Servings

Serving Size:
3 Tbsp

Exchanges

1 Fruit

Ingredients

2 ripe bananas, diced
1/2 cup fresh diced mango or
    papaya
2 Tbsp fresh lime juice
1 jalapeno pepper, minced
2 tsp sugar
2 Tbsp minced red bell pepper
2 tsp minced cilantro

Preparation—10 minutes

Combine all ingredients. Serve at room temperature or chill before serving.

Calories	65
Calories from Fat	3
Total Fat	0 g
Saturated Fat	0 g
Cholesterol	0 mg
Sodium	2 mg
Carbohydrate	17 g
Dietary Fiber	2 g
Sugars	11 g
Protein	1 g

VINEGARS

Rice Vinegar

Rice vinegar is a sweet, mild vinegar used most often in Asian cuisine. I prefer the brown rice variety. Like the name, this variety of rice vinegar has a golden brown color and deep, rich flavor. White rice vinegars tend to have additional sugar added and seem to lack the complex flavor of brown. Purchase brown rice vinegar in natural food stores, gourmet grocery stores, or Asian markets. Brown rice vinegar is great splashed on green salads, used in marinades, and added to sushi.

Butter Lettuce with Toasted Pumpkin Seeds

6 Servings

Serving Size:
1 cup

Exchanges

1 Starch
2 1/2 Fat

Ingredients

6 cups butter lettuce, torn
1 avocado, thinly sliced
1 small red onion, thinly sliced
1/2 cup corn
1 cup halved cherry tomatoes
1/3 cup sherry vinegar
1 Tbsp olive oil
2 Tbsp minced cilantro
2 tsp cumin
2 Tbsp orange juice
Fresh ground pepper
Dash salt (optional)
1/3 cup toasted pumpkin seeds

Preparation—15 minutes

1 Combine the lettuce, avocado, onion, corn, and cherry tomatoes in a salad bowl.
2 Whisk together the remaining ingredients except the pumpkin seeds. Pour the dressing over the salad and toss. Garnish with pumpkin seeds and serve.

Calories	178
Calories from Fat	118
Total Fat	13 g
Saturated Fat	2 g
Cholesterol	0 mg
Sodium	15 mg
Carbohydrate	13 g
Dietary Fiber	5 g
Sugars	5 g
Protein	6 g

 WHY DON'T YOU . . .

Prepare several menu items in advance and freeze. This works great with soups and stews. You can pop them out of the freezer and reheat them as guests arrive.

Mexican Cornbread

6 Servings

Serving Size:
1 2-inch square

Exchanges

1 Very Lean Meat
1 Fat

Ingredients

1 cup yellow cornmeal
1/2 cup unbleached white flour
1 tsp baking powder
2 Tbsp sugar
2 eggs, beaten
1 cup evaporated skim milk
1/2 cup minced onion
2 jalapeno peppers, minced
6 oz shredded low-fat cheddar cheese
1 cup corn
1 Tbsp canola oil

Preparation—20 minutes

1 Preheat the oven to 350 degrees. Combine the cornmeal, flour, baking powder, and sugar in a medium bowl.

2 In a large bowl, combine the remaining ingredients. Stir in the cornmeal mixture. Pour into an 8 X 8-inch nonstick pan and bake until browned, about 35–40 minutes.

Calories	331
Calories from Fat	78
Total Fat	9 g
Saturated Fat	3 g
Cholesterol	87 mg
Sodium	264 mg
Carbohydrate	43 g
Dietary Fiber	3 g
Sugars	10 g
Protein	19 g

Mango Whip

6 Servings

Serving Size:
1/2 cup

Exchanges

2 Fruit
1 Fat

Ingredients

3   large mangoes
3   tsp sugar
1   papaya, peeled, seeded, and cut
    into small pieces
1   cup low-calorie whipped topping
6   Tbsp chopped toasted pecans

Preparation—15 minutes

1   Peel and pit the mangoes. Cut the fruit into pieces and puree in a food processor. Add the sugar and stir in the papaya.
2   Fold in the whipped topping. Top each serving with pecans and serve.

Calories	163
Calories from Fat	52
Total Fat	6 g
Saturated Fat	2 g
Cholesterol	0 mg
Sodium	5 mg
Carbohydrate	29 g
Dietary Fiber	3 g
Sugars	23 g
Protein	1 g

Tropical Meatballs

**Japanese Eggplant Appetizer
Ginger Pineapple Meatballs
Water Chestnut Rice
Sweet and Sour Vegetables
Almond Cookies**

MENU TALK

Eggplant is actually a fruit! There are many varieties of eggplant. Japanese eggplants are thin with a slightly sweeter flesh than regular eggplants. If you can't find Japanese eggplants, look for Italian or baby eggplants, because they also taste sweeter. Peel eggplants just before cooking because their flesh darkens very quickly. Eggplants are extremely low in calories. Hoisin sauce is a must-have ingredient for Asian cooking. It is a reddish brown, thick sauce composed of soybeans, garlic, spices, and chili peppers. Hoisin sauce is found in most supermarkets. It is very flavorful and potent, so use it sparingly.

Oyster sauce is slightly different than hoisin sauce. It is a dark brown sauce composed of oysters, brine, and soy sauce. Oyster sauce is rich, but the flavor mellows while cooking and won't overpower your dishes. Oyster sauce is found in supermarkets and Asian markets. Use this sauce on chicken breasts or shrimp, or use it as a basting sauce for grilled foods.

Have you ever had a fresh water chestnut? It's perfectly acceptable to use canned, but if you're in an Asian grocery store, try a fresh one (just peel the skin before using). Water chestnuts can be tossed into any stir-fry to add crunch and a hint of sweetness. Brown rice should be used within six months of purchase because it contains the rice bran, which can become rancid. Avoid using quick-cooking brown rice. Although it will save time, you'll miss the chewy, nutlike taste of true brown rice. Brown rice has more fiber, vitamins, and minerals than white rice. You may choose from long-grain and short-grain brown rice. I prefer short grain, because it's a little stickier. Be sure to rinse the rice before you cook it. Because of its high starch content, the rice will clump together in a sticky mass if not rinsed. Try this recipe cold as a rice salad.

The sauce topping this menu's vegetables can also be used in stir-frys. Sweet and sour flavors usually come from some combination of sugar and vinegar. This recipe contains significantly less sugar than traditional versions without any loss of flavor.

These almond cookies are an easy slice-and-bake treat. You can prepare this dough weeks in advance, freeze it, defrost it, and slice and bake. You may want to wear rubber gloves as you work with the dough so less heat is conveyed from your hand, which toughens the dough. Almonds provide calcium, fiber, folic acid, riboflavin, and vitamin E.

Pantry List

sesame oil
dry white wine
1 shallot
garlic
hoisin sauce
dry sherry
1 small loaf French or Italian bread
oyster sauce
lite soy sauce
peanut oil
1 can low-fat, low-sodium chicken
   broth
1 small can pineapple juice
brown sugar
pineapple juice concentrate
cornstarch or arrowroot powder
1 bag brown rice
1 6-oz can water chestnuts
sugar
almond extract
yellow food coloring
unbleached white flour
baking soda
sliced almonds

Market List

1/2 lb ground pork tenderloin
1 lb ground turkey breast
1 small Japanese eggplant
1 red pepper
1 carrot
scallions
low-calorie margarine
1 egg

ginger root
cilantro

STEP-BY-STEP COUNTDOWN

1 Prepare the almond cookies. This can be done one day or several days in advance.
2 Prepare the brown rice by boiling 1 1/2 cups rinsed raw brown rice in 3 cups of water. Cover, lower the heat, and simmer for 45 minutes until the water is absorbed.
3 Prepare the first three steps of the meatball recipe. Remove the meatballs from the oven so they won't dry out.
4 Prepare the first two steps of the appetizer recipe.
5 Prepare the vegetables.
6 Finish preparing the rice and turn off the heat.
7 Finish preparing the appetizer and serve.
8 Pour the sauce over the meatballs and bake.
9 Serve the meatballs, vegetables, and rice.
10 Serve the dessert.

Japanese Eggplant Appetizer

6 Servings

Serving Size:
2 pieces

Exchanges

2 Starch

Ingredients

1 tsp sesame oil
1/4 cup dry white wine
1 small Japanese eggplant, diced
1 shallot, minced
2 cloves garlic, minced
1 Tbsp hoisin sauce
2 Tbsp sherry
12 1-oz slices Italian bread
Finely minced red bell pepper

Preparation—15 minutes

1 Heat the oil and wine in a skillet over medium-high heat. Add the eggplant and saute for 5 minutes. Cover and steam for 3 minutes.
2 Add the shallot and garlic and saute for 3 minutes. Add the hoisin sauce and sherry and stir to coat.
3 Toast the bread slices. Place about 1–2 tsp of eggplant on each piece of toast. Garnish with red bell pepper and serve.

Calories	174
Calories from Fat	24
Total Fat	3 g
Saturated Fat	1 g
Cholesterol	1 mg
Sodium	324 mg
Carbohydrate	31 g
Dietary Fiber	3 g
Sugars	6 g
Protein	5 g

❖ ❖ ❖ ❖ ❖

〜 WHY DON'T YOU . . .

Freeze berries in the summer and enjoy them all winter long. Place the berries in a single layer in a plastic container, label them, and freeze.

Orange Ginger Salmon Dinner, see page 145

Southern–Style Supper, see page 203

Rum and Lime Pork Dinner, see page 245

Holiday Roast Pork Dinner, see page 279

Ginger Pineapple Turkey Meatballs

6 Servings

Serving Size:
3 oz

Exchanges

1 Carbohydrate
4 Very Lean Meat

Ingredients

1 lb ground turkey breast (97% fat-free)
1/2 lb ground pork tenderloin
1 Tbsp finely minced ginger
2 Tbsp oyster sauce
1 Tbsp lite soy sauce
2 tsp peanut oil
2 cloves garlic, minced
1 cup diced carrot, peeled
2 cups low-fat, low-sodium chicken broth
1 cup pineapple juice
2 Tbsp pineapple juice concentrate (do not dilute)
2 Tbsp brown sugar
1 Tbsp cornstarch or arrowroot powder
2 Tbsp water

Preparation—20 minutes

1 Preheat the oven to 350 degrees. Combine the turkey, pork, ginger, oyster sauce, and soy sauce in a large bowl and shape into meatballs. Place the meatballs in a nonstick baking dish and bake, covered, for 15 minutes.

2 Heat the oil in a skillet over medium-high heat. Add the garlic and saute for 30 seconds. Add the carrots and saute for 4 minutes. Add the broth and pineapple juice and bring the mixture to a boil.

3 Lower the heat, add the pineapple juice concentrate and brown sugar, and simmer for 5 minutes.

4 Mix the cornstarch or arrowroot powder with the water and add it to the sauce. Cook until thickened, about 3 minutes. Uncover the meatballs and add the sauce. Bake for 10 minutes and serve.

Calories	227
Calories from Fat	38
Total Fat	4 g
Saturated Fat	1 g
Cholesterol	74 mg
Sodium	413 mg
Carbohydrate	18 g
Dietary Fiber	1 g
Sugars	14 g
Protein	29 g

Water Chestnut Rice

6 Servings

Serving Size:
1/2 cup

Exchanges

2 Starch

Ingredients

1 tsp sesame oil
1 clove garlic, minced
2 Tbsp minced green onions
1/2 cup minced onion
3 cups cooked brown rice
1 6-oz can sliced water chestnuts
1/2 cup shredded carrot
1 Tbsp lite soy sauce
Sprigs of cilantro

Preparation—15 minutes

1 Heat the oil in a wok or heavy skillet over medium-high heat. Add the garlic, green onions, and onion and saute for 3 minutes.
2 Add the rice and water chestnuts and saute for 5 minutes. Add the carrots and soy sauce and cook for 5 minutes. Garnish with cilantro and serve.

Calories	143
Calories from Fat	15
Total Fat	2 g
Saturated Fat	0 g
Cholesterol	0 mg
Sodium	112 mg
Carbohydrate	29 g
Dietary Fiber	3 g
Sugars	4 g
Protein	3 g

Sweet and Sour Vegetables

6 Servings

Serving Size:
1/2 cup

Exchanges

1/2 Carbohydrate
1 Vegetable

Ingredients

1/2 cup low-fat, low-sodium
  chicken broth
1/2 cup julienned red bell pepper
1/2 cup trimmed green beans
1/2 cup sliced asparagus
1/2 cup sliced zucchini
1/2 cup sliced mushrooms
1/4 cup tomato sauce
2 Tbsp red wine vinegar
2 Tbsp sugar
Dash salt
2 Tbsp cornstarch or arrowroot
  powder
1/4 cup water

Preparation—15 minutes

1 Heat the broth in a wok or heavy skillet over high heat. Add all the vegetables, cover, and steam until the broth is absorbed, about 5–6 minutes.
2 Combine the tomato sauce, vinegar, sugar, and salt. Add the mixture to the vegetables and stir to coat.
3 Mix the cornstarch or arrowroot powder with the water and add it to the sauce. Cook until thick and bubbly and serve.

Calories	47
Calories from Fat	3
Total Fat	0 g
Saturated Fat	0 g
Cholesterol	0 mg
Sodium	120 mg
Carbohydrate	11 g
Dietary Fiber	1 g
Sugars	6 g
Protein	1 g

Almond Cookies

6 Servings

Serving Size:
2 cookies

Exchanges

1 Carbohydrate
1/2 Monounsatur-
ated Fat

Ingredients

3/4 cup low-calorie margarine
1/3 cup sugar
1 egg
2 tsp almond extract
2 drops yellow food coloring
   (optional)
1 1/4 cups unbleached white flour
1/4 tsp baking soda
Dash salt
1/2 cup sliced almonds

Preparation—15 minutes

1 Preheat the oven to 375 degrees. Cream together the margarine and sugar until fluffy. Add the egg, extract, and food coloring and mix well.
2 Combine the flour, baking soda, and salt and add to the creamed mixture. Mix until a firm dough is formed. Divide the dough in half and shape into a roll, 12 inches long and 1 1/2 inches in diameter. Roll the dough in the sliced almonds, wrap in wax paper, and refrigerate for 3 hours.
3 With a sharp knife, cut the dough into 1/4-inch slices. Place cookies on a nonstick cookie sheet and bake for about 10 minutes. Remove the cookies from the oven and cool completely on a wire rack.

Calories	102
Calories from Fat	51
Total Fat	6 g
Saturated Fat	1 g
Cholesterol	12 mg
Sodium	89 mg
Carbohydrate	11 g
Dietary Fiber	1 g
Sugars	4 g
Protein	2 g

❖ ❖ ❖

Caribbean Chicken

Caribbean Black Bean Soup
Warm Jerk Chicken Salad
Zucchini with Lime Dressing
Sweet Potato Fries
Ugli Fruit, Guava, and Cherimoya Dessert

MENU TALK

Black beans are a staple in Caribbean cuisine. They appear in appetizers, soups, main courses, and side dishes. This soup uses plenty of Caribbean flavorings, such as lime, cumin, ginger, and Caribbean hot sauce. If you cannot find Caribbean hot sauce, use regular hot pepper sauce. This soup freezes well. If you prefer a thinner soup, don't puree the second can of beans.

Jerk seasoning has become very popular among American chefs. It is a dry seasoning consisting primarily of chilis, paprika, garlic, allspice, thyme, and cloves. The mixture can be found in most supermarkets or at specialty shops. You can also create a marinade from jerk seasoning. Just mix the seasoning with water according to your taste and use the mixture to marinate chicken, pork, or seafood. Jerk seasoning is relatively mild, so its flavor can be enjoyed by everyone.

Sweet potatoes are often confused with yams, but they are two different vegetables. Sweet potatoes are slightly smaller and drier when cooked, with a more yellow flesh and skin. Yams are more moist when cooked and have a thicker skin and a more orange flesh. Sweet potatoes are best in the fall and winter months. Look for smooth skins with no evidence of bruising. Sweet potatoes are a much better source of vitamin A than white potatoes. Keep sweet potatoes stored at room temperature.

Use this menu's lime dressing for any green salad, or use it in place of the dressing for the chicken salad. Add a dash of cinnamon or allspice for some extra warmth and sweetness.

Despite its unfortunate name, the ugli fruit is a treat! It also known as a tangelo, a cross between a tangerine and a pomelo (a grapefruit). If ugli fruit is unavailable, use an orange, tangerine, or grapefruit instead. The guava is a sweet tropical fruit. If you are lucky enough to live in an area where you can find guavas, purchase ones that yield to pressure. For the rest of us, canned guavas are available at specialty stores. If neither fresh nor canned is available to you, use a sliced mango or papaya instead.

The cherimoya, also called the custard apple, is a tropical fruit that tastes like a cross between a pineapple and a banana. Shaped like an upside-down pear, it has a scaly green skin that forms a pattern similar to overlapping thumb prints. Cherimoyas grow in California; their best season is November through May. Ripe cherimoyas will yield to pressure. Keep them at room temperature until ripened, and then refrigerate up to four days. To use cherimoyas, cut them in half, scoop out the seeds, and remove the creamy, succulent fruit. If you can't find any, just add more of the other fruit in this recipe. Note that the cherimoya and banana used in this dessert need to be frozen 12 hours ahead of time.

Pantry List

sugar
canola oil
2 cans low-fat, low-sodium chicken
 broth
1 red onion
garlic
2 15-oz cans black beans
cumin
Caribbean hot sauce or hot pepper
 sauce
ground ginger
olive oil
jerk seasoning
brown sugar
mango chutney
2 sweet potatoes
garlic powder
cinnamon

Market List

1 1/2 lb boneless, skinless chicken
 breasts
fresh lime juice
1 red bell pepper
1 green bell pepper
1 carrot
1 cherimoya
1 ugli fruit
1 banana
1 guava
1 large zucchini
green leaf lettuce

STEP-BY-STEP COUNTDOWN

1 Prepare the first step of the chicken recipe.
 This can be done a day in advance.
2 Prepare the soup and turn off the heat.
3 Prepare the sweet potato fries.
4 Finish preparing the chicken.
5 Prepare the dessert and refrigerate.
6 Prepare the zucchini and refrigerate.
7 Reheat and serve the soup.
8 Serve the chicken, zucchini, and fries.
9 Serve the dessert.

Caribbean Black Bean Soup

6 Servings

Serving Size:
I cup

Exchanges

I 1/2 Starch
I Very Lean Meat

Ingredients

1 tsp canola oil
3 1/2 cups low-fat, low-sodium
    chicken broth
1/2 cup minced red onion
2 cloves garlic, minced
1 15-oz can black beans, pureed
1 15-oz can black beans, drained
    and rinsed
1 Tbsp cumin
1 Tbsp fresh lime juice
2 tsp ground ginger
1/2 tsp Caribbean hot sauce or hot
    pepper sauce

Preparation—15 minutes

1 Heat the oil and 1/2 cup broth in a stockpot over medium-high heat. Add the onion and garlic and saute for 5 minutes.
2 Add the beans, 3 cups broth, and cumin. Bring to a boil, lower the heat, and simmer for 20 minutes.
3 Add the lime juice, ginger, and hot sauce to serve.

Calories	157	
Calories from Fat	24	
Total Fat	3	g
Saturated Fat	I	g
Cholesterol	0	mg
Sodium	421	mg
Carbohydrate	26	g
Dietary Fiber	8	g
Sugars	4	g
Protein	II	g

Warm Jerk Chicken Salad

6 Servings

Serving Size:
3 oz chicken
I cup vegetables

Exchanges

I Carbohydrate
I Vegetable
3 Very Lean Meat

Ingredients

1 1/2 lb boneless, skinless chicken
    breasts, sliced into 3-inch strips
2 Tbsp fresh lime juice
1 Tbsp olive oil
2 Tbsp water
1 Tbsp jerk seasoning (available in
    the spice section of your
    supermarket or in gourmet
    cooking stores)
2 tsp brown sugar
1 medium red bell pepper, julienned
1 medium green bell pepper,
    julienned
1/2 cup diced red onion
1 large carrot, thinly sliced
1/4 cup mango chutney
Fresh ground pepper
Dash salt (optional)
Green leaf lettuce

Preparation—20 minutes

1 Combine the chicken strips, lime juice, olive oil, water, jerk seasoning, and brown sugar in a medium bowl. Let the chicken marinate in the refrigerator for at least 2 hours.
2 Grill or broil the chicken strips 6 inches from the heat source, or until the chicken turns opaque.
3 Toss together the bell peppers, onion, carrot, mango chutney, salt, and pepper in a serving bowl. Place lettuce on individual salad plates.
4 Mound the vegetable mixture on each lettuce-lined plate, top with chicken strips, and serve.

Calories	212
Calories from Fat	41
Total Fat	5 g
Saturated Fat	I g
Cholesterol	69 mg
Sodium	187 mg
Carbohydrate	16 g
Dietary Fiber	2 g
Sugars	14 g
Protein	26 g

Zucchini with Lime Dressing

6 Servings

Serving Size:
1/2 cup

Exchanges

1 Vegetable

Ingredients

3 cups thinly sliced zucchini,
   unpeeled
1/3 cup fresh lime juice
1 tsp olive oil
1/2 tsp Caribbean hot sauce or hot
   pepper sauce
1/4 tsp cumin
Fresh ground pepper
Dash salt (optional)

Preparation—10 minutes

1 Steam the zucchini over boiling water for 4 minutes and drain.
2 Whisk together the remaining ingredients and sprinkle over the zucchini. Serve chilled or at room temperature.

Calories	22
Calories from Fat	7
Total Fat	1 g
Saturated Fat	0 g
Cholesterol	0 mg
Sodium	5 mg
Carbohydrate	4 g
Dietary Fiber	1 g
Sugars	2 g
Protein	1 g

WHY DON'T YOU . . .

Grow your own herbs. Herbs need some sunlight, soil, and water—that's it. They are very undemanding plants. Begin with dill, basil, parsley, and chives; then plant more as your interest grows.

Sweet Potato Fries

6 Servings

Serving Size:
1/2 cup

Exchanges

1 1/2 Starch

Ingredients

2 large sweet potatoes, well
   scrubbed, skins on, sliced into
   2-inch rounds
1 tsp olive oil
2 tsp garlic powder
1/2 tsp cinnamon

Preparation—5 minutes

Preheat the oven to 400 degrees. Toss the potatoes with the oil. Sprinkle with the remaining ingredients. Bake until crispy and tender, about 30–40 minutes.

Calories	24
Calories from Fat	8
Total Fat	1 g
Saturated Fat	0 g
Cholesterol	0 mg
Sodium	11 mg
Carbohydrate	28 g
Dietary Fiber	3 g
Sugars	13 g
Protein	2 g

 WHY DON'T YOU . . .

Learn how to change a high-fat favorite into a low-fat dish. Not sure how? Attend a cooking class, subscribe to healthy cooking magazines, or talk to a dietitian.

Ugli Fruit, Guava, and Cherimoya Dessert

6 Servings

Serving Size:
1/2 cup

Exchanges

1 Fruit

Ingredients

1 cherimoya, peeled, seeded, and
  cubed, frozen for 12 hours
2 Tbsp sugar
1 Tbsp lime juice
1 banana, peeled and sliced, frozen
  for 12 hours
1 ugli fruit, peeled and sliced
1 guava, peeled and sliced

Preparation—15 minutes

1 Prepare the cherimoya and banana and freeze in zippered bags for 12 hours.
2 Puree the cherimoya in a blender with the sugar, lime juice, and banana until creamy and thick.
3 Pour the cherimoya mixture into dessert dishes or a hollowed-out pineapple shell. Top with the sliced fruits and serve.

Calories	76
Calories from Fat	3
Total Fat	0 g
Saturated Fat	0 g
Cholesterol	0 mg
Sodium	2 mg
Carbohydrate	19 g
Dietary Fiber	3 g
Sugars	14 g
Protein	1 g

Colorful Crabmeat Salad

Avocados with Cilantro Lime Salsa
Colorful Crabmeat Salad with Orange Cumin Vinaigrette
Chilled Asparagus with Lemon and Parsley
Chili Crisp Toasts
Kiwi and Peaches in Rum

MENU TALK

Cilantro consists of the leaves and stems of the coriander plant. Cilantro is often referred to as Chinese parsley. Cilantro has smaller, more rounded leaves than flat parsley, so be sure not to confuse them. Cilantro is used in Mexican and Asian cooking. Its flavor goes well with very spicy foods. Store cilantro refrigerated as you would a bouquet of flowers, in a glass of water with a plastic bag on top. Try not to use dried cilantro—it has very little of the good flavor that fresh cilantro does. The combination of oranges, onions, and cilantro has been used for centuries in Mexican cooking.

This menu's salad is light and cool and pretty enough to serve to company. You can use cooked medium shrimp, grilled chicken, or cooked scallops—or a combination of all three—instead of crabmeat. Calamari (octopus) is also great in this salad. When buying fresh calamari, look for small ones with clear eyes and a fresh fragrance. Good calamari should be mild and sweet. Calamari can be sliced and steamed or pan-sauted. Be sure not to overcook calamari, or it becomes rubbery.

For a Mediterranean version of this salad, add 1 cup sliced artichoke hearts (packed in water), 1/2 cup roasted red bell pepper, 1 cup blanched sliced asparagus or broccoli, 1/2 cup garbanzo beans, and 1/4 cup chopped basil leaves to the meat or seafood. Omit the corn, oranges, and pumpkin seeds. Use balsamic vinegar instead of sherry in the dressing, and lemon juice instead of lime. Replace the jalapenos, chili powder, and cumin with 2 cloves of minced garlic, 1/2 tsp minced thyme, and 1/4 tsp minced oregano.

You can use broccoli or zucchini instead of asparagus for this menu's vegetable. Asparagus is good served hot or cold. Fresh parsley is an absolute must in this recipe. Try chili powder instead of cayenne pepper on the toast if you want a milder flavor. Do these spicy bread slices at the last minute to ensure crispness.

Peaches and kiwi make an eye-appealing finish to this menu. Dark rum works well with these two fruits. Add rum extract if you do not want to use the real thing, or omit the rum flavor entirely.

Pantry List

2 red onions
olive oil
white wine vinegar
pumpkin seeds
sherry vinegar
chili powder
cumin
red wine vinegar
cayenne pepper
1 small loaf Italian or French bread
paprika
garlic
brown sugar
dark rum

Market List

1 1/2 lb lump crabmeat
cilantro
parsley
fresh lime juice
1 jalapeno pepper
1 large avocado
2 oranges
1 small pkg frozen yellow corn or
    1 ear of corn
1 red bell pepper
fresh orange juice
2 lb fresh spinach leaves
1 bundle asparagus
fresh lemon juice
low-calorie margarine
3 large kiwi
2 peaches

1 Prepare the first step of the appetizer recipe.
2 Prepare the asparagus and refrigerate for 1 hour.
3 Prepare the dessert and refrigerate for 1 hour.
4 Prepare the crabmeat salad and dressing, but do not combine them.
5 Prepare the ingredients for the chili toasts, but do not bake them.
6 Finish preparing the appetizer recipe and serve.
7 Bake the chili toasts.
8 Finish preparing the salad and serve with the asparagus and toasts.
9 Serve the dessert.

Avocados with Cilantro Lime Salsa

6 Servings

Serving Size:
3 slices avocado
1 Tbsp salsa

Exchanges

1/2 Carbohydrate
2 Monounsaturated
 Fat

Ingredients

2 Tbsp minced red onion
2/3 cup minced cilantro
1/4 cup minced parsley
2 Tbsp olive oil
3 Tbsp fresh lime juice
1 1/2 Tbsp white wine vinegar
2 cloves garlic, minced
1 jalapeno pepper, minced
1 large avocado, sliced into 18 thin
   slices
1 medium orange, sectioned
1 small red onion, sliced into rings

Preparation—30 minutes

1 Combine the onion, cilantro, parsley, oil, lime juice, vinegar, garlic, and jalapeno pepper in a small bowl and refrigerate for 2 hours.
2 On individual plates, fan out the avocado slices and top with oranges and red onions. Spoon the salsa on top and serve.

Calories	142
Calories from Fat	105
Total Fat	12 g
Saturated Fat	2 g
Cholesterol	0 mg
Sodium	8 mg
Carbohydrate	10 g
Dietary Fiber	4 g
Sugars	5 g
Protein	2 g

 WHY DON'T YOU . . .

Try a different method of cooking the same old food. Grill your vegetables instead of steaming them, sear your chicken instead of baking it, or bake an apple instead of eating it raw.

Colorful Crabmeat Salad with Orange Cumin Vinaigrette

6 Servings

Serving Size:
1/6 recipe

Exchanges

1 Starch
3 Very Lean Meat
1/2 Monounsatur-
   ated Fat

Ingredients

1 1/2 lb lump crabmeat
1 cup fresh or frozen corn
    kernels (thawed)
1 cup diced red bell pepper
1/4 cup chopped red onion
1/2 cup orange sections
2 Tbsp toasted pumpkin seeds
1/3 cup sherry vinegar
2 Tbsp fresh orange juice
1 Tbsp fresh lime juice
1 tsp minced Jalapeno pepper
Dash chili powder
1 1/2 Tbsp olive oil
2 tsp ground cumin
6 cups fresh washed spinach leaves

Preparation—15 minutes

1 Combine the crabmeat, corn, bell pepper, onion, oranges, and pumpkin seeds in a salad bowl.
2 Whisk together the remaining ingredients except the spinach and pour over the salad. Serve on a bed of spinach leaves.

Calories	205
Calories from Fat	66
Total Fat	7 g
Saturated Fat	1 g
Cholesterol	96 mg
Sodium	316 mg
Carbohydrate	13 g
Dietary Fiber	3 g
Sugars	4 g
Protein	24 g

Chilled Asparagus with Lemon and Parsley

6 Servings

Serving Size:
1/2 cup

Exchanges

1 Vegetable
1/2 Monounsatur-
ated Fat

Ingredients

3 cups diagonally sliced asparagus
1 Tbsp red wine vinegar
1 tsp olive oil
1 Tbsp minced parsley
1 tsp minced garlic
2 Tbsp lemon juice
Dash cayenne pepper
Fresh ground pepper
Dash salt (optional)

Preparation—15 minutes

1 Blanch the asparagus for 3 minutes in a pot of boiling water and drain. Plunge into ice water and drain again.
2 Whisk together the remaining ingredients and pour over the asparagus. Refrigerate for 1 hour before serving.

Calories	36
Calories from Fat	16
Total Fat	2 g
Saturated Fat	0 g
Cholesterol	0 mg
Sodium	11 mg
Carbohydrate	4 g
Dietary Fiber	2 g
Sugars	2 g
Protein	2 g

Chili Crisp Toasts

6 Servings

Serving Size:
1 slice

Exchanges

1 Starch

Ingredients

6 oz sliced French or Italian bread
2 Tbsp low-calorie margarine
1/2 tsp cayenne pepper
1/2 tsp paprika
2 tsp finely minced garlic

Preparation—5 minutes

1 Preheat the oven to 400 degrees. Place the sliced bread on a nonstick cookie sheet in a single layer and toast for 2 minutes.

2 Melt the margarine in a skillet over medium heat. Add in the remaining ingredients. Spread each toasted bread slice with some of the chili mixture and serve.

Calories	85
Calories from Fat	25
Total Fat	3 g
Saturated Fat	1 g
Cholesterol	0 mg
Sodium	165 mg
Carbohydrate	13 g
Dietary Fiber	1 g
Sugars	1 g
Protein	2 g

❧ WHY DON'T YOU . . .

Designate one night a week or month to explore a different cuisine. Or designate one night a week to enjoy your favorite cuisine: "Italian night" or "Mexican night."

Kiwi and Peaches in Rum

6 Servings

Serving Size:
1/2 cup

Exchanges

1 Fruit

Ingredients

1 1/2 cups diced and peeled kiwi
1 1/2 cups sliced peaches
1 Tbsp lime juice
2 tsp brown sugar
1 Tbsp dark rum

Preparation—5 minutes

Combine the kiwi and peaches. Add the lime juice and sugar and let stand for 1/2 hour. Add the rum and let stand for 1 hour. Serve in individual dessert glasses or dishes.

Calories	58
Calories from Fat	2
Total Fat	0 g
Saturated Fat	0 g
Cholesterol	0 mg
Sodium	3 mg
Carbohydrate	13 g
Dietary Fiber	2 g
Sugars	10 g
Protein	1 g

Lean Meats

❖ ❖ ❖ ❖ ❖

Holiday Roast Pork 279

Roasted Butternut Squash Soup with
    Caramelized Red Onion
Roast Pork with Port Wine and Figs
Yukon Gold Mashed Potatoes with Roasted Shallots
Green Beans with Hazelnut Oil and Hazelnuts
Warm Gingerbread

Wild Mushroom Veal 287

Roasted Garlic with Rosemary Toast
Veal with Wild Mushroom Sauce
Carrots with Cognac
Shallot Basmati Rice
Strawberry and Raspberry Ice

Sunday Night Supper 295

Orange Confetti Pork
Potatoes "Low" Gratin
Broccoli with Parmesan Crust
Romaine Salad with Hearts of Palm
Ginger-Baked Pears

Dixieland Dinner 303

Low-Fat Green Goddess Salad
Pork in Bourbon Maple Marinade
Black-Eyed Pea and Corn Salad
Cheesy Vegetables
Peach Blueberry Cobbler

Summer Steak Barbecue 311

Mango Frappe
Simply Great Steak
Skewered Potatoes
Grilled Parmesan Bread
Banana Fool

Elegant British Dinner 319

Pan-Seared Pork on Herbed White Beans
Haricots Verts with Roasted Red Pepper and Lemon
English Cucumber Salad with Cherry Tomatoes
Asparagus with Slivered Garlic
Chocolate Grand Marnier Trifle

Holiday Roast Pork

Roasted Butternut Squash Soup with Caramelized Red Onion
Roast Pork with Port Wine and Figs
Yukon Gold Mashed Potatoes with Roasted Shallots
Green Beans with Hazelnuts and Hazelnut Oil
Warm Gingerbread

MENU TALK

When you're ready to serve an unforgettable meal for the holidays, start the evening off with this colorful butternut squash soup. The hard skin of the butternut squash will allow for longer storage, so you can do some food shopping a few days in advance. Butternut squash is a tan, elongated squash that looks like a long-necked pear. The flesh is sweet and tender, making it appealing to children. I prefer to bake the squash, bringing out all its natural sugars and hearty flavor. After the squash bakes, let it cool down a bit before placing it in the food processor. This soup can be made one day in advance, but add the milk when you are ready to serve. Butternut squash is a good source of vitamin A and fiber. You can substitute acorn squash in this recipe, and serve the soup in acorn squash halves for a really festive presentation.

Port wine is a sweet after-dinner wine, but I think it is ideal for marinating. Prices range from the most expensive vintage ports to more affordable ruby ports. If you do not have port, a dry red wine will also work in this recipe. This sauce can be served over chicken and game hens as well as pork. You can make the sauce several hours before serving.

If you have never had a Yukon gold potato, you are in for a real treat. You can forget about adding any butter to these potatoes, for they have a buttery taste all their own. They are moist, making them ideal for mashed potatoes. Adding the sweet roasted shallots makes these potatoes especially delicious. Yukon gold potatoes are available most of the year. Store them at

See color photo after p. 240.

room temperature. Hazelnuts are very flavorful and go a long way. If you do not have hazelnut oil, substitute walnut or olive oil.

Gingerbread is a must at holiday time. The only fat in this cake is a small amount of canola oil. Increase the amount of spices if you like. Gingerbread can be made a day ahead—a welcome bonus when preparing a holiday feast!

Pantry List

1 yellow onion
2 cans evaporated skim milk
cinnamon
3 cans low-fat, low-sodium chicken
   broth
2 red onions
sugar
olive oil
sherry vinegar
Dijon mustard
garlic
port wine
canola oil
dried figs
5 shallots
cornstarch or arrowroot powder
dry white wine
hazelnut oil
1 small bag hazelnuts
3 Yukon gold or russet potatoes
unbleached white flour
baking powder
baking soda
ginger
allspice
honey
molasses

Market List

1 1/2 lb pork tenderloin
1 large butternut squash
fresh thyme
low-calorie margarine
1 yellow bell pepper

1 small head each red leaf, green
   leaf, and romaine lettuce
1 1/2 lb fresh green beans
1 carton egg substitutes

STEP-BY-STEP COUNTDOWN

1 Marinate the pork overnight.
2 Prepare the first step of the soup recipe.
   This can be done the day before.
3 Prepare the gingerbread. This can also be done
   the day before.
4 Prepare the first step of the mashed
   potato recipe.
5 Prepare and roast the pork.
6 Prepare the salad and dressing, but do not
   combine them.
7 Prepare the second step of the mashed
   potato recipe.
8 Prepare all ingredients for the green beans, but
   do not cook them.
9 Finish preparing the soup and turn off the heat.
10 Prepare the caramelized red onions and turn
   off the heat.
11 Finish preparing the pork recipe.
12 Cook the green beans and turn off the heat.
13 Reheat the soup and serve with the
   caramelized red onion.
14 Toss the salad with the dressing and serve.
15 Whip the potatoes and reheat if necessary
   before serving.
16 Serve the pork, green beans, and potatoes.
17 Warm and serve the gingerbread.

Roasted Butternut Squash Soup with Carmelized Red Onion

6 Servings

Serving Size:
1 cup

Exchanges

1 1/2 Starch
1/2 Skim Milk
1/2 Fat

Ingredients

1 large butternut squash
5 Tbsp low-calorie margarine
1 medium onion, sliced thin
1/2 cup low-fat, low-sodium
    chicken broth
2 cups evaporated skim milk
2 tsp cinnamon
1 small red onion, very thinly sliced
3 tsp sugar

Preparation—25 minutes

1 Preheat the oven to 350 degrees. Cut the butternut squash in half and scoop out the seeds. Place 2 Tbsp margarine, the onion, and broth in a casserole dish. Place the squash halves over the onion mixture and roast, uncovered, until the squash is soft, about 45 minutes to 1 hour.

2 Puree the squash mixture in a blender or food processor and pour into a saucepan. Add the evaporated skim milk and cinnamon and simmer for 5 minutes.

3 Saute the red onion in 3 Tbsp margarine in a skillet over medium heat for 5–6 minutes. Add the sugar and saute until caramelized, about 4–5 minutes. Garnish each serving of soup with caramelized onions.

Calories	185
Calories from Fat	47
Total Fat	5 g
Saturated Fat	1 g
Cholesterol	3 mg
Sodium	185 mg
Carbohydrate	29 g
Dietary Fiber	4 g
Sugars	15 g
Protein	9 g

Roast Pork with Port Wine and Figs

6 Servings

Serving Size:
4 oz

Exchanges

2 1/2 Fruit
4 Very Lean Meat
1 Fat

Ingredients

1 1/2 lb pork tenderloin, rolled and tied
3 cups port wine
1 Tbsp canola oil
2 cups diced dried figs
1/4 cup minced shallots
3 cups low-fat, low-sodium chicken broth
1 Tbsp cornstarch or arrowroot powder
2 Tbsp water
Fresh ground pepper
Dash salt (optional)

Preparation—30 minutes

1 In a nonreactive bowl, combine the pork loin with 2 cups of the port wine and marinate in the refrigerator overnight.
2 The next day, preheat the oven to 400 degrees. Remove the pork loin and discard the wine. Heat 1/2 Tbsp of the oil in a large skillet.
3 Add the pork loin and saute on all sides for about 10 minutes. Place the pork roast on a roasting rack and roast until no pink remains, about 30–40 minutes.
4 Meanwhile, marinate the figs in the remaining 1 cup of port wine. Let stand for 40 minutes, drain, and reserve the port.
5 Heat the remaining oil in a skillet over medium-high heat. Add the shallots and saute for 4 minutes. Add the dried figs and saute for 3 minutes. Add the reserved port and bring the mixture to a boil. Pour in the broth and reduce to 2 cups.
6 Mix the cornstarch or arrowroot powder with the water, add it to the sauce, and cook until thickened, about 1–2 minutes. Add the pepper and salt. Slice the pork roast, surround the slices with the sauce, and serve.

Calories	343
Calories from Fat	76
Total Fat	8 g
Saturated Fat	2 g
Cholesterol	71 mg
Sodium	111 mg
Carbohydrate	38 g
Dietary Fiber	5 g
Sugars	31 g
Protein	29 g

Yukon Gold Mashed Potatoes with Roasted Shallots

6 Servings

Serving Size:
1/2 cup

Exchanges

1 Starch

Ingredients

3 large shallots, peeled
2 tsp olive oil
1/2 cup low-fat, low-sodium
    chicken broth
2 tsp minced thyme
Fresh ground pepper
Dash salt (optional)
3 medium Yukon gold potatoes
    (or russet potatoes), unpeeled,
    cut into chunks
1/2 cup evaporated skim milk

Preparation—20 minutes

1 Preheat the oven to 400 degrees. Place the shallots, oil, broth, thyme, pepper, and salt in a small casserole dish. Cover and roast until the shallots are very soft and brown, about 45 minutes. Remove the casserole from the oven.
2 Cook the potatoes in a large pot of boiling water until they are soft, about 30–35 minutes. Drain the water from the pot. Place the potatoes back in the pot over low heat to dry them a bit.
3 Heat the milk over medium-low heat. Add it to the potatoes and whip. Add the roasted shallots and whip again until the potatoes are the desired consistency.

Calories	96
Calories from Fat	16
Total Fat	2 g
Saturated Fat	0 g
Cholesterol	1 mg
Sodium	39 mg
Carbohydrate	17 g
Dietary Fiber	2 g
Sugars	4 g
Protein	4 g

Green Beans with Hazelnut Oil and Hazelnuts

6 Servings

Serving Size:
1/2 cup

Exchanges

1 Vegetable
1 Monounsaturated
Fat

Ingredients

1 cup low-fat, low-sodium chicken broth
6 cups cut green beans
1/4 cup dry white wine
2 tsp hazelnut oil
1/4 cup chopped, toasted hazelnuts

Preparation—15 minutes

1 Heat the broth in a skillet over medium heat. Add the green beans, cover, and steam for 3 minutes. Remove the green beans.
2 Add the white wine and hazelnut oil to the broth. Bring to a boil and reduce by 1/4.
3 Return the green beans to the skillet, add the hazelnuts, and cook for 1 minute. Serve.

Calories	84
Calories from Fat	47
Total Fat	5 g
Saturated Fat	1 g
Cholesterol	0 mg
Sodium	21 mg
Carbohydrate	8 g
Dietary Fiber	3 g
Sugars	2 g
Protein	3 g

 WHY DON'T YOU . . .

Try an entirely new cuisine once in awhile. Twirl a globe, point your finger, and try the cuisine from that land.

Warm Gingerbread

6 Servings

Serving Size:
1 square

Exchanges

4 Carbohydrate

Ingredients

2 cups unbleached white flour
1 tsp baking soda
1 tsp baking powder
2 tsp ginger
1 tsp cinnamon
1 tsp allspice
1/4 cup honey
1/4 cup molasses
2 Tbsp canola oil
1/2 cup evaporated skim milk
2 egg substitutes, beaten
1/2 cup boiling water

Preparation—20 minutes

1 Preheat the oven to 350 degrees. Combine the dry ingredients in a medium bowl.
2 Combine the remaining ingredients in a large bowl. Add the flour mixture slowly to the wet ingredients, mixing well after each addition.
3 Pour into an 8 X 8-inch nonstick pan and bake for 35–45 minutes. Serve warm.

Calories	303	
Calories from Fat	46	
Total Fat	5	g
Saturated Fat	0	g
Cholesterol	1	mg
Sodium	338	mg
Carbohydrate	56	g
Dietary Fiber	1	g
Sugars	22	g
Protein	8	g

❖ ❖ ❖

Wild Mushroom Veal

Roasted Garlic with Rosemary Toast
Veal with Wild Mushroom Sauce
Carrots with Cognac
Shallot Basmati Rice
Strawberry and Raspberry Ice

MENU TALK

Garlic lovers simply can't get enough of this below-ground bulb, containing 12–24 cloves held together by white, papery skin. There are many varieties of garlic, ranging from Californian white to Mexican pink to Argentinean purple. The large elephant garlic should be avoided—it's too bitter. Look for heads of garlic that feel firm and are held together tightly. Store garlic at room temperature for 2–3 weeks. Roasting garlic is my favorite way to prepare it. When garlic is roasted, the dry heat causes the buds to become sweet and mellow. It is the best substitute I know for butter. The soft, spreadable buds can top toast, baked potatoes, and pasta.

The combination of mushrooms in this menu's entree yields a wide range of flavors. The shiitake, the most intensely flavored of the three mushrooms used, is a large mushroom that is available fresh or dried. The cremini, milder than the shiitake but more intense than the white, is cocoa colored and shaped like a white mushroom. The oyster is the most delicate of all. Fan shaped and light beige, it has a silky texture. Mushrooms should never be washed but simply wiped off with a damp paper towel. Store mushrooms in brown paper bags on a shelf in your refrigerator. Use them within two days. Dried wild mushrooms are also an option to use in this recipe. Although I think some flavor is lost, they are less expensive and keep for a long time. Just rehydrate them in hot water for about 20 minutes, drain, stem, and chop.

Roasting carrots brings out their sweetness. These carrots are tender-crisp and lightly flavored with cognac. Omit the cognac if you prefer. Shallots are a small, brown-skinned member of the onion family. These are slightly sweeter and not as pungent as onions. They are used frequently in Thai cuisine but lend themselves to many other styles of cooking. They grow singly and in clusters. If you cannot find shallots, you can substitute the white part of a green onion. Store them at room temperature. Shallots have lower water content than onions, so they don't turn as mushy in a food processor.

Cool and refreshing frozen fruit makes the best summer dessert. Use any berry you like to substitute for the strawberries and raspberries. While this dessert chills, you are free to create the rest of this meal.

Pantry List

flour
olive oil
2 cans low-fat, low-sodium chicken
    broth
1 can evaporated skim milk
cornstarch or arrowroot powder
walnut oil
cognac
honey
cinnamon
garlic
sugar
4 shallots
basmati rice

Market List

1 1/2 lb veal
1/4 lb each shiitake, cremini, and
    oyster mushrooms
low-fat sour cream
parsley
2 pkg baby carrots
rosemary
3 oz French or Italian bread
1 pint strawberries
1 pint raspberries
mint sprigs
fresh orange juice

STEP-BY-STEP COUNTDOWN

1 Prepare the dessert and freeze.
2 Prepare the appetizer.
3 Prepare and roast the carrots and turn off
   the oven.
4 Prepare all ingredients for the veal, but do not
   cook them.
5 Prepare the rice.
6 Cook the veal.
7 Serve the appetizer.
8 Serve the veal, carrots, and rice.
9 Serve the dessert.

Roasted Garlic with Rosemary Toast

6 Servings

Serving Size:
1-2 cloves garlic
1/2 oz bread

Exchanges

1/2 Starch

Ingredients

1 large garlic bulb
1/2 cup low-fat, low-sodium
  chicken broth
1 sprig fresh rosemary
Fresh ground pepper
3 oz French or Italian bread

Preparation—5 minutes

1 Preheat the oven to 400 degrees. Cut off a slice from the top of the garlic bulb to expose the head of the garlic. Place the bulb in a very small casserole dish or in a double thickness of aluminum foil.
2 Pour broth over the garlic bulb and top it with the rosemary sprig and pepper. Cover or wrap well with the foil. Roast the garlic for 1 hour.
3 Slice the bread and place the slices on a cookie sheet. Toast the slices in the oven for 2–3 minutes.
4 Remove the garlic and bread from the oven. Place the garlic on the table and let each person spread a clove of garlic on the toast.

Calories	45
Calories from Fat	5
Total Fat	1 g
Saturated Fat	0 g
Cholesterol	0 mg
Sodium	77 mg
Carbohydrate	8 g
Dietary Fiber	0 g
Sugars	2 g
Protein	1 g

Veal with Wild Mushroom Sauce

6 Servings

Serving Size:
3 oz

Exchanges

1/2 Starch
4 Lean Meat

Ingredients

1/4 cup flour
Fresh ground pepper
Dash salt (optional)
1 1/2 lb veal, thinly sliced
2 Tbsp olive oil
3 Tbsp low-fat, low-sodium chicken broth
1/2 cup each sliced fresh shiitake, cremini, and oyster mushrooms
1 cup evaporated skim milk
2 tsp cornstarch or arrowroot powder
4 tsp water
2 Tbsp low-fat sour cream
1/2 cup minced parsley

Preparation—15 minutes

1 In a zippered plastic bag, combine the flour, salt, and pepper. Add the veal and shake until each slice of veal is lightly coated with the flour.
2 Heat the oil in a skillet over medium-high heat. Add the veal and saute on both sides for about 4 minutes per side. Remove the veal from the skillet.
3 Pour the broth into the skillet and add the mushrooms. Saute until mushrooms are golden, about 5–6 minutes. Add the milk and reduce the heat to low.
4 Mix the cornstarch or arrowroot powder together with the water and add it to the milk and mushrooms, cooking until the mixture thickens slightly. Return the veal to the skillet and cook for 3 minutes. Add the sour cream and parsley and cook for 1 minute.

Calories	273
Calories from Fat	86
Total Fat	10 g
Saturated Fat	3 g
Cholesterol	120 mg
Sodium	90 mg
Carbohydrate	10 g
Dietary Fiber	1 g
Sugars	4 g
Protein	35 g

Carrots with Cognac

6 Servings

Serving Size:
1/2 cup

Exchanges

2 Vegetable
1/2 Polyunsatur-
   ated Fat

Ingredients

3 cups baby carrots
1 Tbsp walnut oil
1/4 cup cognac
2 tsp honey
1 tsp cinnamon

Preparation—5 minutes

1 Preheat the oven to 400 degrees. Place the carrots on a large sheet of aluminum foil.
2 Combine the remaining ingredients and sprinkle over the carrots.
3 Wrap the carrots up tightly and roast until they are tender, yet crisp, about 25–35 minutes.

Calories	68
Calories from Fat	22
Total Fat	2 g
Saturated Fat	0 g
Cholesterol	0 mg
Sodium	48 mg
Carbohydrate	9 g
Dietary Fiber	2 g
Sugars	5 g
Protein	1 g

Shallot Basmati Rice

6 Servings

Serving Size:
1/2 cup

Exchanges

3 Starch

Ingredients

3 1/4 cups low-fat, low-sodium
        chicken broth
4 shallots, minced
2 cloves garlic, minced
1 1/2 cups basmati rice
1/4 cup minced parsley
Fresh ground pepper
Dash salt (optional)

Preparation—5 minutes

1 Heat 1/4 cup of the broth in a saucepan over medium-high heat.
2 Add the shallots and garlic and saute for 5 minutes. Add the rice and saute for 4 minutes.
3 Add the remainder of the broth and bring to a boil. Lower the heat, cover, and simmer until the rice has absorbed the liquid, about 20 minutes.
4 Fluff with a fork and add parsley. Season with pepper and salt and serve.

Calories	208
Calories from Fat	14
Total Fat	2 g
Saturated Fat	0 g
Cholesterol	0 mg
Sodium	63 mg
Carbohydrate	45 g
Dietary Fiber	2 g
Sugars	2 g
Protein	6 g

Strawberry and Raspberry Ice

6 Servings

Serving Size:
1/3 cup

Exchanges

1 Carbohydrate

Ingredients

3/4 cup strawberries, washed
     and sliced
3/4 cup raspberries, washed
1/4 cup sugar
2 Tbsp fresh orange juice
Mint sprigs

Preparation—5 minutes

1 Puree the berries with the sugar and juice.
Freeze for several hours until almost stiff.
2 Whip the mixture and refreeze for 2 hours.
3 Spoon into dessert dishes, garnish with mint
sprigs, and serve.

Calories	45
Calories from Fat	1
Total Fat	0 g
Saturated Fat	0 g
Cholesterol	0 mg
Sodium	0 mg
Carbohydrate	12 g
Dietary Fiber	1 g
Sugars	10 g
Protein	0 g

❖ ❖ ❖ ❖ ❖ ❖ ❖

 WHY DON'T YOU . . .

*Check out a local farmer's
market for your produce
instead of the supermarket.*

Sunday Night Supper

Orange Confetti Pork
Potatoes "Low" Gratin
Broccoli with Parmesan Crust
Romaine Salad with Hearts of Palm
Ginger-Baked Pears

MENU TALK

Be careful not to overcook this menu's pork. Pork is leaner than it used to be and cooks faster. When pork is cooked beyond 160 degrees it begins to dry out. Luckily, you can camouflage any miscalculations with this tasty sauce. Try this sauce with roast chicken, too.

Au gratin casseroles usually have high-fat cheese or bread-crumb toppings. Compared to its high-fat counterpart, this recipe for potatoes "low" gratin is lower in calories, but just as satisfying. You can satisfy your craving for traditional foods by substituting ingredients lower in fat, but with just as much flavor!

The hearts of romaine are my favorite part of the lettuce. Tender and sweet, it tastes best with light dressings. Some fine restaurants serve long, tender pieces you cut with a knife and fork. Find hearts of romaine in any supermarket. Use the best ruby-red plum tomatoes you can find. Tomatoes are at their peak in the summer, but you can still find good ones through October. Never store tomatoes in the refrigerator. Chilling tomatoes deadens their flavor. Also avoid buying tomatoes that have been stored in refrigerated produce sections.

Good broccoli does not have yellowing buds and split stems. Wash broccoli just before you're ready to cook it—too much water ahead of time causes the broccoli to become soggy. Remove broccoli from the heat as soon as it turns bright green! Do not use color enhancers such as baking soda— it causes the vitamins to leach out into the cooking water.

Serve this menu's dessert either hot or cold. I prefer these pears cold, because the flavor intensifies as they chill. If you happen to overcook these slightly, never fear—the juices become syrupy and delicious. Any kind of pear will do, but try lovely red d'Anjou for a special treat.

Pantry List

1 yellow onion
garlic
shallots
1 can low-fat, low-sodium chicken
    broth
low-sugar orange marmalade
1 can evaporated skim milk
red wine vinegar
Dijon mustard
olive oil
dried basil
dried oregano
paprika
cinnamon
vanilla bean
sugar
dry white wine
dry bread crumbs
cornstarch or arrowroot powder
nonstick cooking spray
unbleached white flour
1 jar hearts of palm

Market List

1 1/2 lb pork tenderloin chops
1 red bell pepper
1 yellow bell pepper
1 bunch green onions
romaine lettuce
4–5 plum tomatoes
1 1/2 lb broccoli
3 large pears
butter
Parmesan cheese

ginger root
low-calorie margarine
lemon juice
3 red potatoes

Orange Confetti Pork

6 Servings

Serving Size:
3 1/2 oz

Exchanges

1/2 Carbohydrate
4 Very Lean Meat
1/2 Fat

Ingredients

2 tsp olive oil
1 1/2 lb boneless pork chops
1/4 cup minced onion
1/2 cup each diced red and yellow
    bell pepper
1 1/2 cups low-fat, low-sodium
    chicken broth
3 Tbsp low-sugar orange
    marmalade
2 Tbsp fresh lemon juice
1 Tbsp cornstarch or arrowroot
    powder
2 Tbsp cold water
1 tsp butter
2 Tbsp minced green onions

Preparation—20 minutes

1 Heat the oil in a large skillet over medium heat. Add the pork chops and saute on each side until lightly browned, about 3–4 minutes per side.
2 Remove the pork from the skillet and set aside. Saute the onion in the pan drippings for about 5 minutes. Add the bell peppers and saute for 4 minutes.
3 Add the broth, marmalade, and lemon juice. Bring to a boil, lower the heat, and simmer for 2 minutes.
4 Mix the cornstarch or arrowroot powder and water together and add it to the skillet. Swirl in the butter and green onions. Return the pork chops to the skillet and cook over low heat for 5–6 minutes.

Calories	200
Calories from Fat	65
Total Fat	7 g
Saturated Fat	2 g
Cholesterol	73 mg
Sodium	92 mg
Carbohydrate	7 g
Dietary Fiber	0 g
Sugars	4 g
Protein	26 g

Potatoes "Low" Gratin

6 Servings

Serving Size:
1/2 cup

Exchanges

1 Starch
1 1/2 Fat

Ingredients

Nonstick cooking spray
3 cups very thinly sliced red
    potatoes, skins on
4 Tbsp low-calorie margarine
2 Tbsp minced onion
3 Tbsp unbleached white flour
1 cup evaporated skim milk
2 oz Parmesan cheese
Fresh ground pepper
Dash salt (optional)

Preparation—15 minutes

1 Preheat the oven to 350 degrees. Spray a casserole dish with nonstick cooking spray. Arrange 1/3 of the potatoes in the bottom of the casserole dish.

2 Heat the margarine in a medium skillet over medium-high heat. Add the onion and saute for 3 minutes.

3 Add the flour and mix until smooth. Add the skim milk and Parmesan cheese. Cook, stirring constantly, until the sauce is smooth and thickened. Add the pepper and salt.

4 Pour 1/3 of the sauce over the potatoes. Add another layer of potatoes and more sauce. Continue for one more layer, ending with sauce. Cover and bake until the potatoes are tender, about 35–40 minutes.

Calories	157
Calories from Fat	60
Total Fat	7 g
Saturated Fat	3 g
Cholesterol	11 mg
Sodium	271 mg
Carbohydrate	17 g
Dietary Fiber	1 g
Sugars	5 g
Protein	9 g

Broccoli with Parmesan Crust

6 Servings

Serving Size:
1/2 cup

Exchanges

1/2 Starch
1 Vegetable
1/2 Monounsaturated Fat

Ingredients

2 tsp olive oil
3 cups broccoli florets
1/2 cup diced shallots
1/2 cup low-fat, low-sodium
    chicken broth
2 Tbsp Parmesan cheese
1/2 cup dry bread crumbs
1 tsp dried basil
1/2 tsp dried oregano
1 tsp paprika
2 tsp melted low-calorie margarine
Fresh ground pepper
Dash salt (optional)

Preparation—25 minutes

1 Heat the oil in a skillet over medium-high heat. Add the broccoli and shallots and saute for 3 minutes. Add the broth, cover, and steam for 3 minutes.
2 Meanwhile, combine the remaining ingredients. Sprinkle the mixture over the cooked broccoli and serve.

Calories	84	
Calories from Fat	32	
Total Fat	4	g
Saturated Fat	1	g
Cholesterol	1	mg
Sodium	138	mg
Carbohydrate	11	g
Dietary Fiber	2	g
Sugars	2	g
Protein	4	g

Romaine Salad with Hearts of Palm

6 Servings

Serving Size:
1 cup

Exchanges

1 Vegetable
1/2 Monounsatur-
ated Fat

Ingredients

6 cups romaine lettuce leaves,
    separated, not torn
12 thick slices plum tomatoes
1 can hearts of palm, drained
1/3 cup red wine vinegar
1 Tbsp olive oil
2 Tbsp Dijon mustard
2 cloves garlic, minced
1 Tbsp minced shallots
Fresh ground pepper
Dash salt (optional)

Preparation—10 minutes

1 Lay a few romaine leaves on each plate. Place 2 tomato slices on each plate. Slice the hearts of palm and distribute evenly among the 6 plates.
2 In a small bowl, whisk together the remaining ingredients. Drizzle a portion over each salad and serve.

Calories	56
Calories from Fat	26
Total Fat	3 g
Saturated Fat	0 g
Cholesterol	0 mg
Sodium	224 mg
Carbohydrate	7 g
Dietary Fiber	3 g
Sugars	3 g
Protein	2 g

❖ WHY DON'T YOU . . .

If you are alone at the holidays, prepare a simple dinner, then enjoy it with candles on the table and soft music playing in the background.

Ginger-Baked Pears

6 Servings

Serving Size:
1/2 large pear

Exchanges

1 1/2 Carbohydrate

Ingredients

1 cup dry white wine
2 Tbsp sugar
1 vanilla bean, split
1 Tbsp very finely minced ginger
1 tsp cinnamon
3 large pears, halved and cored

Preparation—10 minutes

1 Preheat the oven to 350 degrees. Combine the wine, sugar, vanilla, ginger, and cinnamon in a medium saucepan and bring to a boil.
2 Place the pears cut side down in a baking pan. Pour the wine mixture over the pears.
3 Cover and bake until the pears are soft, about 25–30 minutes. Serve pears with juice on top.

Calories	85
Calories from Fat	4
Total Fat	0 g
Saturated Fat	0 g
Cholesterol	0 mg
Sodium	1 mg
Carbohydrate	20 g
Dietary Fiber	2 g
Sugars	17 g
Protein	0 g

❖ ❖ ❖

Dixieland Dinner

Low-Fat Green Goddess Salad
Pork in Bourbon Maple Marinade
Black-Eyed Pea and Corn Salad
Cheesy Vegetables
Peach Blueberry Cobbler

MENU TALK

Green Goddess dressing gets its name from a play running in San Francisco in the 1920s. A chef at the Palace Hotel created it for the lead actor. My version is considerably lower in fat than the traditional recipe, yet I have retained its traditional ingredients, including anchovies and tarragon vinegar. This dressing is good as a sauce for fish, too. Choose any greens you like for the salad—I recommend Bibb and green leaf lettuce.

If you'd like to omit the bourbon from this menu's pork, add an additional 2 Tbsp of ketchup and a little more water instead. This marinade can be used for chicken, shrimp, or beef.

Black-eyed peas originated in Asia. Black-eyed peas, once considered a lowly legume, are now served at some of the finest restaurants. If you do not have black-eyed peas, use black beans instead. Celery seed is a good salt substitute. It mimics the taste of salt, yet there is no sodium to worry about. It has a strong flavor, so use it sparingly.

Using arrowroot powder or cornstarch instead of flour as a thickener produces a smoother sauce. In this menu's vegetables, arrowroot powder is mixed with evaporated skim milk to produce a cream sauce without making a traditional fat-laden roux. Who says you can't have the flavor of rich cheese sauces? With low-fat ingredients, the taste of familiar high-fat foods is only a stir away! When using cheeses for low-fat cooking, it is preferable to purchase finely shredded nonfat or low-fat cheese. Finely shredded cheeses melt much better than cheese that has been shredded coarsely. Add the cheese a little at a time to prevent any lumping. Buy the best quality cheese that you can find—it will melt much more smoothly.

I rely on naturally sweet fruit to flavor this cobbler instead of adding excessive amounts of fat and sugar. Try your favorite fruit, including pears, apples, and berries. The biscuits call for low-fat buttermilk to lend that down-home flavor, but skim milk will work, too. Serve this cobbler warm from the oven and enjoy the rave reviews.

Pantry List

lite mayonnaise
honey
tarragon vinegar
canola oil
1 yellow onion
1 can anchovies or 1 tube
    anchovy paste
capers
garlic
bourbon
maple syrup
catsup
nutmeg
ginger
1 can black-eyed peas
olive oil
red wine vinegar
sugar
celery seed
garlic powder
Dijon mustard
cornstarch or arrowroot powder
1 can evaporated skim milk
peach schnapps
unbleached white flour
baking powder

STEP-BY-STEP COUNTDOWN

1 Marinate the pork overnight.
2 Prepare the dressing for the salad and
   refrigerate. This can be done the day before.
3 Prepare the black-eyed peas and corn
   and refrigerate. This can also be done the
   day before.
4 Prepare the dessert and keep warm.
5 Prepare the ingredients for the vegetables, but
   do not cook them.
6 Finish preparing the pork.
7 Finish preparing the vegetables and turn off
   the heat.
8 Toss the salad with the dressing and serve.
9 Serve the pork, black-eyed peas and corn, and
   cheesy vegetables.
10 Serve the dessert.

Market List

1 1/2 lb pork tenderloin
1 small carton low-fat sour cream
fresh lemon juice
fresh chives
1 small red bell pepper
1 bunch celery
1 1/2 lb mixed greens
8 oz nonfat Swiss or cheddar cheese

1 small pkg frozen yellow corn or
   1 ear corn
1 lb cauliflower, broccoli, green
   beans, or asparagus
3 medium peaches
1/2 pint blueberries
low-fat buttermilk

Low-Fat Green Goddess Salad

6 Servings

Serving Size:
I cup

Exchanges

I Vegetable

Ingredients

1/2 cup lite mayonnaise
1/4 cup low-fat sour cream
1 1/2 Tbsp tarragon vinegar
1 tsp lemon juice
1 Tbsp finely minced onion
1 Tbsp mashed anchovy fillet
(remove the oil) or 1 Tbsp
anchovy paste
1 Tbsp minced fresh chives
1 tsp capers
1 clove garlic, minced
Fresh ground pepper
Dash salt (optional)
6 cups mixed greens of choice

Preparation—20 minutes

1 Combine all ingredients except the mixed greens and refrigerate for 2 hours.
2 Arrange the greens on individual plates. Drizzle with dressing and serve.

Calories	34
Calories from Fat	2
Total Fat	0 g
Saturated Fat	0 g
Cholesterol	I mg
Sodium	237 mg
Carbohydrate	6 g
Dietary Fiber	I g
Sugars	4 g
Protein	2 g

❖ ❖ ❖ ❖ ❖ ❖

🖎 WHY DON'T YOU . . .

Get everyone involved in preparing the holiday meal. Ask some to go to the store, some to help with the preparation, and everyone to help clean up!

Pork in Bourbon Maple Marinade

6 Servings

Serving Size:
3 oz

Exchanges

4 Very Lean Meat

Ingredients

1/4 cup bourbon
2 Tbsp maple syrup
2 Tbsp catsup
1/4 cup water
1/2 tsp nutmeg
1/4 tsp ginger
1 1/2 lb pork tenderloin

Preparation—10 minutes

1 Combine all ingredients except the pork and pour into a nonmetal, shallow dish. Add the pork tenderloin and allow to marinate overnight.
2 The next day, slice the pork tenderloin into 6 serving pieces. Prepare an outdoor grill with the rack set 4–6 inches from the heat source, or prepare an oven broiler.
3 Grill each pork slice until no pink remains and the pork is cooked through, about 6–8 minutes.

Calories	155	
Calories from Fat	40	
Total Fat	4	g
Saturated Fat	1	g
Cholesterol	71	mg
Sodium	70	mg
Carbohydrate	2	g
Dietary Fiber	0	g
Sugars	2	g
Protein	25	g

Black-Eyed Pea and Corn Salad

6 Servings

Serving Size:
1/2 cup

Exchanges

1 1/2 Starch
1/2 Monounsaturated Fat

Ingredients

1/4 cup diced onion
1/2 cup diced red bell pepper
1/2 cup diced celery
2 cups cooked black-eyed peas
1 cup cooked fresh yellow corn
2 Tbsp olive oil
1/3 cup red wine vinegar
2 tsp sugar
1/2 tsp celery seed
1/2 tsp garlic powder
1 tsp Dijon mustard

Preparation—20 minutes

1 Combine the onion, bell pepper, celery, black-eyed peas, and corn in a salad bowl.
2 Whisk together the remaining ingredients and pour over the salad. Refrigerate for 2 hours before serving.

Calories	141
Calories from Fat	45
Total Fat	5 g
Saturated Fat	1 g
Cholesterol	0 mg
Sodium	23 mg
Carbohydrate	20 g
Dietary Fiber	5 g
Sugars	5 g
Protein	5 g

Cheesy Vegetables

6 Servings

Serving Size:
1/2 cup

Exchanges

1/2 Starch
1 Vegetable
1 Very Lean Meat

Ingredients

2 Tbsp cornstarch or arrowroot
 powder
1 cup evaporated skim milk
1/4 tsp dry mustard
Fresh ground pepper
Dash salt (optional)
1 cup shredded nonfat cheese of
 choice (try Swiss or cheddar)
3 cups steamed cauliflower,
 broccoli, green beans, or
 asparagus

Preparation—10 minutes

1 Mix the cornstarch or arrowroot powder with 1/4 cup of the milk. Stir well to blend thoroughly.
2 Heat the remaining milk in a saucepan until little bubbles appear around the rim. Add the cornstarch mixture and cook until the mixture thickens.
3 Add the dry mustard, pepper, salt, and cheese and cook over low heat for a few minutes until the cheese melts. Serve over the steamed vegetables.

Calories	87
Calories from Fat	4
Total Fat	0 g
Saturated Fat	0 g
Cholesterol	4 mg
Sodium	192 mg
Carbohydrate	11 g
Dietary Fiber	2 g
Sugars	6 g
Protein	10 g

Peach Blueberry Cobbler

6 Servings

Serving Size:
1/6 recipe

Exchanges

3 Carbohydrate
1 Monounsaturated
 Fat

Ingredients

2 cups sliced fresh peaches
1 cup fresh blueberries, washed
2 tsp peach schnapps
1/4 cup sugar
1/4 cup water
2 Tbsp lemon juice
1 1/2 Tbsp cornstarch or arrowroot
  powder
3 Tbsp water
1 cup unbleached white flour
2 tsp baking powder
2 Tbsp canola oil
1 Tbsp honey
1/2 cup low-fat buttermilk

Preparation—20 minutes

1 Preheat the oven to 350 degrees. Combine the peaches, blueberries, schnapps, sugar, water, and lemon juice in a large saucepan. Mix well and bring to a boil.
2 Mix the cornstarch or arrowroot powder with the water, and add it to the fruit mixture. Cook over medium heat until thickened. Let cool slightly.
3 Combine the flour and baking powder in a medium bowl. Add the oil and mix well. Add the honey and buttermilk and mix well.
4 Pour the fruit filling in a casserole dish. Drop the dough on top of the filling. Bake, uncovered, until biscuits are browned, about 20–25 minutes.

Calories	223	
Calories from Fat	47	
Total Fat	5	g
Saturated Fat	0	g
Cholesterol	1	mg
Sodium	146	mg
Carbohydrate	42	g
Dietary Fiber	2	g
Sugars	21	g
Protein	3	g

Summer Steak Barbecue

Mango Frappe
Simply Great Steak
Skewered Potatoes
Grilled Parmesan Bread
Banana Fool

MENU TALK

Start this fun summer meal off with a refreshing mango frappe, and invite your guests to socialize while you grill the steaks! Buy club soda with fruit flavorings, but watch for added sugar. Filet mignon comes from the small end of the tenderloin, making it fork-tender. Watch these filets carefully on the grill. Because they lack the fat running through other cuts of steak, they quickly become overcooked and dry.

You can grill many different vegetables. Be sure to soak wooden skewers in warm water for at least 15 minutes before you place them on the grill. This will prevent the skewers from burning on the ends. To grill carrots, parboil thick slices for 5 minutes in boiling water. Wrap the carrots in foil and grill over medium-high heat for 7–8 minutes. For sweet potatoes, parboil thick slices for 10 minutes in boiling water. Brush the sweet potatoes with some olive oil, lay directly on the rack or in a vegetable basket, and grill over medium-high heat for 20–25 minutes. Or try endive: grill halved or whole endive over medium-high heat for 5–8 minutes.

Making good use of the grill adds to the fun. Make room for the bread while the steaks and potatoes cook. Grilled bread is so delicious, you'll want to prepare it this way year-round.

Serve dessert on the patio as the sun sets. Strawberries or peaches may be substituted for the bananas.

Pantry List

sugar
unsweetened coconut
olive oil
cracked peppercorns
24 small red potatoes
1 small loaf Italian or French bread
paprika
garlic
rum

Market List

6 4-oz filet mignons
1 mango
2 bananas
1 bottle orange-flavored club soda
low-calorie margarine
1 papaya
low-calorie whipped topping
Parmesan cheese

Mango Frappe

6 Servings

Serving Size:
1/2 cup

Exchanges

1 Fruit

Ingredients

1 large mango, peeled and cubed
5 cups crushed ice
1 Tbsp sugar
2 cups orange-flavored club soda

Preparation—5 minutes

Combine the mango, ice, and sugar in a blender. Blend well and strain. Pour over club soda and serve.

Calories	53
Calories from Fat	2
Total Fat	0 g
Saturated Fat	0 g
Cholesterol	0 mg
Sodium	18 mg
Carbohydrate	14 g
Dietary Fiber	1 g
Sugars	12 g
Protein	0 g

SPEAKING OF SPICES

Pepper

Pepper grows best in warm, moist climates. The larger the peppercorns, the more developed the flavor. White peppercorns start out as black, then are allowed to fully ripen on the vine. Then they are soaked in water and the shells are removed. White peppercorns taste slightly hotter than black. Green peppercorns are harvested before the peppercorns are mature, and impart a milder flavor to foods. Szechwan peppercorns are not really true peppercorns, but are reddish brown berries with a black inner seed. They are usually placed in a wok on high heat and toasted a bit before grinding.

Simply Great Steak

6 Servings

Serving Size:
3 oz

Exchanges

3 Medium-Fat Meat

Ingredients

6 4-oz filet mignon steaks
1 tsp olive oil
Cracked peppercorns

Preparation—10 minutes

1 Prepare an outdoor grill with the rack set 4–6 inches from the heat source, or prepare an oven broiler. Brush each filet with oil, and press some peppercorns in the top side of each steak.
2 Grill or broil the steaks for 8–12 minutes for medium rare, or longer to taste, turning once.

Calories	206
Calories from Fat	107
Total Fat	12 g
Saturated Fat	4 g
Cholesterol	72 mg
Sodium	53 mg
Carbohydrate	0 g
Dietary Fiber	0 g
Sugars	0 g
Protein	23 g

Skewered Potatoes

6 Servings

Serving Size:
1 skewer

Exchanges

2 Starch

Ingredients

24 small red potatoes, unpeeled
1 1/2 tsp olive oil
1 clove garlic, finely minced

Preparation—10 minutes

1 Boil the potatoes for 5 minutes and drain. When cool enough to handle, thread 4 potatoes onto each of 6 skewers.
2 Combine the oil and garlic and brush onto the potatoes.
3 Prepare an outdoor grill with the rack set 4–6 inches from the heat source, or prepare an oven broiler. Grill or broil the skewers, turning occasionally, until brown, about 10 minutes.

Calories	148
Calories from Fat	11
Total Fat	1 g
Saturated Fat	0 g
Cholesterol	0 mg
Sodium	13 mg
Carbohydrate	32 g
Dietary Fiber	5 g
Sugars	3 g
Protein	4 g

Grilled Parmesan Bread

6 Servings

Serving Size:
I oz

Exchanges

I Starch
1/2 Fat

Ingredients

1 6-oz loaf Italian or French bread
2 Tbsp low-calorie margarine
2 Tbsp Parmesan cheese
2 cloves garlic, finely minced
1/4 tsp paprika

Preparation—5 minutes

1 Split open the bread. Combine the remaining ingredients and brush onto the bread. Wrap the loaf in aluminum foil.

2 Prepare an outdoor grill with the rack set 4–6 inches from the heat source, or prepare an oven broiler. Place the bread on the edge of the grill or broiler and cook until hot, about 5–8 minutes.

Calories	102
Calories from Fat	31
Total Fat	3 g
Saturated Fat	I g
Cholesterol	2 mg
Sodium	214 mg
Carbohydrate	14 g
Dietary Fiber	I g
Sugars	I g
Protein	3 g

Banana Fool

6 Servings

Serving Size:
1/2 cup

Exchanges

1 Carbohydrate
1/2 Saturated Fat

Ingredients

2 medium bananas
1/2 cup diced papaya
1 Tbsp rum (optional)
1 Tbsp sugar
1 cup low-calorie whipped topping
2 Tbsp toasted coconut

Preparation—10 minutes

1 Puree the bananas, papaya, rum, and sugar in a blender. Fold the banana mixture into the whipped topping and refrigerate for 1 hour.
2 Spoon the banana fool into individual dessert dishes, garnish with toasted coconut, and serve.

Calories	93
Calories from Fat	19
Total Fat	2 g
Saturated Fat	2 g
Cholesterol	0 mg
Sodium	8 mg
Carbohydrate	18 g
Dietary Fiber	1 g
Sugars	13 g
Protein	1 g

 WHY DON'T YOU . . .

Bake only healthy goodies for gifts at the holidays. Your recipients will appreciate this.

❖ ❖ ❖

Elegant British Dinner

Pan-Seared Pork on Herbed White Beans
Haricots Verts with Roasted Red Pepper and Lemon
English Cucumber Salad with Cherry Tomatoes
Asparagus with Slivered Garlic
Chocolate Grand Marnier Trifle

M E N U   T A L K

If you'd like to use fresh beans in this recipe, soak them at least 8 hours in two to three times their volume of water to soften them. After soaking, replace the water with fresh water and cook the beans over a low flame. Canellini beans and garbanzo beans take about 2 hours to cook. Make sure your heat is on low, otherwise the beans will be tough and the skins will come off and float everywhere. Cooked beans should be firm, yet soft enough to chew. Beans are a wonderful fat-free source of protein and complex carbohydrates. If you use canned beans, rinse them well under cold running water to lower their sodium content. A bit of seaweed (kombu, found in Asian grocery stores) added to the cooking water may improve the digestibility of the beans. The herb mixture for the pork can be eaten by itself as a salad. Make sure the pork is pounded thin enough so it cooks quickly. You want the pork to be very tender, yet thoroughly cooked.

The haricot vert is a French green bean. Haricots verts are elegant and slimmer than string beans and are often sold in supermarkets. They cook more quickly than string beans, but are more expensive. They should be bright green and very crisp after cooking. If they are unavailable, use string beans. I think they taste better served at room temperature.

The English cucumber is a delightful cucumber about twice the length of a regular cucumber. It is also known as a hothouse cucumber. It is seedless, making it ideal to add to salads, where excess moisture from the seeds causes sogginess. If it is unavailable, use a regular cucumber, but seed it

319

first. The flavored walnut or hazelnut oil really perks up this salad, but you may use olive or canola oil instead.

Asparagus and garlic are a natural combination. The woodsy taste of asparagus and the pungent flavor of garlic work well together. Serve this dish hot or cold. Use broccoli or zucchini instead of asparagus if you like.

Trifle is a traditional English dessert, and it is so easy to prepare! My version is much lower in fat—I substitute nonfat pudding for custard and use fat-free pound cake. Use a trifle bowl or a glass bowl with straight sides. Press the cake against the glass, revealing the jewel-colored jam layers. Fresh raspberries add flavor, but no fat. Omit the Grand Marnier if you like.

Pantry List

olive oil
dry white wine
1 red onion
garlic
1 can garbanzo beans
1 can canellini beans
balsamic vinegar
cracked black peppercorns
1 small jar roasted red bell pepper
white wine vinegar
Dijon mustard
walnut or hazelnut oil
1 4-serving-size pkg fat-free,
    artificially sweetened, instant
    chocolate pudding
2 cans evaporated skim milk
sugar
1 fat-free pound cake
all-fruit preserve of choice
Grand Marnier
cocoa powder
vanilla

Market List

1 1/2 lb boneless pork tenderloin
1 bunch basil
oregano
chives
parsley
1 1/2 lb green beans
fresh lemon juice
3 heads butter lettuce leaves
1 English cucumber
1 pkg white mushrooms

1 pint cherry tomatoes
1 bundle asparagus
1 pint fresh raspberries
1 container low-calorie whipped
    topping

STEP-BY-STEP COUNTDOWN

1 Prepare the dessert and refrigerate.
2 Prepare the salad and dressing, but do not combine them.
3 Prepare the pork recipe. Keep the beans in the skillet. Wrap the pork in foil and place in a very low oven.
4 Prepare the haricots verts.
5 Prepare the asparagus.
6 Toss the salad with the dressing and serve.
7 Serve the pork on the white beans with the haricots verts and asparagus.
8 Serve the dessert.

Pan-Seared Pork on Herbed White Beans

6 Servings

Serving Size:
3 oz pork
1/2 cup beans

Exchanges

1 1/2 Starch
4 Very Lean Meat
1 Monounsaturated
  Fat

Ingredients

1 Tbsp olive oil
2 Tbsp dry white wine
1/2 cup minced red onion
1 clove garlic, minced
1 1/2 cups canned garbanzo beans,
  drained and rinsed
1 1/2 cups canned canellini beans,
  drained and rinsed
2 Tbsp minced basil
2 tsp minced oregano
1/2 tsp minced chives
2 Tbsp minced Italian parsley
1 Tbsp balsamic vinegar
Fresh ground pepper
Dash salt (optional)
3 tsp cracked black peppercorns
1 1/2 lb boneless pork tenderloin,
  cut into 6 pieces, 1/4 inch thick

Preparation—20 minutes

1 Heat 1 tsp oil and wine in a skillet over medium-high heat. Add the onion and saute for 4 minutes. Add the garlic and saute for 2 minutes.
2 Add the beans, herbs, 1 Tbsp parsley, and balsamic vinegar and heat through. Season with pepper and salt and set aside.
3 Heat 2 tsp oil in a skillet. Press some peppercorns onto each piece of pork. Sear the pork in the hot oil on each side until cooked through, about 4 minutes per side.
4 Mound a portion of the herbed beans on a plate and top with sliced pork. Garnish with the remaining parsley to serve.

Calories	308
Calories from Fat	71
Total Fat	8 g
Saturated Fat	2 g
Cholesterol	71 mg
Sodium	58 mg
Carbohydrate	25 g
Dietary Fiber	5 g
Sugars	4 g
Protein	34 g

Haricots Verts with Roasted Red Pepper and Lemon

6 Servings

Serving Size:
1 cup

Exchanges

2 Vegetable
1/2 Monounsaturated Fat

Ingredients

6   cups fresh haricots verts,
     sliced lengthwise
1   cup diced roasted red bell pepper
2   Tbsp fresh lemon juice
1   tsp grated lemon peel
2   tsp olive oil

Preparation—10 minutes

1   Blanch the beans for 2 minutes in a pot of boiling water. Drain and rinse with cold water.
2   Toss the beans with the remaining ingredients and serve at room temperature.

Calories	65
Calories from Fat	18
Total Fat	2 g
Saturated Fat	0 g
Cholesterol	0 mg
Sodium	92 mg
Carbohydrate	12 g
Dietary Fiber	4 g
Sugars	3 g
Protein	3 g

 VINEGARS

Herb Vinegars

Herb vinegars are wine or fruit vinegars with different herbs added to steep in the bottles. Tarragon vinegar is one of the most popular flavors. Tarragon, a licorice-tasting herb, is quite strong; just a little tarragon vinegar goes a long way. Herb vinegar often contain slices of garlic and black peppercorns. They make a wonderful gift and are calorie- and fat-free!

English Cucumber Salad with Cherry Tomatoes

6 Servings

Serving Size:
1 cup

Exchanges

2 Vegetable
1/2 Polyunsaturated
   Fat

Ingredients

24 large butter lettuce leaves
1 English cucumber, cut into matchstick pieces (or use a regular cucumber)
10 large, well-cleaned white mushrooms, sliced (use an egg slicer for perfect slices)
1 pint cherry tomatoes, stemmed and halved
1/4 cup white wine vinegar
2 tsp Dijon mustard
1 Tbsp walnut or hazelnut oil
Fresh ground pepper
Dash salt (optional)

Preparation—10 minutes

1 Place 4 lettuce leaves on individual plates. Decoratively place the cucumber, mushrooms, and cherry tomatoes.
2 Whisk together the remaining ingredients. Drizzle evenly over each salad.

Calories	61
Calories from Fat	27
Total Fat	3 g
Saturated Fat	0 g
Cholesterol	0 mg
Sodium	34 mg
Carbohydrate	8 g
Dietary Fiber	3 g
Sugars	5 g
Protein	2 g

Asparagus with Slivered Garlic

6 Servings

Serving Size:
1/2 cup

Exchanges

1 Vegetable

Ingredients

3 cups diagonally sliced fresh
  asparagus
1 tsp olive oil
2 Tbsp dry white wine
2 cloves garlic, slivered
2 Tbsp minced red onion
1 Tbsp lemon juice
Fresh ground pepper
Dash salt (optional)

Preparation—5 minutes

1 Blanch the asparagus for 3 minutes in a pot of boiling water and drain.
2 Heat the oil and wine in a skillet over medium heat. Add the garlic and onion and saute for 4 minutes.
3 Toss the mixture with the asparagus. Sprinkle lemon juice, pepper, and salt to serve.

Calories	35
Calories from Fat	10
Total Fat	1 g
Saturated Fat	0 g
Cholesterol	0 mg
Sodium	11 mg
Carbohydrate	5 g
Dietary Fiber	2 g
Sugars	2 g
Protein	2 g

Chocolate Grand Marnier Trifle

6 Servings

Serving Size:
1/3 cup

Exchanges

2 1/2 Carbohydrate

Ingredients

1 4-serving-size pkg fat-free,
   artificially sweetened, instant
   chocolate pudding
2 cups evaporated skim milk
1 1/2 tsp vanilla
1 1/2 cups fresh raspberries
1 Tbsp sugar
6 1/3-inch slices fat-free pound cake
1/4 cup all-fruit preserve of choice
1 Tbsp Grand Marnier
1 1/2 cups low-calorie whipped
   topping
cocoa powder

Preparation—20 minutes

1 Prepare the pudding mix according to package directions, using the evaporated skim milk and adding the vanilla. Refrigerate to set.
2 Mix together the raspberries and sugar and set aside.
3 Spread some jam on each slice of cake. Sprinkle each slice with Grand Marnier.
4 In a small trifle bowl or another glass bowl, press the cake slices, jam side up, on the sides of the bowl. Top with some of the fruit. Add some of the pudding. Repeat with the pudding and fruit.
5 Top the entire pudding with whipped topping. Sprinkle with cocoa powder and serve.

Calories	173	
Calories from Fat	5	
Total Fat	1	g
Saturated Fat	0	g
Cholesterol	3	mg
Sodium	248	mg
Carbohydrate	33	g
Dietary Fiber	3	g
Sugars	19	g
Protein	8	g

Mediterranean Magic

❖ ❖ ❖ ❖ ❖

Hills of Tuscany Pasta 329

Tomato Florentine Soup with Mozzarella Croutons
Field Greens with Toasted Pine Nuts
Penne with Broccoli Rabe and White Beans
Spicy Veal Patties
Berries and Cream

Trattoria Chicken 337

Mediterranean Chicken
Mustard and Wine Potatoes
Zucchini and Yellow Squash Saute
Plum Tomato and Escarole Salad with Parmesan
Balsamic Dressing
Low-Fat Tiramisu

Wine-Seared Scallops 345

Arugula and Beet Salad
Vine-Ripened Tomatoes Provençal
Seared Sea Scallops with Wine Sauce
Herb and Lemon Rice
Melon and Berries in Sauternes

Roman Candlelight Supper 353

Sun-Dried Tomato Crostini
Shells in Alfredo Sauce
White Mushroom Salad with Parmesan Shards
Asparagus Almondine
Italian Cheesecake Squares

Penne Carbonara 361

Red Chard Soup
Penne Carbonara
Broccoli and Cherry Tomato Salad
Artichoke Hearts Braised with Garlic
Figs Stuffed with Almonds and Chips

Hills of Tuscany Pasta

Tomato Florentine Soup with Mozzarella Croutons
Field Greens with Toasted Pine Nuts
Penne with Broccoli Rabe and White Beans
Spicy Veal Patties
Berries and Cream

M E N U   T A L K

Low-fat cream soups are easy to make with evaporated skim milk. Add this at the end of the cooking time and no one will know that the soup is not made with heavy cream. Sage is great with tomato-based foods. Dried sage has more intense flavor than fresh.

Field greens or mesclun are classic salad ingredients favored in the south of France. You can find this tasty salad mixture in most supermarkets. The youngest, most tender leaves of oakleaf lettuce, arugula, chervil, romaine, frisee, dandelion, and endive are included. These young leaves spoil quickly, so use them soon after purchase. Dress field greens very lightly—try spritzing on the dressing with a plant sprayer.

Broccoli rabe, also known as rapini, is a turnip green found on the dining tables in Tuscany. It is mildly bitter but has the familiar broccoli taste. I prefer to discard the stalks and just use the leaves. A traditional way to serve broccoli rabe is to combine it with pasta. If you cannot find broccoli rabe, use broccoli florets. The beans in this recipe provide more fiber and protein. You can also skip the pasta and just serve the broccoli rabe and white beans as a side dish.

Fennel has been cultivated for centuries. The Romans used it for culinary purposes and they, in turn, introduced fennel to the English. In Italian cuisine, you will find it used primarily to flavor sausages and tomato sauces. The English use it in fish dishes. You may even want to chew on a few fennel seeds after dinner to aid in digestion. You

See color photo after p. 368.

329

may substitute ground pork, beef, chicken, or turkey for the veal in this recipe.

Toasting nuts is a good way to bring out the flavor. Despite their high fat content, you can still use some nuts in cooking. Try to use really flavorful ones, like the hazelnuts used here, so that you only need a small amount. To toast them, simply place the nuts in a dry skillet over medium-high heat, and shake the pan until the nuts are toasted. This dessert tastes like the inside of an Italian cannoli. For an extra treat, sprinkle just a few mini chocolate chips on top of this dessert before serving.

Pantry List

sage
rosemary
basil
oregano
sugar
Marsala wine
hazelnuts
garlic
fennel seeds
crushed red pepper
1 can low-fat, low-sodium chicken
   broth
2 cans canellini beans
1 jar roasted red peppers
1 box penne pasta
1 yellow onion
1 red onion
red wine vinegar
1 shallot
olive oil
Dijon mustard
pine nuts
1 32-oz can crushed tomatoes
1 can evaporated skim milk
3 oz Italian bread
dried Italian seasoning

Market List

12 oz ground veal
1 pkg spinach
part-skim mozzarella cheese
1 1/2 lb field greens
1 red bell pepper
1 yellow bell pepper

parsley
1 lb broccoli rabe
Parmesan cheese
1 pint strawberries
1 pint blueberries
1 container part-skim ricotta cheese

1 Prepare the veal patties and refrigerate.
   You may do this the night before.
2 Prepare the salad and dressing, but do not
   combine them.
3 Prepare the dessert and refrigerate.
4 Prepare the soup and keep warm.
5 Boil the pasta and prepare the bean and rabe
   mixture, but do not combine them.
6 Cook the veal patties and place in a low oven.
   Or, cook them the night before and refrigerate.
7 Toast the bread and serve on the soup.
8 Toss the salad with the dressing and serve.
9 Combine the beans and rabe with the cooked
   pasta. Serve with the veal patties.
10 Serve the dessert.

Tomato Florentine Soup with Mozzarella Croutons*

6 Servings

Serving Size:
1 cup

Exchanges

2 Starch
1 Monounsaturated
Fat

Ingredients

1 Tbsp olive oil
1 onion, chopped
3 cloves garlic, minced
1 Tbsp minced sage
1 32-oz can crushed tomatoes
2 cups low-fat, low-sodium chicken broth
2 cups fresh spinach, washed and torn
1 Tbsp minced rosemary
2 tsp minced basil
1 cup evaporated skim milk
Fresh ground pepper
6 1/2-oz slices Italian bread
1 tsp olive oil
1 tsp dried Italian seasoning
3 oz part-skim mozzarella cheese

Preparation—10 minutes

1 Heat the oil in a stockpot over medium-high heat. Add the onion and garlic and saute for 5 minutes.
2 Add the sage, tomatoes, broth, and spinach. Bring to a boil, lower the heat, and simmer for 10 minutes.
3 Preheat the oven to 400 degrees. Add the rosemary, basil, and milk to the soup and simmer for 5 minutes. Season with pepper.
4 Spread each slice of bread with oil and Italian seasoning. Toast in the oven for 2 minutes. Top with cheese and continue to bake until the cheese melts, about 2 minutes. Place a bread slice on each serving of soup.

Calories	202
Calories from Fat	42
Total Fat	5 g
Saturated Fat	0 g
Cholesterol	4 mg
Sodium	686 mg
Carbohydrate	28 g
Dietary Fiber	5 g
Sugars	14 g
Protein	13 g

* This recipe is relatively high in sodium.

Field Greens with Toasted Pine Nuts

6 Servings

Serving Size:
I cup

Exchanges

I Vegetable
I Monounsaturated
  Fat

Ingredients

6 cups field greens (also known as
  European salad mix or mesclun)
1/2 small red bell pepper, julienned
1/2 yellow bell pepper, julienned
1 small red onion, sliced into thin
  rings
1/4 cup red wine vinegar
1 Tbsp minced shallots
1 Tbsp olive oil
2 tsp sugar
1 Tbsp Dijon mustard
2 Tbsp toasted pine nuts

Preparation—15 minutes

1 In a large bowl, combine the field greens, red
and yellow peppers, and onion.
2 In a medium bowl, whisk together the
remaining ingredients except the pine nuts.
3 Toss the salad with the dressing and garnish
with toasted pine nuts.

Calories	66
Calories from Fat	38
Total Fat	4 g
Saturated Fat	1 g
Cholesterol	0 mg
Sodium	40 mg
Carbohydrate	7 g
Dietary Fiber	1 g
Sugars	5 g
Protein	2 g

Penne with Broccoli Rabe and White Beans

6 Servings

Serving Size:
1 cup pasta
1/2 cup beans
1/4 cup broccoli
rabe

Exchanges

4 Starch
1 Vegetable
1 Very Lean Meat

Ingredients

1   Tbsp olive oil
2   cloves garlic, minced
1   lb broccoli rabe, washed and
    coarsely chopped
1   cup low-fat, low-sodium
    chicken broth
1   tsp minced fresh oregano
3   cups canellini (white) beans,
    drained and rinsed
2   Tbsp minced Italian parsley
1/4 cup roasted red bell pepper
6   cups cooked penne pasta
Fresh ground pepper
Dash salt (optional)
1/4 cup grated fresh Parmesan
    cheese

Preparation—20 minutes

1   Heat the oil in a heavy skillet over medium
heat. Add the garlic and saute for 30 seconds. Add
the broccoli rabe and saute for 2 minutes.
2   Add the broth, cover, and cook until the rabe
wilts. Add the oregano and simmer for 1 minute.
Add the beans and simmer for 2 minutes. Add the
parsley and roasted peppers.
3   Combine the rabe and beans with the cooked
pasta. Add the pepper and salt and garnish with
grated fresh Parmesan cheese.

Calories	401
Calories from Fat	49
Total Fat	5 g
Saturated Fat	1 g
Cholesterol	3 mg
Sodium	275 mg
Carbohydrate	69 g
Dietary Fiber	8 g
Sugars	6 g
Protein	21 g

Spicy Veal Patties

6 Servings

Serving Size:
2 oz

Exchanges

2 Very Lean Meat

Ingredients

12 oz ground veal
1/2 cup finely minced onion
3 cloves garlic, finely minced
1/2 tsp fennel seeds
1 tsp crushed red pepper
2 Tbsp minced Italian parsley

Preparation—10 minutes

1 Combine all ingredients and refrigerate for at least 1 hour.
2 Shape into patties and cook in a nonstick dry skillet on each side until crispy and browned, a total of 7–8 minutes for each patty.

Calories	88
Calories from Fat	28
Total Fat	3 g
Saturated Fat	1 g
Cholesterol	47 mg
Sodium	44 mg
Carbohydrate	2 g
Dietary Fiber	0 g
Sugars	1 g
Protein	12 g

 WHY DON'T YOU . . .

Join a food co-op in your city, if one is available. Prices are usually cheaper than in regular supermarkets.

Berries and Cream

6 Servings

Serving Size:
1/2 cup

Exchanges

1 Carbohydrate

Ingredients

1 1/2 cups sliced fresh strawberries
1 1/2 cups blueberries (or raspberries)
1 cup part-skim ricotta cheese
1 Tbsp evaporated skim milk
1 Tbsp sugar
1 1/2 Tbsp Marsala wine
1 1/2 Tbsp toasted hazelnuts

Preparation—10 minutes

1 Layer the fruits in 6 individual serving dishes.
2 Using electric beaters, whip together the ricotta cheese, milk, sugar, and wine.
3 Spoon a portion of the cream over each fruit serving, top with toasted hazelnuts, and serve.

Calories	86
Calories from Fat	13
Total Fat	1 g
Saturated Fat	0 g
Cholesterol	13 mg
Sodium	38 mg
Carbohydrate	12 g
Dietary Fiber	3 g
Sugars	8 g
Protein	6 g

 WHY DON'T YOU . . .

Purchase really long, tapered candles. They're all you need to adorn your dinner table.

Trattoria Chicken

Mediterranean Chicken
Mustard and Wine Potatoes
Zucchini and Yellow Squash Saute
Plum Tomato and Escarole Salad with Parmesan Balsamic Dressing
Low-Fat Tiramisu

M E N U   T A L K

When preparing chicken for a low-fat meal, I think it is best to pan-sear it for added flavor. The pan searing produces a golden crust while keeping the chicken tender. If you don't have fresh tomatoes for this recipe, using canned plum tomatoes is fine. The Kalamata olives add a special touch, so do seek them out. They are highly flavored, tasting rich and fruity, so you will need less to season this dish. Use the sauce in this recipe for other foods, such as seafood, pork, beef, turkey, and pasta.

When purchasing potatoes, look for ones that are rock-hard and blemish-free. Potatoes are more volatile than some people think. They need to be stored at the correct temperature (about 45 degrees) and light level (dim). Check your potatoes for signs of sprouting, which indicates they are going bad. Although the refrigerator will preserve a potato, unfortunately the starch turns to sugar and the potato flavor will be off. Roasting potatoes is my favorite way to fix them. The dry heat gives the potato great taste and texture.

Zucchini and yellow squash are extremely fast-cooking vegetables. Served together, they can make a side dish much more colorful. Zucchini and yellow squash appear on many Italian dinner tables and are often combined with tomatoes and basil. Keep squash in plastic bags in the refrigerator for a maximum of five days.

Escarole is a green that can take a strong dressing, such as this one with Parmesan cheese. Slightly bitter when raw, escarole is tamed by the addition of balsamic vinegar, romaine, and bibb lettuces. Cooking escarole mellows it still further.

When my husband and I were in Italy several years ago, we ate creamy tiramisu almost every night! I was determined to come up with a low-fat version of this classic dessert. By using just a small amount of mascapone cheese, the rich cheese that gives tiramisu its special flavor, combining it with low-fat ricotta cheese, and lowering the sugar content, I came up with something you won't be able to tell from the real thing.

Pantry List

olive oil
dry white wine
Kalamata olives
2 red potatoes
2 russet potatoes
Dijon mustard
garlic
1 each red and yellow onion
paprika
Kahlua
sugar
cocoa powder
instant coffee
fat-free pound cake
balsamic vinegar
1 can low-fat, low-sodium
   chicken broth
1 jar roasted red bell peppers

Market List

1 1/2 lb boneless, skinless
   chicken breasts
thyme
basil
Italian parsley
green onions
marscapone cheese
part-skim ricotta cheese
low-calorie whipped topping
fresh raspberries or strawberries
1 head escarole
1 head romaine lettuce
1 head bibb lettuce
3 tomatoes

4–5 plum tomatoes
lemon juice
1 zucchini
1 yellow squash
Parmesan cheese

Mediterranean Chicken

6 Servings

Serving Size:
1/2 breast

Exchanges

1 Vegetable
4 Very Lean Meat
1/2 Monounsaturated Fat

Ingredients

2 tsp olive oil
2 Tbsp dry white wine
3 whole boneless, skinless chicken breasts, halved
3 cloves garlic, minced
1/2 cup diced onion
3 medium tomatoes, coarsely chopped
2 tsp minced thyme
1 Tbsp minced basil
1/2 cup dry white wine
1/2 cup Kalamata olives
1/4 cup minced Italian parsley
Fresh ground pepper
Dash salt (optional)

Preparation—20 minutes

1 Heat the oil and wine in a heavy skillet over medium heat. Add the chicken breasts and saute until golden on each side, about 4–6 minutes a side. Remove the chicken from the skillet.
2 Saute the garlic for 30 seconds in the pan drippings. Add the onion and saute for 3 minutes. Add the tomatoes and bring to a boil.
3 Lower the heat, add the wine, and simmer for 10 minutes. Add the thyme and basil and simmer for 5 minutes.
4 Return the chicken to the skillet and cover. Cook over low heat until the chicken is cooked through.
5 Add the olives and parsley and cook 1 minute. Season with pepper and salt and serve.

Calories	191
Calories from Fat	53
Total Fat	6 g
Saturated Fat	1 g
Cholesterol	69 mg
Sodium	165 mg
Carbohydrate	7 g
Dietary Fiber	2 g
Sugars	4 g
Protein	26 g

Mustard and Wine Potatoes

6 Servings

Serving Size:
1/2 cup

Exchanges

1 Starch

Ingredients

3 Tbsp Dijon mustard
1 cup dry white wine
2 Tbsp minced green onions
2 tsp minced garlic
2 Tbsp minced onion
2 tsp paprika
1 1/2 cups cubed red potatoes,
    skins on
1 1/2 cups cubed russet potatoes,
    skins on

Preparation—10 minutes

1 Preheat the oven to 350 degrees. Combine all ingredients except the potatoes in a large bowl. Add the potatoes and toss so the potatoes are well coated.
2 Place into a casserole dish and bake, uncovered, until the potatoes are soft and slightly crisp on the outside, about 45 minutes.

Calories	89
Calories from Fat	4
Total Fat	0 g
Saturated Fat	0 g
Cholesterol	0 mg
Sodium	103 mg
Carbohydrate	18 g
Dietary Fiber	3 g
Sugars	3 g
Protein	3 g

Zucchini and Yellow Squash Saute

6 Servings

Serving Size:
1/2 cup

Exchanges

1 Vegetable

Ingredients

2 tsp olive oil
1/2 red onion, diced
1 clove garlic, minced
1 cup diced zucchini, skin on
1 cup diced yellow squash, skin on
1 cup roasted red bell peppers
1/2 cup low-fat, low-sodium
    chicken broth
1 Tbsp minced basil

Preparation—15 minutes

1 Heat the oil in a skillet over medium-high heat. Add the onion and garlic and saute for 2 minutes.
2 Add the zucchini and squash and saute for 3 minutes. Add the peppers, broth, and basil. Cover, steam for 4 minutes, and serve.

Calories	37
Calories from Fat	16
Total Fat	2 g
Saturated Fat	0 g
Cholesterol	0 mg
Sodium	11 mg
Carbohydrate	5 g
Dietary Fiber	1 g
Sugars	3 g
Protein	1 g

Plum Tomato and Escarole Salad with Parmesan Balsamic Dressing

6 Servings

Serving Size:
I cup

Exchanges

I Vegetable
1/2 Monounsatur-
ated Fat

Ingredients

2 cups escarole, washed and torn
2 cups romaine lettuce, washed and torn
2 cups bibb lettuce
12 slices plum tomatoes
1/2 cup balsamic vinegar
1 Tbsp olive oil
1 Tbsp Parmesan cheese
2 cloves garlic, minced
1 Tbsp fresh lemon juice
1/4 cup low-fat, low-sodium chicken broth
Fresh ground pepper
Dash salt (optional)

Preparation—10 minutes

1 In a salad bowl, combine the greens and tomatoes.
2 In a separate bowl, whisk together the remaining ingredients. Toss the salad with the dressing and serve immediately.

Calories	47
Calories from Fat	26
Total Fat	3 g
Saturated Fat	I g
Cholesterol	I mg
Sodium	31 mg
Carbohydrate	5 g
Dietary Fiber	2 g
Sugars	3 g
Protein	2 g

 WHY DON'T YOU . . .

Have a contest in the family to see who can prepare the tastiest dish.

Low-Fat Tiramisu

6 Servings

Serving Size:
1/2 cup

Exchanges

1 1/2 Carbohydrate
1 Lean Meat
2 Saturated Fat

Ingredients

3 1-oz slices fat-free pound cake
2 Tbsp Kahlua
1/3 cup marscapone cheese
3/4 cup part-skim ricotta cheese
1/2 cup low-fat cream cheese
1/4 cup sugar
1 Tbsp cocoa powder
2 Tbsp instant coffee granules
1/2 cup low-calorie whipped
    topping
Cocoa powder
Fresh raspberries or strawberries

Preparation—20 minutes

1 Drizzle the cake slices with the liqueur. Let them soak for 10 minutes.
2 Combine the cheeses, sugar, cocoa powder, and coffee.
3 Crumble some of the cake into each of 6 serving dishes. Add a layer of the cheese mixture. Add a layer of crumbled cake.
4 Top each serving with some whipped topping and a dusting of cocoa, then garnish with berries to serve.

Calories	252
Calories from Fat	120
Total Fat	13 g
Saturated Fat	8 g
Cholesterol	39 mg
Sodium	199 mg
Carbohydrate	26 g
Dietary Fiber	1 g
Sugars	18 g
Protein	7 g

Wine-Seared Scallops

Arugula and Beet Salad
Vine-Ripened Tomatoes Provençal
Seared Sea Scallops with Wine Sauce
Herb and Lemon Rice
Melon and Berries in Sauternes

MENU TALK

The beet, with its striking ruby-red color, is one of the prettiest vegetables. Most people are familiar with the canned variety, but try a fresh beet—you won't believe the taste! Small and medium beets are usually the best. The greens attached to the beets are edible and are loaded with vitamins. Try them torn into salads or steamed with a little lemon juice on top. Wash beets before you cook them and peel them afterward, when they have cooled. Cook beets in boiling water for about 30 minutes or until they are tender.

The crumb mixture used in this menu's vegetable can be used as a topping for broccoli, asparagus, green beans, and cauliflower. Try serving this dish in the summer when tomatoes are at their peak. Good, fresh tomatoes will have a juicy texture and will still retain their sweet taste when baked. You can make up the crumb mixture in advance and store it in the refrigerator for several days.

There are many types of scallops, but scallops are generally classified as either bay or sea scallops. Bay scallops found on the East coast are smaller, sweeter, and more tender than sea scallops. They are generally more expensive because they are not as plentiful as sea scallops. The best time for sea scallops is mid-fall to mid-spring. Use scallops the same day you buy them. Cook them carefully and briefly, just until they turn white. I think the best cooking method is pan-sauteing.

Use fresh herbs in the rice for the best flavor. Rice is relatively bland, so don't be afraid to boldly season this rice dish. I find rice cooked in broth to be much more flavorful than in plain water.

Sauternes is an elegant wine from the Sauternes region of western France. It is made from Sauvignon Blanc or Semillon grapes. You may use dry white wine, nonalcoholic wine, or even white grape juice in this dessert.

Pantry List

walnut oil
red wine vinegar
Dijon mustard
3 cans low-fat, low-sodium
    chicken broth
garlic
plain bread crumbs
dry white wine
capers
1 onion
1 bag brown rice
sauternes or dessert wine
canola oil
olive oil

Market List

1 1/2 lb sea scallops
2 lb arugula
4 fresh beets (or 1 can beets)
1 head romaine lettuce
6 medium tomatoes
fresh lemon juice
1 lemon
parsley
chives
thyme
unsalted butter
1 carrot
basil
1/2 honeydew or cantaloupe
2 pints fresh blueberries

1 Prepare the dessert and refrigerate.
2 Prepare the rice.
3 Prepare the salad and dressing, but do not
    combine them.
4 Prepare steps 1 and 2 of the tomato recipe.
5 Prepare the scallops and turn off the heat.
6 Bake the tomatoes and leave in a warm oven.
7 Toss the salad with the dressing and serve.
8 Serve the scallops, tomatoes, and rice.
9 Serve the dessert.

Arugula and Beet Salad

6 Servings

Serving Size:
1 cup

Exchanges

1 Vegetable
1/2 Polyunsaturated
   Fat

Ingredients

4 cups arugula, torn
1 1/2 cups sliced cooked beets
1 cup romaine lettuce, torn
1 Tbsp walnut oil
2 Tbsp red wine vinegar
1 Tbsp Dijon mustard
1 Tbsp fresh lemon juice
2 Tbsp low-fat, low-sodium
   chicken broth

Preparation—15 minutes

1 Combine the arugula, beets, and lettuce in a salad bowl.
2 Whisk together the remaining ingredients, pour over the salad, and serve.

Calories	47
Calories from Fat	24
Total Fat	3 g
Saturated Fat	0 g
Cholesterol	0 mg
Sodium	72 mg
Carbohydrate	6 g
Dietary Fiber	1 g
Sugars	3 g
Protein	1 g

❖ ❖ ❖ ❖ ❖ ❖ ❖

⤳ WHY DON'T YOU . . .

Get a nice wok. Serve a stir-fry directly from the wok!

Vine-Ripened Tomatoes Provençal

6 Servings

Serving Size:
1 tomato

Exchanges

1/2 Starch
1 Vegetable
1/2 Monounsatur-
  ated Fat

Ingredients

6 medium vine-ripened tomatoes,
   cut in half
2 Tbsp minced parsley
2 Tbsp fresh lemon juice
2 tsp olive oil
1 Tbsp finely minced garlic
2 tsp minced chives
1 tsp minced thyme
2 Tbsp low-fat, low-sodium
   chicken broth
1/2 cup plain dried bread crumbs
Fresh ground pepper
Dash salt (optional)

Preparation—10 minutes

1 Preheat the oven to 400 degrees. Prepare the tomatoes and set aside.

2 Combine the remaining ingredients except for the bread crumbs, pepper, and salt. Add the bread crumbs and mix well. Season with pepper and salt and spread the mixture evenly over each tomato half.

3 Place the tomatoes in a baking dish and bake until the top is slightly browned, about 10 minutes.

Calories	85
Calories from Fat	23
Total Fat	3 g
Saturated Fat	0 g
Cholesterol	0 mg
Sodium	95 mg
Carbohydrate	15 g
Dietary Fiber	2 g
Sugars	5 g
Protein	3 g

Seared Sea Scallops with Wine Sauce

6 Servings

Serving Size:
3–4 oz

Exchanges

3 Very Lean Meat
1 Monounsaturated
   Fat

Ingredients

1 1/2 Tbsp canola oil
1 1/2 lb sea scallops
2 cups dry white wine
3 Tbsp fresh lemon juice
1/2 Tbsp unsalted butter
2 Tbsp capers
2 Tbsp minced fresh parsley
Fresh ground pepper

Preparation—15 minutes

1 Heat the oil in a heavy skillet over high heat. When the oil is very hot, quickly add the scallops to the pan and sear for 1 minute.

2 Add 1/2 cup of the wine, lower the heat, and simmer for 2 minutes. Remove the seared scallops from the pan.

3 Add the remaining wine and lemon juice. Bring to a boil and reduce by half. Add the butter, capers, and parsley. Season with pepper.

4 Place the cooked scallops on a plate, surround with the wine sauce, and serve.

Calories	162
Calories from Fat	48
Total Fat	5 g
Saturated Fat	1 g
Cholesterol	37 mg
Sodium	305 mg
Carbohydrate	3 g
Dietary Fiber	0 g
Sugars	3 g
Protein	19 g

Herb and Lemon Rice

6 Servings

Serving Size:
1/2 cup

Exchanges

2 1/2 Starch

Ingredients

1/4 cup low-fat, low-sodium
  chicken broth
1 clove garlic, minced
2 Tbsp minced onion
1/4 cup minced carrot
1 1/2 cups short-grain brown rice
3 cups low-fat, low-sodium chicken
  broth
1–2 Tbsp minced basil
2 tsp minced parsley
1 Tbsp lemon juice
1/4 tsp lemon rind

Preparation—15 minutes

1 Heat the broth in a saucepan over medium-high heat. Add the garlic and onion and saute for 3 minutes. Add the carrot and saute for 3 minutes. Add the rice and saute for 2 minutes.
2 Add the broth, bring to a boil, lower the heat, cover, and simmer until the water is absorbed, about 40–45 minutes. Add the remaining ingredients and serve.

Calories	190
Calories from Fat	23
Total Fat	3 g
Saturated Fat	1 g
Cholesterol	0 mg
Sodium	66 mg
Carbohydrate	38 g
Dietary Fiber	2 g
Sugars	1 g
Protein	6 g

Melon and Berries in Sauternes

6 Servings

Serving Size:
1/2 cup

Exchanges

1 Carbohydrate

Ingredients

1 1/2 cups diced honeydew melon
         (or use cantaloupe)
1 1/2 cups fresh blueberries
1   cup sauternes or other
         dessert wine

Preparation—5 minutes

Toss all ingredients together and refrigerate for
1–2 hours. Serve in clear glasses.

Calories	96
Calories from Fat	2
Total Fat	0 g
Saturated Fat	0 g
Cholesterol	0 mg
Sodium	10 mg
Carbohydrate	14 g
Dietary Fiber	1 g
Sugars	11 g
Protein	1 g

🦅 SPEAKING OF SPICES

Saffron

Saffron is the most valuable spice in the world. Despite its initial cost, it is fairly inexpensive to use, since only a small amount imparts rich color and flavor to foods. Saffron is made from the crocus flower. Some cooks substitute turmeric for saffron, but I don't recommend this, because the flavors are different: turmeric is slightly peppery and is a perennial closely related to the ginger family. Turmeric is used in commercial mustards, more for its color than its flavor.

Roman Candlelight Supper

Sun-Dried Tomato Crostini
Shells in Alfredo Sauce
White Mushroom Salad with Parmesan Shards
Asparagus Almondine
Italian Cheesecake Squares

MENU TALK

Crostini means toast in Italian. In Italy, toast is topped with many inventive combinations. In this recipe, the flavor of sun-dried tomatoes enhances every bite. You can find anchovy paste in most supermarkets. It comes in a tube and is very easy to use. Anchovy paste gives foods a rich taste, and a little goes a long way.

The best way to create creamy sauces without the fat is to use evaporated skim milk. Using plain skim milk does not yield the rich creaminess that evaporated skim milk does. Make sure to simmer sauces with milk for a short period, otherwise the sauce will curdle. Try evaporated skim milk in coffee, too.

Making Parmesan cheese shards for this menu's salad is a great way to serve it. Make sure you have a good vegetable peeler, and with a firm hand, make long peels from a wedge of Parmesan. Allow 3 strips per person. Wrap the remaining cheese in cheesecloth. Avoid using preshredded or grated Parmesan—although it's convenient, if you want authentic flavor, you will enjoy long peels of the real stuff!

Always try to obtain fresh asparagus. Look for stalks that are neither too thin not too wide. Break off the tough bottoms with your hands. Asparagus is packed with fiber, vitamins, and minerals. Be careful not to overcook it. Store asparagus as you would a bouquet of flowers: bundle the stalks together, place them in a jar with an inch of water in the bottom, cover loosely with a plastic bag, and refrigerate.

The part-skim ricotta cheese makes this Italian cheesecake a lovely low-fat version of a classic favorite. Try serving this cheesecake with fresh berries in the summer. It's good with strawberries, blackberries, or boysenberries instead of raspberries, if you can find fresh ones.

Pantry List

sun-dried tomatoes
1 tube anchovy paste
small capers
olive oil
balsamic vinegar
1 small loaf French or Italian bread
1 can evaporated skim milk
1 jar roasted red bell peppers
almond extract
garlic
1 box pasta shells
1 small pkg sliced almonds
vanilla extract
lemon extract
sugar
cornstarch or arrowroot powder

Market List

basil
thyme
low-fat sour cream
Parmesan cheese
1 pint white mushrooms
1 bunch celery
fresh lemon juice
1 bundle asparagus
low-calorie margarine
part-skim ricotta cheese
low-fat cream cheese
2 pints raspberries
pineapple juice concentrate
1 carton egg substitutes

STEP-BY-STEP COUNTDOWN

1 Prepare the dessert. This can be done the day before.
2 Prepare the first step of the appetizer recipe.
3 Prepare the salad and dressing, but do not combine them.
4 Prepare the asparagus and almonds, but do not cook the asparagus.
5 Prepare the pasta and turn off the heat when completed.
6 Finish preparing the appetizer and serve.
7 Cook the asparagus, top with almonds, and turn off the heat.
8 Toss the salad with the dressing and serve.
9 Serve the pasta and asparagus.
10 Serve the dessert.

Sun-Dried Tomato Crostini

6 Servings

Serving Size:
1/2 oz bread
1 Tbsp spread

Exchanges

1/2 Starch

Ingredients

10 sun-dried tomatoes, rehydrated
(do not use oil-packed tomatoes)
2 tsp anchovy paste
1 tsp small capers
1 tsp olive oil
2 tsp balsamic vinegar
2 tsp minced basil
1 tsp minced thyme
3 oz sliced French or Italian bread

Preparation—15 minutes

1 Preheat the oven to 350 degrees. In a food processor, combine all ingredients except the bread and pulse on and off until the mixture is blended, but still a little coarse.
2 Toast the bread slices in the oven on each side for a total of 2–3 minutes.
3 Spread each slice with some of the tomato mixture and serve.

Calories	59
Calories from Fat	14
Total Fat	2 g
Saturated Fat	0 g
Cholesterol	2 mg
Sodium	257 mg
Carbohydrate	9 g
Dietary Fiber	1 g
Sugars	1 g
Protein	2 g

Shells in Alfredo Sauce

6 Servings

Serving Size:
1 cup

Exchanges

3 Starch
1/2 Skim Milk
1 1/2 Saturated Fat

Ingredients

1   tsp olive oil
2   cloves garlic, minced
1   cup low-fat sour cream
1   12-oz can evaporated skim milk
1/4   cup Parmesan cheese (or use
        Romano for a stronger flavor)
2   Tbsp minced basil
Fresh ground pepper
Dash salt (optional)
6   cups cooked shell pasta

Preparation—20 minutes

1   Heat the oil in a skillet over medium-high heat. Add the garlic and saute for 30 seconds. Add the sour cream and milk and mix until smooth.
2   Lower the heat and simmer for 5 minutes. Add the cheese, basil, pepper, and salt. Toss with the hot cooked shells and serve.

Calories	364
Calories from Fat	80
Total Fat	9 g
Saturated Fat	5 g
Cholesterol	32 mg
Sodium	176 mg
Carbohydrate	53 g
Dietary Fiber	1 g
Sugars	11 g
Protein	15 g

❖   ❖   ❖   ❖   ❖   ❖
🦅   WHY DON'T YOU . . .

Have a healthy recipe exchange party. Invite some of your friends over to share the finished products, or if you have a big kitchen, cook together!

White Mushroom Salad with Parmesan Shards

6 Servings

Serving Size:
1/2 cup

Exchanges

1 Vegetable
1/2 Fat

Ingredients

2 cups sliced white mushrooms
1/2 cup sliced celery
1/2 cup sliced roasted red bell
  pepper
1/4 cup balsamic vinegar
1 Tbsp lemon juice
2 tsp olive oil
2 cloves garlic, finely minced
Fresh Parmesan cheese shards

Preparation—15 minutes

1 Combine the mushrooms, celery, and pepper in a salad bowl.
2 Whisk together the vinegar, lemon juice, oil, and garlic. Pour over the salad, and let the salad sit for 1/2 hour.
3 Serve the salad on individual plates. Top each serving with parmesan shards.

Calories	57
Calories from Fat	35
Total Fat	4 g
Saturated Fat	2 g
Cholesterol	8 mg
Sodium	171 mg
Carbohydrate	3 g
Dietary Fiber	1 g
Sugars	2 g
Protein	4 g

Asparagus Almondine

6 Servings

Serving Size:
1/2 cup

Exchanges

1 Vegetable
1 Monounsaturated
  Fat

Ingredients

3 cups diagonally sliced asparagus
2 Tbsp low-calorie margarine
1/4 cup sliced almonds
Fresh ground pepper
Dash salt (optional)

Preparation—10 minutes

1 Blanch the asparagus in boiling water for 2 minutes and drain.
2 Melt the margarine in a skillet over medium-high heat. Add the almonds and saute until the almonds are toasted, about 3 minutes. Top the asparagus with the almonds. Season with pepper and salt and serve.

Calories	65
Calories from Fat	41
Total Fat	5 g
Saturated Fat	1 g
Cholesterol	0 mg
Sodium	40 mg
Carbohydrate	5 g
Dietary Fiber	2 g
Sugars	2 g
Protein	3 g

 WHY DON'T YOU . . .

Try one exotic fruit when it is in season—a mango, papaya, Asian pear, or pomegranate.

Italian Cheesecake Squares

6 Servings

Serving Size:
One 1 1/2-inch
square

Exchanges

1 1/2 Carbohydrate
2 Very Lean Meat

Ingredients

2 cups part-skim ricotta cheese
1 cup low-fat cream cheese (use the
   bar type only)
3 egg substitutes
1 Tbsp vanilla extract
1/2 tsp almond extract
1 tsp lemon juice
1/4 cup sugar
1 1/2 cups fresh raspberries
1/4 cup pineapple juice concentrate,
   thawed
1 Tbsp sugar
1/2 cup water
2 Tbsp cornstarch or arrowroot
   powder

Preparation—20 minutes

1 Preheat the oven to 350 degrees. Combine
the cheeses, egg substitute, vanilla extract, almond
extract, lemon juice, and 1/4 cup sugar and
mix well.
2 Pour into a 9-inch nonstick square pan. Bake
until a tester inserted in the center comes out clean,
about 50 minutes. Refrigerate for several hours.
3 In a saucepan over medium heat, combine the
raspberries, pineapple juice concentrate, 1 Tbsp
sugar, and 1/4 cup of the water. Bring to a boil,
lower the heat, and simmer for 5 minutes.
4 Mix the cornstarch or arrowroot powder with
the remaining water and add to the saucepan. Cook
over low heat until the mixture thickens. Cool the
mixture in a bowl for several hours.
5 Spread the topping over the squares, cut,
and serve.

Calories	173
Calories from Fat	2
Total Fat	0 g
Saturated Fat	0 g
Cholesterol	32 mg
Sodium	365 mg
Carbohydrate	21 g
Dietary Fiber	2 g
Sugars	12 g
Protein	21 g

❖ ❖ ❖

Penne Carbonara

Red Chard Soup
Broccoli and Cherry Tomato Salad
Penne Carbonara
Artichoke Hearts Braised with Garlic
Figs Stuffed with Almonds and Chips

MENU TALK

Red chard is a member of the beet family and is prized for its looks. Bright red stalks with ruby-red veins outline each leaf. Chard is a cruciferous, cancer-fighting vegetable. The red chard, unlike the green chard, can be torn in pieces and eaten raw in salads. Store chard in the refrigerator in a plastic bag for up to three days. If you cannot find chard, use fresh spinach to prepare this soup. Blanch the chard first to reduce its crunchiness. Be sure to plunge the chard into the boiling water for just a few seconds so you can preserve its bright red color. Plunging it immediately into ice water "shocks" the vegetable, stops the cooking process, and helps retain the color.

Carbonara is a term to describe a mixture of pasta with cream, eggs, Parmesan cheese, and bacon. It is a rather rich entree that can be loaded with fat! Here is a lighter version made with evaporated skim milk, low-fat sour cream, Canadian bacon, and just a little cheese. This sauce is also great on chicken or seafood.

This menu's salad also requires the blanching technique. I prefer to blanch vegetables rather than always steam them, because I believe this produces a crisper, brighter vegetable with a higher nutrient content. Use the blanching water as a base for soup or stews. Use asparagus or zucchini instead of broccoli in this salad if you wish.

Braising is a slow method of cooking that tenderizes meat while the flavor develops. But try braising vegetables—it really draws out their natural flavors, especially with the addition of fresh garlic!

Figs were brought to this country by Spanish Franciscan missionaries who traveled to California—hence the name Mission fig. There are many varieties of figs, such as the green-skinned Calimyra fig, the Turkish Smyrna, the green-skinned Adriatic, the small yellow-green Kadota, and the purplish black Mission. They are all sweet and succulent. I love to eat juicy Calimyras off my friend's tree in sunny California. The season for fresh figs is from June through October. They are very perishable, so do refrigerate and eat them quickly. If fresh figs are not available, use dried in this recipe. Figs are a good source of fiber, iron, calcium, and phosphorus.

Pantry List

1 small bag mini chocolate chips
1 small bag almond slivers
orange liqueur or Marsala wine
dry white wine
3 cans low-fat, low-sodium chicken
    broth
1 yellow onion
garlic
1 can evaporated skim milk
1 box penne pasta
Dijon mustard
red wine vinegar
olive oil
2 cans artichoke hearts packed in
    water
1 jar roasted red bell peppers

Market List

5 oz Canadian bacon
2 large bunches red chard
1 bunch basil leaves
Parmesan cheese
1 carton low-fat sour cream
1 lb broccoli
1 pint cherry tomatoes
3 green onions
fresh lemon juice
6 medium figs
fresh rosemary

Red Chard Soup

6 Servings

Serving Size:
1 cup

Exchanges

1/2 Starch
1/2 Fat

Ingredients

2　large bunches of red chard, washed thoroughly
1/4　cup dry white wine
2　cloves garlic, minced
1/2　cup minced onion
5　cups low-fat, low-sodium chicken broth
1/2　cup minced basil leaves
2　Tbsp Parmesan cheese
Fresh ground pepper
Dash salt (optional)

Preparation—15 minutes

1 Remove the stems from the chard and cut the stems and leaves into pieces. Blanch the chard for 15 seconds, drain, plunge into ice water, and drain again.
2 Heat the wine in a stockpot over medium-high heat. Add the garlic and onion and saute for 5 minutes. Add the broth and bring to a simmer. Add the chard and simmer for 10 minutes.
3 Add the basil and cheese. Season with pepper and salt and serve.

Calories	53
Calories from Fat	23
Total Fat	3 g
Saturated Fat	1 g
Cholesterol	2 mg
Sodium	244 mg
Carbohydrate	6 g
Dietary Fiber	2 g
Sugars	2 g
Protein	5 g

Broccoli and Cherry Tomato Salad

6 Servings

Serving Size:
1/2 cup

Exchanges

1 Vegetable
1/2 Monounsatur-
    ated Fat

Ingredients

1 1/2 cups broccoli florets
1 1/2 cups halved cherry tomatoes
3 green onions, minced
1 Tbsp Dijon mustard
2 Tbsp red wine vinegar
2 tsp lemon juice
1 Tbsp olive oil
2 tsp Parmesan cheese

Preparation—15 minutes

1 Blanch the broccoli in boiling water for
2 minutes. Drain, plunge into ice water, and drain
again. Toss the broccoli with the tomatoes and
green onions.
2 Whisk together the remaining ingredients.
Pour the dressing over the salad and refrigerate for
1 hour before serving.

Calories	43
Calories from Fat	25
Total Fat	3 g
Saturated Fat	0 g
Cholesterol	0 mg
Sodium	53 mg
Carbohydrate	4 g
Dietary Fiber	1 g
Sugars	2 g
Protein	1 g

Penne Carbonara

6 Servings

Serving Size:
1 cup

Exchanges

3 Starch
1/2 Skim Milk
1 Medium-Fat Meat

Ingredients

2 tsp olive oil
2 cloves garlic, minced
1/2 cup minced onion
5 oz Canadian bacon
1 12-oz can evaporated skim milk
1/2 cup low-fat sour cream
2 Tbsp Parmesan cheese
6 cups cooked penne pasta
1/4 cup minced fresh basil

Preparation—15 minutes

1 Heat the oil in a skillet over medium-high heat. Add the garlic and onion and saute for 4 minutes. Add the bacon and saute until the bacon is crisp, about 4 minutes. Crumble the bacon.
2 Remove the garlic-bacon mixture from the skillet. Add the evaporated milk and sour cream to the skillet. Cook over low heat until thickened (do not curdle).
3 Add the cheese and the garlic-bacon mixture to the skillet. Toss the sauce with the hot cooked penne, top with basil, and serve.

Calories	361
Calories from Fat	72
Total Fat	3 g
Saturated Fat	3 g
Cholesterol	22 mg
Sodium	420 mg
Carbohydrate	53 g
Dietary Fiber	2 g
Sugars	10 g
Protein	18 g

Artichoke Hearts Braised with Garlic

Ingredients

2 15-oz cans artichoke hearts,
   packed in water, drained, left
   whole
6 cloves garlic, peeled, left whole
2 sprigs fresh rosemary
1/2 cup low-fat, low-sodium
   chicken broth
1/2 cup dry white wine
1 tsp olive oil
1/4 cup diced roasted red bell
   pepper (optional)
Fresh ground pepper
Dash salt (optional)

Preparation—15 minutes

1 Place the artichokes, garlic, rosemary, broth, wine, and oil in a skillet over medium-high heat. Cover the skillet and braise until liquid is reduced by half, about 10 minutes.

2 Uncover and cook until almost all the liquid is evaporated, about 5 minutes. Add the roasted red bell peppers, if desired. Season with pepper and salt and serve at room temperature.

Calories	47	
Calories from Fat	12	
Total Fat	1	g
Saturated Fat	0	g
Cholesterol	0	mg
Sodium	242	mg
Carbohydrate	7	g
Dietary Fiber	2	g
Sugars	3	g
Protein	2	g

Figs Stuffed with Almonds and Chips

6 Servings

Serving Size:
1 stuffed fig

Exchanges

1 Carbohydrate
1/2 Monounsatur-
   ated Fat

Ingredients

6 medium figs or dates
2 Tbsp mini chocolate chips
1/4 cup toasted slivered almonds
1 Tbsp orange liqueur or
   Marsala wine

Preparation—15 minutes

1 Preheat the oven to 350 degrees. Cut each fig in half. Combine the remaining ingredients.
2 Spoon about 2 tsp of the stuffing into each fig half. Bake on a cookie sheet for 10 minutes.
3 If you can't find fresh figs, then stuff the mixture inside dried figs. Cut a little opening in the top of the fig and spoon in the stuffing. Proceed with the recipe.

Calories	93
Calories from Fat	36
Total Fat	4 g
Saturated Fat	1 g
Cholesterol	0 mg
Sodium	2 mg
Carbohydrate	15 g
Dietary Fiber	3 g
Sugars	8 g
Protein	1 g

Hills of Tuscany Pasta, see page 329

Banana Bread Brunch, see page 403

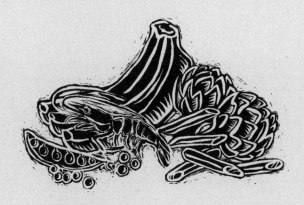

Light Bites

❖ ❖ ❖ ❖

Artichoke Pasta 371

Light Red and Green Lentil Soup
Tomato and Roasted Red Pepper Salad
Pasta with Artichokes and Basil
Asparagus and Zucchini in Garlic
Quick Amaretto Mousse

Smoked Turkey Salad 379

Chicken, Greens, and Noodle Soup
Bulgur Wheat Salad with Smoked Turkey
Vegetable Plate
Savory Herb Muffins
Hot Walnut Sundae

Southern Shrimp Gumbo 387

Southern Shrimp Gumbo
Buttermilk Cornbread Muffins
Carrot Coleslaw
Green Beans with White Wine and
    Garlic Vinaigrette
Clove-Scented Pears

Pasta Pie 395

Italian Vegetable Antipasto
Pasta Pie
Chilled Green Beans and Carrot Slivers
Basil and Tomato Bread
Grapes with Mint

Banana Bread Brunch 403

Very Berry Drink
Poppyseed Fruit Salad
Baked Banana Bread French Toast
Spicy Pork Sausages
Orange Syrup

Turkey Tenderloin Picnic 411

Cucumber Dill Dip
Creamy Peach Soup
Roast Turkey Tenderloins with Kiwi Slaw
Garlic New Potato Salad
Mint Tea

Artichoke Pasta

Light Red and Green Lentil Soup
Tomato and Roasted Red Pepper Salad
Pasta with Artichokes and Basil
Asparagus and Zucchini in Garlic
Quick Amaretto Mousse

MENU TALK

Although popular in Europe, the Middle East, and India, the lentil didn't capture our attention in this country until vegetarian cooking became popular. There are several varieties of lentils, including the red lentil, which is smaller than the brown or yellow lentil. Red lentils are found in speciality grocery stores. Lentils will keep up to a year when placed in a tightly sealed jar or bag. Lentils are a good source of iron and vitamins A and B. The spinach for this menu's soup is slivered (the culinary term is chiffonade, which translates to "made of rags"). Vegetables chiffonade are cut into thin strips or shreds. This soup is very light, in spite of the lentils. If you want to serve this soup as a main course, add 1 more cup of lentils and 2 more cups of liquid. You can puree half the soup to give it a thicker texture.

Although you can use jarred roasted red peppers in this recipe, I've provided instructions for roasting your own. Try to do this yourself— it's fun, and you'll enjoy the fresh-roasted pepper flavor. You can make a batch of them to use in several different recipes. Simply refrigerate them in a sealed plastic container with 2 Tbsp of white wine vinegar. They'll keep for 1–2 weeks. Even if you are not an anchovy fan, try them in this dressing. Anchovies packed in oil, once opened, can be stored in the refrigerator for 2 months. Since you will probably not go through a can of anchovies in 2 months, an alternative is to use 2 tsp anchovy paste for this dressing.

The artichoke is the bud of a large plant from the thistle family. Fresh artichokes are a true delight, but canned artichokes work just as well for this menu's entree. I would advise against frozen artichoke hearts—they tend to be mushy. This sauce can be used to top chicken, beef, or seafood or poured over rice or a baked potato. Be sure to simmer the sauce for only a short amount of time. Despite what you may have been told, tomato sauces are really best when allowed to simmer only 20 minutes.

Greek for "joy of the mountain," oregano did not make its way to most American dining tables until after World War II. Oregano belongs to the mint family and is related to both thyme and marjoram, but it is stronger than marjoram. Fresh Mediterranean oregano is available in many supermarkets. Choose bright green bunches that have not yellowed. Dried oregano is always available. Oregano works very well with tomato-based dishes and vegetables such as the asparagus and zucchini used here.

Amaretto is an almond-tasting liqueur. A very small amount provides a pleasing flavor to this pudding, but you may omit it if you like. Evaporated skim milk makes this pudding richer without unwanted fat.

Pantry List

olive oil
dry white wine
1 red onion
garlic
1 4-serving-size pkg artificially
  sweetened, nonfat, instant
  chocolate pudding
2 cans evaporated skim milk
Amaretto liqueur
shallots
1 pkg dry green lentils
1 pkg dry red lentils
4 cans low-fat, low-sodium chicken
  broth
balsamic vinegar
1 pkg anchovies
1 can crushed tomatoes
1 pkg sun-dried tomatoes
1 can artichoke hearts
1 box penne pasta
crushed red pepper

Market List

fresh spinach
1 medium red bell pepper
1 medium yellow bell pepper
6 bunches watercress
6 plum tomatoes
Parmesan cheese
rosemary
Italian parsley
1 large portobello mushroom
basil
oregano

1 bunch asparagus
1 zucchini
1 cup raspberries
low-calorie whipped topping

STEP-BY-STEP COUNTDOWN

1 Prepare the first step of the salad recipe.
2 Prepare the dessert and refrigerate.
3 Prepare the first step of the soup recipe.
4 Prepare all the ingredients for the pasta
   and asparagus recipes.
5 Boil the pasta and drain.
6 Finish preparing the salad and refrigerate.
7 Finishing preparing the pasta recipe.
8 Finish preparing the asparagus.
9 Finish preparing the soup and serve.
10 Serve the salad
11 Serve the pasta and asparagus.
12 Serve the dessert.

Light Red and Green Lentil Soup

6 Servings

Serving Size:
1 cup

Exchanges

1 1/2 Starch
1 Very Lean Meat

Ingredients

2 tsp olive oil
1/2 cup minced shallots
1 clove garlic, minced
1/2 cup each red and green dry
      lentils, rinsed
7 cups low-fat, low-sodium chicken
      broth
1 cup fresh spinach leaves, slivered
      and stems removed
Fresh ground pepper
Dash salt (optional)

Preparation—10 minutes

1 Heat the oil in a stockpot over medium-high heat. Add the shallots and saute for 5 minutes. Add the garlic and saute for 2 minutes.
2 Add the lentils and broth. Bring to a boil, lower the heat, and simmer until lentils are tender, about 35–45 minutes.
3 Divide the spinach leaves among 6 individual soup bowls. Pour the soup over the spinach, add pepper and salt, and serve.

Calories	160	
Calories from Fat	41	
Total Fat	5	g
Saturated Fat	1	g
Cholesterol	0	mg
Sodium	136	mg
Carbohydrate	23	g
Dietary Fiber	10	g
Sugars	4	g
Protein	13	g

Tomato and Roasted Pepper Salad

6 Servings

Serving Size:
1 cup watercress
1/2 cup vegetables

Exchanges

2 Vegetable
1/2 Fat

Ingredients

1 each medium red and yellow bell peppers
6 cups watercress
6 medium plum tomatoes, thinly sliced
1/3 cup balsamic vinegar
2 anchovy filets, drained of oil and mashed
1 Tbsp Parmesan cheese
2 tsp olive oil
1 Tbsp finely minced red onion
2 cloves garlic, finely minced
Fresh ground pepper
Dash salt (optional)
1/2 cup finely minced Italian parsley
6 rosemary sprigs

Calories	58
Calories from Fat	20
Total Fat	2 g
Saturated Fat	0 g
Cholesterol	2 mg
Sodium	90 mg
Carbohydrate	9 g
Dietary Fiber	2 g
Sugars	5 g
Protein	3 g

Preparation—15 minutes

1 Place the bell peppers on a broiler pan and broil 3–4 inches from the heat source until the skin is blackened. Or, if you have a gas stove, spear each pepper with a meat fork (or hold with tongs) and roast over a high flame, turning, until the peppers are blackened. Place the blackened peppers into a zippered plastic bag, seal, and let cool.
2 When the peppers are cool, rub off the skin with your fingertips. Discard the seeds and membrane. Slice each pepper into thin strips. Combine the yellow and red bell peppers.
3 Place a cup of watercress on individual plates. Place a few slices of tomatoes on the watercress, then a spoonful of roasted peppers.
4 Combine the remaining ingredients except the rosemary and parsley. Drizzle some dressing over each salad.
5 To serve, sprinkle each salad with parsley and spear a rosemary sprig inside the mound of peppers so it looks like a feather.

Pasta with Artichokes and Basil

6 Servings

Serving Size:
1 cup pasta
1/2 cup sauce

Exchanges

3 Starch
2 Vegetable
1/2 Monounsaturated Fat

Ingredients

2 Tbsp olive oil
1/4 cup dry white wine
3 cloves garlic, minced
1/2 cup minced red onion
1 cup diced portobello mushroom
1 1/2 cups crushed tomatoes
1 cup sliced rehydrated sun-dried
    tomatoes
1 cup artichoke hearts, halved
    (packed in water and drained)
1/4 cup slivered basil leaves
1 tsp minced oregano
Fresh ground pepper
1/4 tsp crushed red pepper
6 cups cooked penne or rigatoni
    pasta

Preparation—25 minutes

1 Heat the oil and wine in a skillet over medium-high heat. Add the garlic and onion and saute for 4 minutes. Add the portobello mushroom and saute for 4 minutes. Add the tomatoes.
2 Bring the mixture to a boil, lower the heat, and simmer for 5–6 minutes. Add the artichokes and simmer for 5 minutes. Add the basil, oregano, pepper, and crushed red pepper. Simmer for 2 minutes.
3 Toss the pasta with the sauce and serve.

Calories	312
Calories from Fat	55
Total Fat	6 g
Saturated Fat	1 g
Cholesterol	0 mg
Sodium	375 mg
Carbohydrate	54 g
Dietary Fiber	5 g
Sugars	7 g
Protein	10 g

Asparagus and Zucchini in Garlic

6 Servings

Serving Size:
1/2 cup

Exchanges

1 Vegetable

Ingredients

1 tsp olive oil
1/4 cup dry white wine
4 cloves garlic, minced
1 1/2 cups asparagus,
     diagonally sliced
1 1/2 cups zucchini, sliced
1 tsp minced oregano
Fresh ground pepper
Dash salt (optional)

Preparation—10 minutes

1 Heat the oil and wine in a skillet over medium-high heat. Add the garlic and saute for 1 minute.
2 Add the asparagus and zucchini and saute for 5 minutes. Cover and steam for 4 minutes.
3 Add the seasonings and serve.

Calories	29
Calories from Fat	8
Total Fat	1 g
Saturated Fat	0 g
Cholesterol	0 mg
Sodium	6 mg
Carbohydrate	4 g
Dietary Fiber	1 g
Sugars	2 g
Protein	1 g

❧ WHY DON'T YOU . . .

*In summer, buy plastic
sunglasses and attach a dinner
placecard to the glasses.*

Quick Amaretto Mousse

6 Servings

Serving Size:
1/2 cup

Exchanges

1 1/2 Carbohydrate

Ingredients

1 4-serving-size pkg artificially
   sweetened, nonfat, instant
   chocolate pudding mix
2 cups evaporated skim milk
1 Tbsp Amaretto liqueur
1/2 cup low-calorie whipped
   topping
1 cup fresh raspberries

Preparation—5 minutes

1 Prepare the pudding according to package
directions using the evaporated skim milk. Add the
Amaretto.
2 Let the pudding set for 10 minutes. Fold in the
whipped topping.
3 Alternate layers of raspberries and mousse in
parfait glasses, ending with raspberries, and serve.

Calories	123	
Calories from Fat	9	
Total Fat	1	g
Saturated Fat	1	g
Cholesterol	3	mg
Sodium	173	mg
Carbohydrate	20	g
Dietary Fiber	2	g
Sugars	11	g
Protein	7	g

Smoked Turkey Salad

Chicken, Greens, and Noodle Soup
Bulgur Wheat Salad with Smoked Turkey
Vegetable Plate
Savory Herb Muffins
Hot Nut Sundae

MENU TALK

The secret to this quick, easy-to-make soup is adding previously cooked chicken to a broth base and vegetables. Spinach boosts the nutrition content, as would escarole, chard, or kale. Chicken soup should be seasoned mildly. You can use leftover cubed turkey instead of chicken, if available, or omit the chicken entirely and substitute 1 cup canned garbanzo or kidney beans instead.

Bulgur wheat is a staple of Middle Eastern cuisine. It consists of wheat that has been steamed, dried, and crushed. The beauty of bulgur wheat lies in its cooking method. All you need to do is pour boiling water or broth over the grains and set it aside for 45–60 minutes. Bulgur wheat can be found in all supermarkets, but you can use cooked rice or couscous in this salad. Bulgur wheat also makes a great substitute for ground beef in chili. Just add the bulgur wheat dry to the liquid and cook the chili until the bulgur wheat is soft.

Prepare the vegetables and serve them with dinner if you like. Snacking on raw vegetables is good for you, because raw vegetables usually contain more vitamins and fiber than cooked ones. Be sure to include at least one or two servings of raw vegetables a day. If you prefer cooked vegetables, try to just blanch or very lightly steam them to preserve the nutrients. The creamy dressing that accompanies these vegetables is great over leafy green salads as well.

Savory is an herb closely related to the mint family. There are two varieties, summer and winter. Summer savory is slighter milder, but both types are strong and should be used gingerly. Savory tastes like a cross between thyme and mint. Either dried or fresh savory will work for this chewy muffin.

End this menu with everyone's favorite: an ice-cream sundae! Have your guests scoop out their favorite flavor of nonfat frozen yogurt and a spoonful of warm nut topping. This recipe is an adaptation of a similar one by Nikki and David Goldbeck.

Pantry List

4 cans low-fat, low-sodium chicken broth
1 onion
dried thyme
black peppercorns
pure maple syrup
1 box penne pasta
1 small pkg chopped walnuts
1 pkg bulgur wheat
rice vinegar
lite soy sauce
sugar
dry sherry
garlic
sesame oil
unbleached white flour
baking powder
1 can evaporated skim milk
savory

Market List

6 oz boneless, skinless chicken breasts
1 1/2 lb smoked turkey breasts
3 carrots
celery
thyme
parsley
1/2 lb fresh spinach
1 cucumber
green onions
1 red bell pepper
1 bag baby carrots
1 zucchini

1 broccoli head
1 small cauliflower
1 carton low-fat sour cream
1 small pkg low-fat cream cheese
1 small pkg Roquefort cheese
buttermilk
chives
1 egg
low-calorie margarine
fat-free, sugar-free frozen yogurt

STEP-BY-STEP COUNTDOWN

1 Prepare the bulgur wheat and let stand 1 hour.
2 Prepare the rest of the salad ingredients and set aside.
3 Prepare the salad dressing and set aside.
4 Prepare steps 1 and 2 of the soup recipe.
5 Prepare the muffins and bake.
6 Prepare the vegetable plate and dressing.
7 Finish preparing the salad.
8 Remove the muffins from the oven.
9 Prepare the first step of the dessert recipe and leave in the skillet.
10 Finish preparing the soup and serve.
11 Serve the salad, vegetable plate, and muffins.
12 Finish preparing the dessert and serve.

Chicken, Greens, and Noodle Soup

6 Servings

Serving Size:
1 cup

Exchanges

1 Starch
1 Very Lean Meat
1/2 Fat

Ingredients

6 cups low-fat, low-sodium
   chicken broth
1 carrot, diced
1/2 cup diced onion
1/2 cup sliced celery
2 sprigs thyme
3 sprigs parsley
3 black peppercorns
2 cloves garlic
6 oz cooked, cubed chicken
1 cup cooked penne pasta
1 1/2 cups spinach leaves, torn,
   stems removed
Fresh ground pepper
Dash salt (optional)

Preparation—15 minutes

1 Heat the broth with the carrot, onion, and celery in a stockpot over medium heat for 10 minutes.
2 Bundle together the thyme, parsley, peppercorns, and garlic in a piece of cheesecloth. Bring the soup to a boil, lower the heat to simmer, and cook for 20 minutes.
3 Add the chicken, pasta, and spinach and cook for 5 minutes. Remove the cheesecloth, add pepper and salt, and serve.

Calories	133
Calories from Fat	42
Total Fat	5 g
Saturated Fat	1 g
Cholesterol	26 mg
Sodium	176 mg
Carbohydrate	13 g
Dietary Fiber	2 g
Sugars	3 g
Protein	14 g

Bulgur Wheat Salad with Smoked Turkey*

6 Servings

Serving Size:
1 cup

Exchanges

1 Starch
1 Vegetable
3 Very Lean Meat

Ingredients

2 cups boiling low-fat, low-sodium
  chicken broth
1 cup dry bulgur wheat
2 green onions, minced
2 medium carrots, peeled and sliced
1/2 cup diced cucumber
2 Tbsp minced parsley
1 1/2 lb smoked turkey breasts,
  cubed (or use cooked, cubed
  fresh turkey)
1/2 cup rice vinegar
1 Tbsp lite soy sauce
1 tsp sugar
1 Tbsp dry sherry
2 cloves garlic, minced
1 tsp sesame oil

Preparation—20 minutes

1 Pour boiling broth over the bulgur wheat into a heatproof bowl and let stand for 1 hour. Drain any excess liquid. Combine the bulgur wheat with the green onions, carrots, cucumber, parsley, and cubed turkey.
2 In a blender or food processor, process the remaining ingredients, pour over the salad, and serve.

Calories	223
Calories from Fat	28
Total Fat	3 g
Saturated Fat	1 g
Cholesterol	52 mg
Sodium	1512 mg
Carbohydrate	25 g
Dietary Fiber	6 g
Sugars	5 g
Protein	27 g

* This recipe is extremely high in sodium!

Vegetable Plate

6 Servings

Serving Size:
1/2 cup

Exchanges

2 Vegetable

Ingredients

1 cup sliced red bell peppers
1/2 cup baby carrots
1/2 cup sliced zucchini
1/2 cup broccoli florets
1/2 cup cauliflower florets
1/2 cup low-fat sour cream
1/4 cup low-fat cream cheese
1 Tbsp Roquefort cheese
1 Tbsp nonfat buttermilk
1 Tbsp minced chives
1 clove garlic, finely minced
1 Tbsp minced parsley

Preparation—20 minutes

1 Arrange the vegetables decoratively on a platter.
2 Whip together the remaining ingredients in a food processor, or use electric beaters. Put the dip in a small bowl in the center of the platter and serve.

Calories	45
Calories from Fat	4
Total Fat	0 g
Saturated Fat	0 g
Cholesterol	2 mg
Sodium	127 mg
Carbohydrate	6 g
Dietary Fiber	1 g
Sugars	4 g
Protein	4 g

Savory Herb Muffins

6 Servings

Serving Size:
1 muffin

Exchanges

1 1/2 Starch

Ingredients

2 cups unbleached white flour
1/4 cup sugar
1 Tbsp baking powder
1 egg, beaten
1 cup evaporated skim milk
1/4 cup low-calorie
    margarine, melted
1/4 tsp savory
1/2 tsp dried thyme
1/4 tsp salt

Preparation—30 minutes

1 Preheat the oven to 425 degrees. Combine the flour, sugar, and baking powder in a small bowl.
2 Combine the remaining ingredients in a medium bowl. Add the dry ingredients slowly to the medium bowl, mixing until blended after each addition. Do not overbeat.
3 Fill nonstick muffin cups 2/3 full and bake for 20–25 minutes. Let cool for 10 minutes in the pan. Turn out to completely cool before serving.

Calories	133
Calories from Fat	23
Total Fat	3 g
Saturated Fat	1 g
Cholesterol	18 mg
Sodium	199 mg
Carbohydrate	23 g
Dietary Fiber	1 g
Sugars	6 g
Protein	4 g

Hot Walnut Sundae

6 Servings

Serving Size:
1/3 cup frozen
    yogurt
1 Tbsp topping

Exchanges

1 Carbohydrate
1 1/2 Polyunsatur-
    ated Fat

Ingredients

2 Tbsp low-calorie margarine
1/2 cup chopped walnuts
2 Tbsp pure maple syrup
1 1/2 Tbsp water
2 cups artificially sweetened, nonfat
    frozen yogurt (flavor of choice)

Preparation—10 minutes

1 Melt the margarine in a skillet. Add the nuts
and toast over low heat. Add the syrup and water
and toss with the nuts to coat.
2 Top each portion of frozen yogurt with warm
nuts and serve.

Calories	158
Calories from Fat	72
Total Fat	8 g
Saturated Fat	1 g
Cholesterol	0 mg
Sodium	75 mg
Carbohydrate	18 g
Dietary Fiber	1 g
Sugars	7 g
Protein	4 g

❖ ❖ ❖ ❖ ❖ ❖ ❖

☞ WHY DON'T YOU . . .

*Set up a picnic indoors. Instead
of eating at the table, place a
large blanket on the floor and
serve picnic style, even if it's
raining or snowing outside!*

Southern Shrimp Gumbo

Southern Shrimp Gumbo
Buttermilk Cornbread Muffins
Carrot Coleslaw
Green Beans with White Wine and Garlic Vinaigrette
Clove-Scented Pears

MENU TALK

Gumbo is a thick, stewlike mixture made with okra and many different ingredients. Okra is a small green vegetable with ridged skin. You will always find okra on supermarket shelves in the South, but for the rest of the country, it is best purchased from May to October. Okra serves to thicken the gumbo. I think fresh okra is best, but frozen or canned will also work. File powder is made from ground, dried leaves of the sassafras tree. It is added after food has been cooked and removed from the heat. You can find file powder in most supermarkets.

The simplicity of a good coleslaw suits this hearty soup dinner. A food processor is most useful for large jobs, such as shredding carrots and cabbage for coleslaw. You can purchase prepared slaw mixtures from the supermarket, but the nutrient content will be lower. Prepackaged mixes are cut hours, if not days, before you purchase them and packaged in clear bags that are exposed to light. Prolonged exposure to light can decrease the vitamin and mineral content of fresh vegetables. Cabbage is part of the cruciferous, cancer-fighting family. A head of cabbage will last in the refrigerator for 1–2 weeks.

Turn this menu's green beans into a traditional three-bean salad by adding canned kidney and garbanzo beans. Or blanch any other vegetable, such as carrots, broccoli, zucchini, or peppers, and use the same tasty white wine vinaigrette.

387

I love sweet cornbread, and this recipe is my favorite. Buttermilk adds moistness to the batter, while the honey provides a delicious , more flavorful sweetness. Bake this cornbread in an iron skillet or corn stick molds. If you make muffins, be sure to blend the batter until the ingredients are just combined. Prolonged mixing will result in a tough cornbread.

Cloves start out as pinkish flower buds from the evergreen clove plant. They are dried in the sun and turn a reddish brown. Cloves are used primarily in baking, but try them in a beef stew or homemade gravies. I purchase whole cloves and grind them myself in an electric coffee grinder for about 30 seconds. There is nothing like the aroma of freshly ground cloves!

Pantry List

1 yellow onion
2 cans low-fat, low-sodium chicken
 broth
1 can diced tomatoes
Worcestershire sauce
bay leaf
hot pepper sauce
1 pkg yellow cornmeal
unbleached white flour
baking powder
baking soda
honey
canola oil
1 shallot
garlic
white wine vinegar
olive oil
lite mayonnaise
sugar
whole cloves
brown rice
gumbo file

Market List

1 lb boneless, skinless chicken
 breasts or 1 lb medium shrimp,
 peeled and deveined
1 green bell pepper
1 bunch celery
1/4 lb fresh okra
1 small pkg frozen chopped spinach
2 eggs
1 carton low-fat buttermilk
1 lb green beans

fresh lemon juice
2 large carrots
1 small head green cabbage
1/2 head red cabbage
skim milk
6 pears

STEP-BY-STEP COUNTDOWN

1 Prepare the coleslaw and refrigerate.
2 Prepare the gumbo and simmer.
3 Prepare the cornbread and bake.
4 Prepare the dessert and turn off the heat
 when finished.
5 Prepare the green beans and keep at
 room temperature.
6 Serve the soup, cornbread, coleslaw, and
 green beans.
7 Serve the dessert hot or at room temperature.

Southern Shrimp Gumbo

6 Servings

Serving Size:
1 cup

Exchanges

1 Starch
1 Vegetable
2 Very Lean Meat
1 Fat

Ingredients

1 Tbsp canola oil
1 medium onion, diced
1/4 cup diced green bell pepper
2 stalks celery, diced
4 cups low-fat, low-sodium chicken
    broth
2 cups diced canned tomatoes,
    undrained
1/2 cup brown rice, rinsed
1 cup sliced fresh okra
1/2 cup chopped frozen spinach,
    thawed and drained
2 cups cooked diced chicken or
    shrimp
2 tsp Worcestershire sauce
1 bay leaf
Hot pepper sauce to taste
1 tsp gumbo file powder

Preparation—20 minutes

1 Heat the oil in a stockpot over medium-high heat. Add the onion and saute for 5 minutes.
2 Add the remaining ingredients and simmer until the rice is tender, about 40 minutes.
3 Add the hot pepper sauce to taste. Add in the file powder just before serving.

Calories	225
Calories from Fat	73
Total Fat	8 g
Saturated Fat	2 g
Cholesterol	42 mg
Sodium	289 mg
Carbohydrate	22 g
Dietary Fiber	3 g
Sugars	5 g
Protein	19 g

Buttermilk Cornbread Muffins

6 Servings

Serving Size:
1 muffin

Exchanges

1 1/2 Starch
1/2 Monounsatur-
ated Fat

Ingredients

1 cup yellow cornmeal
1 cup unbleached white flour
2 tsp baking powder
1 tsp baking soda
2 eggs, beaten
3/4 cup low-fat buttermilk
1/4 cup honey
2 Tbsp canola oil

Preparation—10 minutes

1 Preheat the oven to 375 degrees. Combine the cornmeal, flour, baking powder, and baking soda in a large bowl.
2 Combine the remaining ingredients and add to the dry ingredients. Mix until blended. Pour into nonstick muffin cups and bake until golden, about 25 minutes. Remove from the tins and let cool.

Calories	142
Calories from Fat	32
Total Fat	4 g
Saturated Fat	1 g
Cholesterol	36 mg
Sodium	193 mg
Carbohydrate	24 g
Dietary Fiber	1 g
Sugars	7 g
Protein	4 g

Carrot Coleslaw

6 Servings

Serving Size:
1/2 cup

Exchanges

1 Vegetable

Ingredients

2 medium carrots, shredded
1 cup shredded green cabbage
1/2 cup shredded red cabbage
1/2 cup lite mayonnaise
1 Tbsp skim milk
1 Tbsp lemon juice
1/2 tsp sugar
Fresh ground pepper
Dash salt (optional)

Preparation—20 minutes

Combine the vegetables together in a large bowl. Whisk together the remaining ingredients and pour over the salad. Refrigerate for 1 hour before serving.

Calories	37
Calories from Fat	1
Total Fat	0 g
Saturated Fat	0 g
Cholesterol	0 mg
Sodium	157 mg
Carbohydrate	8 g
Dietary Fiber	1 g
Sugars	5 g
Protein	1 g

Green Beans with White Wine and Garlic Vinaigrette

6 Servings

Serving Size:
1/2 cup

Exchanges

1 Vegetable

Ingredients

3 cups fresh green beans, trimmed
2 Tbsp finely minced shallots
2 cloves garlic, minced
1/4 cup white wine vinegar
2 tsp olive oil
1 Tbsp lemon juice
Fresh ground pepper
Dash salt (optional)

Preparation—10 minutes

1 Blanch the green beans in boiling water for 2 minutes and drain. Plunge them into cold water and drain again.
2 Whisk together the remaining ingredients and add to the green beans. Toss and serve.

Calories	38
Calories from Fat	15
Total Fat	2 g
Saturated Fat	0 g
Cholesterol	0 mg
Sodium	3 mg
Carbohydrate	6 g
Dietary Fiber	2 g
Sugars	2 g
Protein	1 g

OILS

Olive Oil

Choose domestic or imported olive oil. Try to purchase cold-pressed oils; this process uses less heat and no chemicals. The result is a very clean-tasting oil. The fruitiest of the olive oils is extra virgin olive oil. This oil ranges in color from straw to deep green. I like a very green olive oil; it has deep flavor and you use less. Extra virgin olive oils have a low acid level, making them the tastiest. Virgin olive oil has a higher level of acidity. Fine olive oil is a blend of extra virgin and virgin. Light olive oil is just a lighter-colored and lighter-tasting olive oil; it is not any lower in fat than extra virgin olive oils. It has very little authentic flavor. Olive oil is best in cold food preparation and light sauteing.

Clove-Scented Pears

6 Servings

Serving Size:
1 medium pear

Exchanges

1 1/2 Fruit

Ingredients

2 Tbsp sugar
1 cup water
4 whole cloves
6 medium pears, sliced

Preparation—5 minutes

In a saucepan, combine the sugar, water, and cloves and bring to a boil. Add the pears, lower the heat, and simmer until the pears are soft, about 20 minutes. Add more water if necessary.

Calories	100
Calories from Fat	5
Total Fat	1 g
Saturated Fat	0 g
Cholesterol	0 g
Sodium	0 mg
Carbohydrate	26 g
Dietary Fiber	3 g
Sugars	22 g
Protein	1 g

 WHY DON'T YOU . . .

In spring, use individual seed packets for vegetables or flowers, attach a dinner placecard to the packet, and encourage guests to take the seeds home and plant them.

Pasta Pie

Italian Vegetable Antipasto
Pasta Pie
Chilled Green Beans and Carrot Slivers
Basil and Tomato Bread
Grapes with Mint

MENU TALK

Antipasto literally means before the pasta. Antipasto can consist of meats, cheeses, pickled foods, and vegetables. This menu begins with a healthy antipasto that can be left on the table for people to graze on all through dinner. The dressing can also be used as a marinade or tossed with a leafy green salad. To serve the antipasto as a main meal, add a low-fat bean salad and lean turkey slices. Serve with fresh Italian bread and dessert.

This pasta pie frittata is appropriate to serve for brunch or a weekday dinner. A frittata is a flat, rather than folded, Italian omelet. The frittata is flipped or can be finished under a broiler and is served in wedges like a pie. This recipe makes good use of any leftover pasta you might have in your refrigerator. You can serve the frittata in the same attractive iron skillet you used to cook it. Almost anything can go into a frittata—use your imagination! If you prefer, you can make this frittata with all egg whites.

The carrot is a member of the parsley family. I think the best-tasting carrots are thin, long, and sold in bunches with their tops on. Avoid carrots with splits or that are too soft. Store your carrots in a plastic bag in the refrigerator. Carrots that have become a little limp can be revived in a bowl of ice water.

Basil, a member of the mint family, was called the royal herb by the ancient Greeks. Basil is an essential ingredient in Italian cooking, but it should not be allowed to cook for a long time in foods. The delicate, sweet taste is destroyed by prolonged heat. It is best to add basil toward the end of preparing a tomato sauce, for example. Basil grows best in the summer, but with good sunshine, basil can be grown in a pot in the windowsill during the winter. If you want to grow your own herbs, start with basil—it grows like wildfire! Be aware that basil spoils quickly. To preserve it best, place the leaves, stem side down, in a glass of water and place a plastic bag on top. Put the glass in the refrigerator and change the water every other day. The basil should last for several days.

Grapes are grown throughout the world. Green and red grapes are equally delicious. When purchasing green grapes, look for smooth skins with a light green color. Red grapes should have no sign of green. Store grapes unwashed in a plastic bag in the refrigerator.

There are many varieties of mint. We are most familiar with peppermint and spearmint. The former has a stronger flavor and the latter is more mild. Mint is best purchased in the summer, but it is available all year—or grow your own. Try chewing on a piece of mint after a meal to refresh your palate.

Pantry List

1 can artichoke hearts
honey
balsamic vinegar
olive oil
anchovies
capers
garlic
tomato paste
1 red onion
1 box spaghetti
garlic powder
dried basil
dried oregano
red wine vinegar
crushed red pepper
3 oz Italian bread

Market List

1 bunch asparagus
1 bunch broccoli
1 each red, green, and yellow bell
   peppers
1 zucchini
4 plum tomatoes
2 tomatoes
1 carton egg substitutes
green onions
1/2 lb green beans
2 carrots
low-calorie margarine
basil
1 bunch green grapes
mint
lemon juice

Italian Vegetable Antipasto

6 Servings

Serving Size:
1 cup
1 Tbsp dressing

Exchanges

2 Vegetable
1/2 Monounsaturated Fat

Ingredients

1/2 cup halved canned artichoke
    hearts, drained and rinsed
4 plum tomatoes, cut into thirds
12 asparagus spears
1 cup broccoli florets
1/2 each red and yellow bell
    peppers, julienned
1 small zucchini, cut into chunks
1/2 cup balsamic vinegar
1 Tbsp olive oil
2 anchovies, well drained
1 tsp capers
2 tsp minced garlic
2 tsp tomato paste
Fresh ground pepper
Dash salt (optional)

Preparation—15 minutes

1 Place a small dip bowl in the center of a large platter. Arrange the artichokes and tomatoes on the platter in spoke fashion around the dip bowl.
2 Blanch the asparagus spears and broccoli for 2 minutes in a pot of boiling water. Drain, plunge into ice water, and drain again. Arrange the asparagus, broccoli, bell peppers, and zucchini on the platter in rows around the dip bowl, continuing the spoke pattern.
3 Combine the remaining ingredients in a blender and process for 1 minute. Pour into the dip bowl in the center of the platter. Serve with toothpicks.

Calories	68	
Calories from Fat	26	
Total Fat	3	g
Saturated Fat	0	g
Cholesterol	1	mg
Sodium	133	mg
Carbohydrate	10	g
Dietary Fiber	3	g
Sugars	5	g
Protein	3	g

Pasta Pie

6 Servings

Serving Size:
1/6 recipe

Exchanges

1 Starch
1 Vegetable
1 Very Lean Meat

Ingredients

2 tsp olive oil
1/2 cup diced red onion
2 Tbsp each minced red and green
   bell pepper
12 egg substitutes (or 4 eggs,
   beaten, and 6 egg whites)
1 1/2 cups cooked broken spaghetti,
   linguine, or fettucine
2 tsp garlic powder
2 tsp dried basil
1 tsp dried oregano
2 medium tomatoes
2 Tbsp minced green onions

Preparation—15 minutes

1 Heat the oil in a large oven-proof nonstick skillet over medium heat. Add the onion and saute for 5 minutes. Add the bell peppers and saute for 5 minutes.
2 Mix together the egg substitute, pasta, and dried seasonings and pour over the onions and peppers. Let the mixture cook for 6–7 minutes, lifting to allow the top uncooked portion to flow to the bottom. Cook a little longer if you need to.
3 Slice the tomatoes and place on top of the eggs in a circular pattern. Sprinkle with green onions.
4 Set the oven to broil. Place the pan 6–7 inches from the heat source. Broil the frittata until the top is browned (watch carefully!) and the eggs are set, about 5 minutes. Cut into wedges and serve.

Calories	154
Calories from Fat	18
Total Fat	2 g
Saturated Fat	0 g
Cholesterol	0 mg
Sodium	226 mg
Carbohydrate	18 g
Dietary Fiber	2 g
Sugars	5 g
Protein	15 g

Chilled Green Beans and Carrot Slivers

6 Servings

Serving Size:
1/2 cup

Exchanges

1/2 Carbohydrate
1 Vegetable

Ingredients

1/3 cup red wine vinegar
2 Tbsp honey
1/2 tsp crushed red pepper
2 cloves garlic, minced
1 1/2 cups trimmed green beans
1 1/2 cups slivered carrots

Preparation—15 minutes

1   In a small bowl or measuring cup, combine the vinegar, honey, red pepper, and garlic. Let the dressing stand for 1 hour.
2   Blanch the green beans and carrots for 2 minutes in a pot of boiling water. Drain, plunge into ice water, and drain again. Mix the green beans and carrots with the dressing and marinate for 1 hour before serving.

Calories	47
Calories from Fat	1
Total Fat	0 g
Saturated Fat	0 g
Cholesterol	0 mg
Sodium	11 mg
Carbohydrate	12 g
Dietary Fiber	2 g
Sugars	9 g
Protein	1 g

Basil and Tomato Bread

6 Servings

Serving Size:
1/2 oz

Exchanges

1/2 Starch
1/2 Fat

Ingredients

2 Tbsp finely minced seeded tomato
2 cloves garlic, finely minced
1 tsp capers
1 tsp balsamic vinegar
2 Tbsp low-calorie margarine
1 Tbsp minced basil
Fresh ground pepper
Dash salt (optional)
3 oz Italian bread, sliced

Preparation—15 minutes

1 Preheat the oven to 400 degrees. Mix together all ingredients except the bread. Spread the mixture evenly on the bread slices.
2 Bake until the bread is toasted, about 2–3 minutes.

Calories	56
Calories from Fat	21
Total Fat	2 g
Saturated Fat	0 g
Cholesterol	0 mg
Sodium	126 mg
Carbohydrate	7 g
Dietary Fiber	0 g
Sugars	1 g
Protein	1 g

OILS

Peanut Oil

Peanut oil's primary use is in stir-frying because of its high smoking point. Try Chinese peanut oil; it has a nuttier taste than American peanut oil. Keep peanut oil refrigerated to prevent it from becoming rancid.

Grapes with Mint

6 Servings

Serving Size:
1/2 cup

Exchanges

1 Fruit

Ingredients

3 cups halved seedless green grapes
1 Tbsp honey
2 Tbsp lemon juice
1 Tbsp minced mint

Preparation—10 minutes

Combine all ingredients. Refrigerate for 1 hour before serving.

Calories	69
Calories from Fat	4
Total Fat	0 g
Saturated Fat	0 g
Cholesterol	0 mg
Sodium	3 mg
Carbohydrate	17 g
Dietary Fiber	1 g
Sugars	15 g
Protein	1 g

❖ ❖ ❖ ❖ ❖ ❖

➥ WHY DON'T YOU . . .

Keep track of all your family's favorites on paper or a computer. This way you can look back to the recipes you really liked and make them again. Any failures? You'll know not to repeat them!

❖ ❖ ❖
Banana Bread Brunch

Very Berry Drink
Poppyseed Fruit Salad
Baked Banana Bread French Toast
Spicy Pork Sausages
Orange Syrup

MENU TALK

Start the day off right with an eye-opening, vitamin C-rich drink. Raspberries and strawberries make great, colorful drinks. I think raspberries have the best flavor. The red variety is the most common, but black and golden raspberries are also available. Look for berries that have no mold and look bright. Handle the berries very carefully—they are soft and fragile. Rinse them lightly. Strawberries have grown wild for centuries in both America and Europe. Generally, the smaller berries are more flavorful. Although strawberries are available all year in a few parts of the United States, I think it is best to purchase them from April through June. Or plan a berry-picking day and enjoy the fresh air!

Poppy seeds are the dried, bluish gray seeds of the poppy plant. In India, the poppy seeds are yellow; in Turkey, they are brown. We are most familiar with the gray ones used as a topping for bagels, baked goods, and tossed into salads. Store poppy seeds in an airtight container in the refrigerator for about six months. Gala apples are crisp and sweet. Serve them unpeeled—their bright red and yellow streaks make an attractive addition to fruit salads. Make fruit salad just before you plan to serve it.

See color photo after p. 368.

Have the butcher cut fresh pork tenderloin to ensure a lean product. The loin comes from the area on both sides of the backbone from the shoulder to the leg. Cook pork to a temperature between 155 and 165 degrees. Make sure you thoroughly wash your hands and all utensils and cutting boards after they have been in contact with raw pork.

French toast or, as the French call it, pain perdu (lost bread) is, after many years, the most popular way to use up stale bread. This is a unique recipe incorporating fresh-baked, then dried, banana bread. The bread can dry out for 1–3 days. This French toast is baked instead of fried, which lowers the fat content. This casserole-style dish frees you up to concentrate on other parts of the menu or on your guests! It can stay in the oven for a bit if your guests are late or your family wants to sleep in.

Pantry List

almond extract
honey
cinnamon
canola oil
poppy seeds
raisins
fennel seeds
crushed red pepper
1 red onion
garlic
unbleached white flour
baking powder
baking soda
cinnamon
nutmeg
unsweetened applesauce
vanilla
1 can evaporated skim milk

Market List

1 lb ground pork tenderloin
1 pint raspberries or strawberries
skim milk
2 Gala apples
4 bananas
1 bunch green grapes
orange juice
lemon juice
cilantro
parsley
2 eggs
1 carton egg substitute
butter
low-calorie margarine

Very Berry Drink

6 Servings

Serving Size:
1 cup

Exchanges

1 Carbohydrate

Ingredients

2 cups fresh raspberries,
strawberries, or a combination
of the two
2 cups cold skim milk
1 tsp almond extract
1 Tbsp honey
1 tsp cinnamon
5 large ice cubes

Preparation—5 minutes

Combine all ingredients in a blender until smooth. To serve, pour from a tall pitcher into chilled glasses.

Calories	57
Calories from Fat	3
Total Fat	0 g
Saturated Fat	0 g
Cholesterol	1 mg
Sodium	42 mg
Carbohydrate	11 g
Dietary Fiber	2 g
Sugars	9 g
Protein	3 g

❖ ❖ ❖ ❖ ❖ ❖

 SPEAKING OF SPICES

Paprika

Paprika can be used as a garnish and as a seasoning. The Hungarian variety is considered the finest. Paprika is made by grinding sweet red pepper pods. California paprika is more mild than Hungarian. Both varieties are found in some supermarkets and specialty stores. Look for paprika packaged in a tin.

Poppyseed Fruit Salad

6 Servings

Serving Size:
1/2 cup

Exchanges

2 Fruit
1 Monounsaturated
  Fat

Ingredients

2 Gala apples, chopped (or use
   red delicious)
2 bananas, sliced
1 cup green grapes
2 Tbsp raisins
2 Tbsp honey
2 Tbsp canola oil
1/3 cup orange juice
1 Tbsp poppy seeds
1 tsp lemon juice

Preparation—10 minutes

Combine the apples, bananas, grapes, and raisins in
a serving bowl. Whisk together the remaining
ingredients and pour over the fruit. Refrigerate for
1–2 hours before serving.

Calories	171
Calories from Fat	48
Total Fat	5 g
Saturated Fat	1 g
Cholesterol	0 mg
Sodium	2 mg
Carbohydrate	33 g
Dietary Fiber	3 g
Sugars	27 g
Protein	1 g

Baked Banana Bread French Toast

6 Servings

Serving Size:
1 1-inch slice

Exchanges

4 Carbohydrate
1/2 Fat

Ingredients

2   cups unbleached white flour
2   tsp baking powder
1/2 tsp baking soda
1   tsp cinnamon
1/2 tsp nutmeg
2   eggs, beaten
1/2 cup unsweetened applesauce
1   Tbsp canola oil
1/4 cup honey
2   bananas, ripe and mashed
2   tsp vanilla
4   egg substitutes
1/2 cup evaporated skim milk
2   tsp cinnamon
2   tsp butter

Preparation—30 minutes

1   Preheat the oven to 350 degrees. Combine the flour, baking powder, baking soda, cinnamon, and nutmeg in a medium bowl.

2   Mix together the eggs, applesauce, and oil in a large bowl and beat well. Add the honey, bananas, and vanilla. Add the flour mixture slowly to the banana mixture. Mix well, but do not overbeat. Pour the mixture into a nonstick loaf pan. Bake until a toothpick inserted in the center comes out clean, about 35–45 minutes.

3   Let the banana bread cool for 10 minutes in the pan. Remove the bread from the pan and let it cool completely, then slice into 1-inch thick slices. Let the banana bread dry out overnight.

4   The next day, beat together the egg substitute, milk, and cinnamon. Place the banana bread slices into a casserole dish. Pour the egg mixture over the banana bread slices and place in the refrigerator for several hours.

5   Dot the banana bread with the butter. Bake the banana bread slices until golden brown, about 15–17 minutes.

Calories	347
Calories from Fat	54
Total Fat	6 g
Saturated Fat	2 g
Cholesterol	75 mg
Sodium	361 mg
Carbohydrate	61 g
Dietary Fiber	2 g
Sugars	24 g
Protein	13 g

Spicy Pork Sausages

6 Servings

Serving Size:
2 oz

Exchanges

2 Lean Meat

Ingredients

1 lb lean ground pork tenderloin
1/4 cup minced cilantro
1 tsp fennel seeds
2 tsp crushed red pepper
2 cloves garlic, minced
2 tsp minced parsley
2 tsp minced red onion

Preparation—10 minutes

1 Preheat the oven to 350 degrees. Combine all ingredients in a food processor. Refrigerate overnight.
2 The next day, form into patties. Bake on a nonstick cookie sheet until the pork is cooked through, about 20 minutes.

Calories	102
Calories from Fat	27
Total Fat	3 g
Saturated Fat	0 g
Cholesterol	47 mg
Sodium	35 mg
Carbohydrate	1 g
Dietary Fiber	0 g
Sugars	0 g
Protein	17 g

Orange Syrup

6 Servings

Serving Size:
1 oz

Exchanges

1/2 Other
Carbohydrate

Ingredients

1/2 cup orange juice
2 Tbsp sugar
1 Tbsp low-calorie margarine
2 tsp cornstarch or arrowroot powder

Preparation—5 minutes

Combine all ingredients in a saucepan and cook over medium heat for 5 minutes.

Calories	34
Calories from Fat	9
Total Fat	1 g
Saturated Fat	0 g
Cholesterol	0 mg
Sodium	15 mg
Carbohydrate	6 g
Dietary Fiber	0 g
Sugars	6 g
Protein	0 g

 WHY DON'T YOU . . .

*In winter, buy pine cones,
spray paint them gold,
and use them as holders for
dinner placecards.*

Turkey Tenderloin Picnic

Cucumber Dill Dip
Creamy Peach Soup
Roast Turkey Tenderloins with Kiwi Slaw
Garlic New Potato Salad
Mint Tea

MENU TALK

Dill has been around for thousands of years. The green leaves of the dill plant are called dill weed. Dill is best when fresh. It should be added to hot foods at the end of the cooking time, because its heady fragrance is lost in prolonged heat. The cucumber dill dip can be thinned with some low-fat buttermilk to make a creamy salad dressing. Use the cucumber dill dip to top salmon filets or even a baked potato.

Cooking with alcohol is a wonderful way to impart flavor to foods; however, feel free to omit the wine and orange liqueur from this soup recipe if you like. Add some kind of extract, such as vanilla or almond, to give the soup a boost. Honeydew melon, plums, nectarines, and berries also make great bases for cold soups. Serve fruit soups as appetizers or desserts.

The kiwi is cultivated in both California and New Zealand, making kiwi available to us all year long. The exquisite-looking interior with its bold green color and edible black seeds adds eye appeal to any fruit platter. Another fun way to eat a kiwi is to slice off the top and scoop out the flesh with a grapefruit spoon. Kiwis can last up to three weeks in the refrigerator and are a good source of vitamin C. In this recipe, kiwi adds sweetness to traditional coleslaw. When selecting a head of cabbage, choose one that is firm, feels heavy for its size, and has crisp-looking leaves. Cabbage is a good cruciferous, cancer-fighting vegetable that should be included in your diet whenever possible. If you can't find turkey tenderloins, turkey breast portions will do. The turkey tenderloin is the tender underside of the turkey breast. The tenderloins are lean but juicy.

New potatoes are the natural choice for making potato salads, because they retain their shape so well after being cooked. New potatoes are young potatoes that have a waxy texture and very thin skins. Mix the potatoes with the other ingredients while the potatoes are still warm. The heat will help all the flavors to blend. Then refrigerate the salad so the flavors develop further. Potato salads are like a blank canvas—you can add so many interesting ingredients to them! Experiment with Indian spices such as cumin and fennel, or make an Italian potato salad by adding drops of balsamic vinegar and strips of roasted red pepper. There's more to potato salad than just mayonnaise!

Tea has become so popular in recent years that some major cities offer teahouses as well as trendy coffeehouses. Tea was cultivated in China over 4000 years ago and popularized in Europe by the British. The ritualistic high tea gives you an indication just how seriously the Europeans take tea drinking. Everything from black teas to Asian green teas to aromatic herb teas can produce fine ice tea. For truly special tea, purchase the teas loose and place the leaves in a tea ball. Your tea will probably be stronger in taste using this method compared with just using tea bags. Teas have essential oils, so be sure to keep them tightly covered in glass jars or tins.

Pantry List

decaffeinated tea
sugar
1 1/2 lb new potatoes
Dijon mustard
garlic
canola oil
olive oil
honey
lite mayonnaise
1 shallot
apple cider vinegar
dry white wine
orange liqueur

Market List

1 1/2 lb turkey tenderloins
4 medium peaches
1 container low-fat buttermilk
   or plain yogurt
part-skim ricotta cheese
mint
1 medium cucumber
low-fat sour cream
low-fat yogurt
fresh dill
parsley
thyme
fresh lime juice
1 small head green cabbage
1 carrot
2 kiwis
green onions
1 orange
1 lemon

STEP-BY-STEP COUNTDOWN

1 Prepare the mint tea and allow it to steep.
2 Prepare the potato salad and refrigerate.
3 Prepare the soup and refrigerate.
4 Prepare the dip and refrigerate.
5 Prepare the turkey and slaw.
6 Serve the dip.
7 Serve the turkey, slaw, and potato salad.
8 Serve the soup for dessert. Serve tea throughout the meal, but be sure to strain it first.

Cucumber Dill Dip

6 Servings

Serving Size:
2 Tbsp
Exchanges

1/2 Starch

Ingredients

1/2 medium cucumber, peeled,
    seeded, and finely diced
3/4 cup low-fat sour cream
2 Tbsp plain low-fat yogurt
1/4 cup lite mayonnaise
2 cloves garlic, minced
2 Tbsp minced shallots
1 Tbsp minced fresh dill
2 tsp minced parsley
1/2 tsp minced thyme
2 tsp apple cider vinegar

Preparation—10 minutes

Combine all ingredients by hand until smooth.
Serve with raw vegetables or crackers.

Calories	42
Calories from Fat	0
Total Fat	0 g
Saturated Fat	0 g
Cholesterol	0 mg
Sodium	135 mg
Carbohydrate	7 g
Dietary Fiber	0 g
Sugars	5 g
Protein	3 g

 WHY DON'T YOU . . .

*In fall, use mini pumpkins and
prop dinner placecards against
the pumpkins.*

Creamy Peach Soup

6 Servings

Serving Size:
1/2 cup

Exchanges

1 1/2 Carbohydrate

Ingredients

4 medium peaches, peeled, pitted, and cut into chunks
1/2 cup dry white wine
1 cup low-fat buttermilk or plain yogurt
1/2 cup part-skim ricotta cheese
2 tsp orange liqueur
2 Tbsp honey
Mint leaves

Preparation—10 minutes

1 Puree the peaches and wine in a blender and pour into a chilled bowl. Add the remaining ingredients and mix well. Refrigerate for 1 hour.
2 Divide among 6 individual chilled serving bowls. Garnish each bowl with a mint leaf and serve.

Calories	109
Calories from Fat	10
Total Fat	1 g
Saturated Fat	1 g
Cholesterol	10 mg
Sodium	77 mg
Carbohydrate	20 g
Dietary Fiber	2 g
Sugars	17 g
Protein	5 g

Roast Turkey Tenderloins with Kiwi Slaw

6 Servings

Serving Size:
3 oz turkey
1/2 cup coleslaw

Exchanges

1/2 Fruit
1 Vegetable
4 Very Lean Meat
1 Monounsaturated
  Fat

Ingredients

1 1/2 lb turkey tenderloins
Olive oil for brushing turkey
3 Tbsp fresh lime juice
2 Tbsp canola oil
1 Tbsp honey
2 cups shredded cabbage
1 cup shredded carrots
2 kiwi fruits, peeled and diced

Preparation—25 minutes

1   Grill the turkey tenderloins 6 inches from the heat source, about 4–5 minutes per side, brushing with the olive oil. Remove the turkey and let cool.
2   Combine the lime juice, oil, and honey. Toss in the cabbage and carrots. Add the kiwi and toss again.
3   Serve the turkey at room temperature with the slaw.

Calories	229
Calories from Fat	71
Total Fat	8 g
Saturated Fat	1 g
Cholesterol	75 mg
Sodium	59 mg
Carbohydrate	11 g
Dietary Fiber	2 g
Sugars	8 g
Protein	28 g

Garlic New Potato Salad

6 Servings

Serving Size:
1/2 cup

Exchanges

1 1/2 Starch

Ingredients

1 1/2 lb new potatoes, well
       scrubbed, halved, skins on
3/4 cup lite mayonnaise
1/2 cup low-fat sour cream
1/4 cup low-fat plain yogurt
2 Tbsp finely minced garlic
2 Tbsp minced green onions
2 Tbsp Dijon mustard

Preparation—25 minutes

1 Boil the potatoes in water until tender, about 15–20 minutes, and drain.
2 Combine the potatoes with the remaining ingredients and refrigerate for at least 1 hour before serving.

Calories	134
Calories from Fat	3
Total Fat	0 g
Saturated Fat	0 g
Cholesterol	0 mg
Sodium	330 mg
Carbohydrate	28 g
Dietary Fiber	3 g
Sugars	7 g
Protein	5 g

❖ ❖ ❖ ❖ ❖ ❖

↩ WHY DON'T YOU . . .

Let guests know when the party is over with a very polite yawn.

Mint Tea

6 Servings

Serving Size:
1 cup

Exchanges

Free Food

Ingredients

4 decaffeinated or herbal tea bags
1 orange, sliced
1 lemon, sliced
1/4 cup mint leaves
Sweetener of choice (optional)

Preparation—5 minutes

1 Put the tea bags in a large pitcher. Pour 6 cups of boiling water over the tea bags and let them steep for 5 minutes.
2 Add the orange, lemon, and mint. Continue to steep for 1 hour. To serve, strain the tea and pour over ice into individual serving glasses.
3 If desired, add your favorite sweetener to taste.

Calories	3
Calories from Fat	0
Total Fat	0 g
Saturated Fat	0 g
Cholesterol	0 mg
Sodium	5 mg
Carbohydrate	1 g
Dietary Fiber	0 g
Sugars	0 g
Protein	0 g

❖ ❖ ❖ ❖ ❖

➥ WHY DON'T YOU . . .

Relax and let people into your kitchen. People are curious about food and how you're preparing it. Your kitchen is a workplace, so don't worry about a dirty pot or pan here and there.

❖ ❖ ❖

Index

Z
Zucchini

ABOUT THE AUTHOR

Robyn Webb is an award-winning nutritionist and the owner of *A Pinch Of Thyme Cooking School* in Alexandria, Virginia, the first all low-fat cooking school in the Washington, D.C., area. She has been featured in *Woman's Day* magazine, *Cosmopolitan, USA Today,* and the Associated Press, among others. She has appeared on the TV Food Network, "Working Woman," "CBS News," ESPN, and QVC. In addition, she hosts "Food Focus," a segment of food and health news on Washington's News Channel 8's Cable Ace award-winning show, "Healthline." Robyn is the author of three best-selling books, *A Pinch Of Thyme: Easy Lessons For A Leaner Life* (1994), *Diabetic Meals in 30 Minutes or Less* (1996), and *Flavorful Seasons Cookbook* (1996).

❖ ❖ ❖

Cookbooks & Meal Planners from the American Diabetes Association

N E W !   *The Diabetes Carbohydrate and Fat Gram Guide*
Calories are important, but knowing the fat and carbohydrate content of the foods you eat is the key to eating right. Registered dietitian Lee Ann Holzmeister shows you how to count carbohydrate and fat grams and exchanges and why it's important. Dozens of charts list foods, serving sizes, and nutrient data for hundreds of products.
Softcover. #CMPCFGG
Nonmember: $11.95/ADA Member: $9.95

N E W !   *Brand-Name Diabetic Meals in Minutes*
Save time cooking with these popular taste-tested recipes from the kitchens of Campbell Soup, Kraft Foods, Weetabix, Dean Foods, Eskimo Pie, and Equal. Features more than 200 recipes from appetizers to desserts that will help make your meals tastier and your life easier. Nutrient information included.
Softcover. #CCBBNDM
Nonmember: $12.95/ADA Member: $10.95

N E W !   *How to Cook for People with Diabetes*
Finally, a collection of reader favorites from the delicious, nutritious recipes featured every month in *Diabetes Forecast*. But you don't only get ideas for pizza, chicken, unique holiday foods, vegetarian recipes, and more; you also get nutrient analysis and exchanges for each recipe.
Softcover. #CCBCFPD
Nonmember: $11.95/ADA Member: $9.95

N E W ! *Magic Menus*
Now you can plan all your meals from more than 50 breakfasts, 50 lunches, 75 dinners, and 30 snacks. Like magic, this book figures fats, calories, and exchanges for you automatically. The day's calories will still equal 1,500. Thousands of combinations are possible.
Softcover. #CCBMM
Nonmember: $14.95/ADA Member: $12.95

N E W ! *World-Class Diabetic Cooking*
Travel around the world at every meal with a collection of 200 exciting new low-fat, low-calorie recipes. Features recipes from Thailand, Italy, Greece, Spain, China, Japan, Africa, Mexico, Germany, and more. Appetizers, soups, salads, pastas, meats, breads, and desserts are highlighted.
Softcover. #CCBWCC
Nonmember: $12.95/ADA Member: $10.95

N E W ! *Southern-Style Diabetic Cooking*
This cookbook takes traditional Southern dishes and turns them into great-tasting recipes you'll come back to again and again. Features more than 100 recipes, including appetizers, main dishes, and desserts; complete nutrient analysis with each recipe; and suggestions for modifying recipes to meet individual nutritional needs.
Softcover. #CCBSSDC
Nonmember: $11.95/ADA Member: $9.95

Flavorful Seasons Cookbook
Warm up your winter with recipes for Christmas, welcome spring with an Easter recipe, and cool off those hot summer days with more recipes for the Fourth of July. More than 400 unforgettable choices that combine great taste with all the good-for-you benefits of a well-balanced meal. Cornish Game Hens, Orange Sea Bass, Ginger Bread Pudding, many others.
Softcover. #CCBFS
Nonmember: $16.95/ADA Member: $14.95

Diabetic Meals In 30 Minutes—Or Less!
Put an end to bland, time-consuming meals with more than 140 fast, flavorful recipes. Complete nutrition information accompanies every recipe. A number of "quick tips" will have you out of the kitchen and into the dining room even faster! Salsa Salad, Oven-Baked Parmesan Zucchini, Roasted Red Pepper Soup, Layered Vanilla Parfait, and more.
Softcover. #CCBDM
Nonmember: $11.95/ADA Member: $9.95

Diabetes Meal Planning Made Easy
Learn quick and easy ways to eat more starches, fruits, vegetables, and milk; make changes in your eating habits to reach your goals; and understand how to use the Nutrition Facts on food labels. You'll also master the intricacies of each food group in the new Diabetes Food Pyramid.
Softcover. #CCBMP
Nonmember: $14.95/ADA Member: $12.95

Month of Meals
When celebrations begin, go ahead—dig in! Includes a Special Occasion section that offers tips for brunches, holidays, and restaurants to give you delicious dining options anytime, anywhere. Menu choices include Chicken Cacciatore, Oven-Fried Fish, Sloppy Joes, Crab Cakes, and many others.
Softcover. #CMPMOM
Nonmember: $12.50/ADA Member: $10.50

Month of Meals 2
Automatic menu planning goes ethnic! Tips and meal suggestions for Mexican, Italian, and Chinese restaurants are featured. Quick-to-fix and ethnic recipes are also included: Beef Burritos, Chop Suey, Veal Piccata, Stuffed Peppers, and others.
Softcover. #CMPMOM2
Nonmember: $12.50/ADA Member: $10.50

Month of Meals 3

Enjoy fast food without guilt! Make delicious choices at McDonald's, Wendy's, Taco Bell, and other fast-food restaurants. Special sections offer valuable tips such as reading ingredient labels, preparing meals for picnics, and meal planning when you're ill.
Softcover. #CMPMOM3
Nonmember: $12.50/ADA Member: $10.50

Month of Meals 4

Meat and potatoes menu planning! Enjoy with old-time family favorites like Meatloaf and Pot Roast, Crispy Fried Chicken, Beef Stroganoff, and many others. Hints for turning family-size meals into delicious leftovers will keep generous portions from going to waste. Meal plans for one or two people are also featured. Spiral-bound.
Softcover. #CMPMOM4
Nonmember: $12.50/ADA Member: $10.50

Month of Meals 5

Meatless meals picked fresh from the garden. Choose from a garden of fresh vegetarian selections like Eggplant Italian, Stuffed Zucchini, Cucumbers with Dill Dressing, Vegetable Lasagna, and many others. Plus, you'll reap all the health benefits of a vegetarian diet.
Softcover. #CMPMOM5
Nonmember: $12.50/ADA Member: $10.50

Great Starts & Fine Finishes

Try Crab-Filled Mushrooms, Broiled Shrimp or Baked Scallops for an appetizer. Dig into Cherry Cobbler or Chocolate Chip Cookies for dessert.
Softcover. #CCBGSFF
Nonmember: $8.95/ADA Member: $7.15

Easy & Elegant Entrees

Enjoy Fettucine with Peppers and Broccoli, Steak and Brandied Onions, Shrimp Creole, many more. You'll also enjoy peace of mind knowing your meals are low in fat and calories.
Softcover. #CCBEEE
Nonmember: $8.95/ADA Member: $7.15

Savory Soups & Salads

Pasta-Stuffed Tomato Salad, Mediterranean Chicken Salad, Seafood Salad, many others. Hungry for soup? Try a bowl of Clam Chowder, Gazpacho, Mushroom and Barley, others.
Softcover. #CCBSSS
Nonmember: $8.95/ADA Member: $7.15

Quick & Hearty Main Dishes

Try Spicy Chicken Drumsticks, Apple Cinnamon Pork Chops, Chicken and Turkey Burgers, Macaroni and Cheese, Beef Stroganoff, and dozens more.
Softcover. #CCBQHMD
Nonmember: $8.95/ADA Member: $7.15

Simple & Tasty Side Dishes

Sauted Sweet Peppers, Onion-Seasoned Rice, Parsley-Stuffed Potatoes, Brown Rice with Mushrooms, Broccoli with Lemon Butter Sauce, and a pantry of others.
Softcover. #CCBSTSD
Nonmember: $8.95/ADA Member: $7.15

To order call: 1-800-232-6733

To join ADA call: 1-800-806-7801